PENGU

DUTCH PHRASE BOOK

OTHER PENGUIN PHRASE BOOKS

French
German
Greek
Italian
Portuguese
Russian
Spanish
Turkish

DUTCH
PHRASE BOOK

THIRD EDITION

JILL NORMAN

PAUL BREMAN

PENGUIN BOOKS

PENGUIN BOOKS

Published by the Penguin Group
27 Wrights Lane, London W8 5TZ, England
Viking Penguin Inc., 40 West 23rd Street, New York, New York 10010, USA
Penguin Books Australia Ltd, Ringwood, Victoria, Australia
Penguin Books Canada Ltd, 2801 John Street, Markham, Ontario, Canada L3R 1B4
Penguin Books (NZ) Ltd, 182–190 Wairau Road, Auckland 10, New Zealand

Penguin Books Ltd, Registered Offices: Harmondsworth, Middlesex, England

First published 1972
Second edition 1978
Third edition 1989
1 3 5 7 9 10 8 6 4 2

Filmset in Monotype Lasercomp Ehrhardt by
Santype International Limited, Salisbury, Wilts

Made and printed in Great Britain by
Richard Clay Ltd, Bungay, Suffolk

CONTENTS

INTRODUCTION

In this series of phrase books only those words and phrases that might be called essential to a traveller have been included, but the definition of 'traveller' has been made very wide, to include both the business traveller and the holiday maker, whether travelling alone, with a group or the family, for short or longer stays. Each type of traveller has his or her own requirements, and for easy use the phrases are arranged in sections which deal with specific situations.

Pronunciation is given for each phrase and for all words in the extensive vocabulary. An explanation of the system used for the pronunciation guide is to be found on pages xiii–xix. It is essential to read that section carefully before starting to use this book.

Some of the Dutch phrases are marked with an asterisk* – these attempt to give an indication of the kind of reply you might get to your question, and of questions you may be asked in your turn.

For those who would like to know a little more about the Dutch language, a brief survey of the main points of its grammar is provided at the end of the book (pages 212–222).

PRONUNCIATION

The pronunciation guide is intended for people with no knowledge of Dutch. As far as possible, the system is based on English sounds. This means that complete accuracy will sometimes be lost for the sake of simplicity, but the reader should be able to understand Dutch pronunciation, and make himself understood, if he reads this section carefully and practises the sounds. Each word in the book has a transcription into English symbols, according to the rules set out below, and each word is broken into syllables according to common Dutch practice. Stressed syllables are printed in **bold** type in the pronunciation guide.

VOWELS

Pronounce:

open **a**, **aa** as a in are, but with the sound made just behind the teeth instead of back in the throat

symbol **ā** kamer – room (**kā**-muhr) slaap – sleep (slāp)

closed **a** as **a** in father, but shorter

a dag – day (dakh)

open e, ee as **a** in able (but modified before **r** to a much flatter sound)	**ay**	eten – to eat (ay-tuhn) heet – hot (hayt)
closed e as e in wet	**e**	weg – road (wekh)
final el often as **le** in apple, esp. after **p** or **t**	**'l**	mantel – coat (**man-t'l**)
final en often as **en** in open, esp. after **d**, **k**, **p** or **t**	**'n**	kopen – to buy (kō-p'n)
final er often as **re** in theatre, esp. after **d**, **k** or **t**	**'r**	water – water (wä-t'r)
muted e as a in ago	**uh**	aarde – earth (är-duh)
open i, ie as i in machine	**ee**	benzine – petrol (ben-zee-nuh) vriend – friend (vreent)
closed i as i in inn	**i**	in – in (in)
open o, oo as o in open	**ō**	lopen – to walk (lō-p'n) boot – boat (bōt)
but before r as **oo** in **door**		horen – to hear (hō-ruhn) voor – for (vōr)
closed o as o in pot	**o**	zon – sun (zon)

open **u, uu**	not an English sound: say **ee** with the lips pushed forward and rounded as for **oo**	**ü**	huren – to rent (hü-ruhn) uur – hour (ür)
closed **u**	as **a** in ago	**uh**	druk – busy (druhk)

DIPHTHONGS

ai (in words borrowed from French) as **ai** in air	symbol **è**	populair – popular (po-pü-lèr)
au(w), ou(w) as **ou** in loud	**ow**	gauw – soon (khow) oud – old (owt)
except in words borrowed from French		auto – motorcar (ō-tō)
ei, ij as **i** in fine, but with the lips spread to make a flatter sound	**y**	mei – May (my) rijden – to drive (ry-duhn)
eu as **e** in her, but longer and with the lips well rounded and forward	**œ**	leuk – nice (lœk)
oe as **oo** in moon (but short in closed syllables)	**oo**	hoed – hat (hoot)

ui unlike any English sound, and difficult to produce: it is like **ou** in mouse said far forward, with the lips rounded into a tight circle, and the sound sliding to **ee**

ui huis – house (hui

VOWEL GROUPS

aai, ooi, oei unchanged main vowel or diphthong sound, with a slide towards **ee** at the end of a syllable, or to **y** (as in yes) at the beginning of one

symbol **āee,** **ā-y** haai – shark (hāee

ā-y aaien – to stroke (**ā**-yuhn)

ōee, ō-y mooi – beautiful (m**ō**ee)

gooien – to throw (kh**ō**-yuhn)

ooee, oo-y moeite – trouble (mooee-tuh)

roeien – to row (roo-yuhn)

eeuw, ieuw unchanged open vowel sound, ending on **w**

ayw leeuw – lion (layw

eew nieuw – new (neew)

eau (in words borrowed from French) is pronounced as **o** in open

ō cadeau – gift (ka-d**ō**)

CONSONANTS

Most consonants have approximately the same sound as in English, but they tend to be crisper and more firmly pronounced. Some exceptions are noted below: where necessary the transcriptions will always indicate the true pronunciation.

d as in English — symbol **d** — moeder – mother (**moo**-duhr)

except at the end of a word — **t** — hoed – hat (hoot)

often dropped when between two vowels — **y** — goedendag – hello (khoo-yuhn-dakh)

f often nearer to **v** in above than to **f** in foot

g as **ch** in Scottish loch, quite sharp; — **kh** — goed – good (khoot)

but softer in middle of word — zagen – to saw (zā-khuhn)

j as **y** as a first letter in English, e.g. in yes — **y** — jas – coat (yas)

n final **n** is often dropped in colloquial Dutch – where appropriate, the pronunciation guide follows common practice, but in the Vocabulary the **n** is always voiced — **n** — mijn fiets – my bicycle (muh **feets**: emphasis on the object **feets**; **myn** feets: emphasis on possession)

r always pronounced, often strongly, rolling off the tip of the tongue	**r** erger — worse (**er**-khur)
s always as in soft, never as in rose	**s** suiker — sugar (**sui**-kuhr)
v usually nearer to f in foot than to v in verb	**v** voet — foot (voot)
w much less rounded than in English	**w** water — water (wā-t'r)

Double consonants usually retain their separate sounds (**kn**, for example, never has silent **k** as in English) – often with such force that their pronunciation seems to create a new syllable: dorp (village) **do**-ruhp. There are two exceptions

ch as **ch** in Scottish loch	symbol **kh** schrijven — to write (**skhry**-vuhn)
but initial **ch** in words borrowed from French is like **sh** in ship and in the ending -isch the **ch** is not pronounced at all	**sh** chocola — chocolate (shō-kō-lā) technisch — technical (tekh-nees)
ng as in ring, never as in finger	haring — herring (hā-ring)

PRONOUNCING THE DUTCH ALPHABET

A	ā	N	en
B	bay	O	ō
C	say	P	pay
D	day	Q	kü
E	ay	R	er
F	ef	S	es
G	khay	T	tay
H	hā	U	ü
I	ee	V	vay
J	yay	W	way
K	kā	X	iks
L	el	Y	y
M	em	Z	zet

ESSENTIALS

FIRST THINGS

Yes	**Ja**	yā
No	**Nee**	nay
Please/Here you are	**Alstublieft**	als-tü-bleeft
Thank you	**Dank u (wel)**	dank ü (wel)
You're welcome	**Graag gedaan**	khrākh khuh-dān
No, thank you	**Nee, dank u**	nay, dank ü
Sorry	**Pardon**	par-don

LANGUAGE PROBLEMS

| I'm English/American | **Ik kom uit Engeland/Amerika** | ik kom uit **eng-uh-lant**/a-**may-ree-kā** |
| Do you speak English? | **Spreekt u Engels?** | spraykt ü **eng-uhls** |

Does anybody here speak English?	**Spreekt hier iemand Engels?**	spraykt heer ee-mant eng-uhls
I don't speak Dutch	**Ik spreek geen Nederlands**	ik sprayk khayn nay-duhr-lants
I speak a little Dutch	**Ik spreek een beetje Nederlands**	ik sprayk 'n bayt-yuh nay-duhr-lants
Do you understand (me)?	***Begrijpt u (mij)?**	buh-khrypt ü my
I (don't) understand	**Ik begrijp het (niet)**	ik buh-khryp uht (neet)
Would you say that again, please?	**Wilt u dat herhalen?**	wilt ü dat her-hā-luhn
Please speak more slowly	**Kunt u langzamer praten?**	kuhnt ü lang-zā-muhr prā-t'n
What does that mean?	**Wat betekent dat?**	wat buh-tay-kuhnt dat
Can you translate this for me?	**Kunt u dit voor me vertalen?**	kuhnt ü dit vōr my vuhr-tā-luhn
Please write it down	**Wilt u het even opschrijven?**	wilt ü uht ay-vuhn op-skhry-vuhn
What do you call this in Dutch?	**Hoe heet dat in het Nederlands?**	hoo hayt dat in uht nay-duhr-lants
How do you say that in Dutch?	**Hoe zeg je dat in het Nederlands?**	hoo zekh yuh dat in uht nay-duhr-lants
I will look it up in my phrase book	**Ik zoek het even op in mijn boekje**	ik zook uht ay-vuhn op in myn book-yuh
Please show me the word in this book	**Wilt u me het woord in dit boekje aanwijzen?**	wilt ü muh uht wōrt in dit book-yuh ān-wy-zuhn

QUESTIONS

Who?	Wie?	wee
Where (is/are ...)?	Waar (is/zijn ...)?	wār (is/zyn)
When?	Wanneer?	wan-nayr
Why?	Waarom?	wār-om
How much/many?	Hoeveel?	hoo-vayl
How far/long?	Hoe ver/lang?	hoo ver/lang
What's this?	Wat is dat?	wat is dat
What do you want?	Wat wilt u?	wat wilt ü
What must I do?	Wat moet ik doen?	wat moot ik doon
Have you .../Do you sell ...?	Hebt u ...?	hebt ü
Is/Are there ...?	Is/Zijn er ...?	is/zyn 'r
Have you seen ...?	Hebt u ... gezien?	hebt ü ... khuh-zeen
May I have ...?	Mag ik ... hebben?	makh ik ... he-buhn
Where can I find ...?	Waar kan ik ... vinden?	wār kan ik ... vin-duhn
I want/should like ...	Ik zou graag willen ... (*verb*)	ik zow khrākh wil-luhn
	Ik zou graag ... (*noun*) willen hebben	ik zow khrākh ... wil-luhn he-buhn
I don't want ...	Ik wil niet ... (*verb*)	ik wil neet
	Ik wil geen ... (*noun*)	ik wil khayn

What is the matter?	**Wat is er aan de hand?**	wat is uhr ān duh hant
Can I help you?	***Kan ik u helpen?**	kan ik ü **hel**-puhn
Can you help me?	**Kunt u mij helpen?**	kuhnt ü my **hel**-puhn
Can you tell me ...?	**Kunt u me zeggen ...?**	kuhnt ü muh **ze**-khuhn
Can you give/show me ...?	**Kunt u me ... geven/laten zien**	kuhnt ü muh ... **khay**-vuhn/**lā**-t'n zeen

USEFUL STATEMENTS

It is(n't)	**Het is (niet)**	uht is (neet)
I have	**Ik heb**	ik heb
I don't have ...	**Ik heb niet ...** (*verb*)	ik heb neet
	Ik heb geen ... (*noun*)	ik heb khayn
I want ...	**Ik wil/Ik zoek ...**	ik wil/ik zook
I would like ...	**Ik wou graag ...**	ik wow khrākh
I need ...	**Ik heb ... nodig**	ik heb ... nō-duhkh
I'm lost	**Ik ben de weg kwijt**	ik ben duh wekh kwyt
We're looking for ...	**We zoeken naar ...**	wuh zoo-k'n nār
Here is/are ...	**Hier is/zijn**	heer is/zyn
There they are	**Daar zijn ze**	dār zyn zuh
You are right/wrong	**U hebt gelijk/ongelijk**	ü hebt khlyk/**on**-khlyk

You are mistaken	**U vergist zich**	ü vuhr-**khist** zikh
It's important/urgent	**Het is belangrijk/dringend**	uht is buh-**lang-ryk/dring-**uhnt
I like it	**Het bevalt me**	uht buh-**valt** muh
I don't like them	**Ze bevallen me niet**	zuh buh-**val-**luhn muh neet
OK/That's fine	**Goed/Dat is goed**	khoot/dat is khoot
I (don't) know	**Ik weet het (niet)**	ik wayt uht (neet)
I did(n't) know	**Ik wist het (niet)**	ik wist uht (neet)
I think (that) ...	**Ik geloof (dat) ...**	ik khuh-**lōf** (dat)
I'm hungry/thirsty	**Ik heb honger/dorst**	ik heb **hong-**uhr/dorst
I'm tired/ready	**Ik ben moe/klaar**	ik ben moo/klār
I'm in a hurry	**Ik heb haast**	ik heb hāst
Leave me alone	**Laat me met rust**	lāt muh met ruhst
Just a minute	***Een ogenblik(je)**	uhn ō-khuhn-blik-(yuh)
This way, please	***Deze kant op, alstublieft**	day-zuh kant op, als-tü-bleeft
Take a seat	***Neemt u plaats/Gaat u zitten**	naymt ü plāts/gāt ü zi-t'n
Come in!	***Binnen!**	bin-nuh
It's cheap	**Het is goedkoop**	uht is khoot-kōp
It's (too) expensive	**Het is (te) duur**	uht is (tuh) dür
That's all	**Dat is alles**	dat is al-luhs

GREETINGS

Hello/Good day	(Goeden) dag	(khoo-yuhn)-dakh
Good morning	Goeiemorgen	khoo-yuh-mor-khuh
Good afternoon	Goeiemiddag	khoo-yuh-mi-dakh
Good evening	Goeienavond	khoo-yuhn-ā-vont
Good night/Sleep well	Welterusten	wel-tuh-ruhs-tuhn
Good-bye	Tot ziens	tot zeens
How are you?	Hoe maakt u het?	hoo mākt ü uht
Very well, thank you	Goed, dank u	khoot, dank ü
See you soon/tomorrow	Tot gauw/morgen	tot khow/mor-khuhn
Have a good journey	Goede reis	khoo-yuh rys
Good luck/all the best	Het beste	uht bes-tuh
Have a nice time	Veel plezier	vayl pluh-zeer

POLITE PHRASES

Sorry	Pardon	par-don
Excuse me	Neem me niet kwalijk	naym muh neet kwā-luhk
Excuse me (*to pass*)	Pardon	par-don
That's all right	't is wel goed	tis wel khoot

Not at all	**Helemaal niet**	hay-luh-**māl** neet
Don't mention it/You're welcome	**Graag gedaan**	khrākh khuh-**dān**
Everything all right?	**Alles in orde?**	**al**-luhs in **or**-duh
Can't complain	**(Ik) mag niet mopperen**	(ik) makh neet **mop**-puh-ruh
Don't worry	**Maakt u zich geen zorgen**	mākt ü zikh khayn **zor**-khuhn
It doesn't matter	**Het geeft niet**	uht khayft neet
I beg your pardon?	**Wat zegt u?**	wat zekht ü
Am I disturbing you?	**Stoor ik?**	stōr ik
I'm sorry to have troubled you	**Het spijt me dat ik u zoveel last bezorgd heb**	uht spyt muh dat ik ü zō-vayl last buh-**zorkht** heb
Good/That's fine	**Goed/Dat is in orde**	khoot/dat is in **or**-duh
That is very kind of you	**Dat is heel vriendelijk van u**	dat is hayl **vreen**-duh-luhk van ü
That's nice	**Dat is aardig/fijn**	dat is **ār**-duhkh/fyn
Thank you very much for all your trouble	**Hartelijk dank voor al uw moeite**	har-tuh-luhk dank vōr al üw **mooee**-tuh

OPPOSITES

| before/after | **voor/na** | vōr/nā |
| early/late | **vroeg/laat** | vrookh/lāt |

first/last	eerste/laatste	ayr-stuh/lāt-stuh
now/later	nu/later	nü/lā-tuhr
far/near	ver/dichtbij	ver/dikht-by
here/there	hier/daar	heer/dār
in/out	in/uit	in/uit
inside/outside	binnen/buiten	bin-nuh/bui-tuh
under/over	onder/boven	on-duhr/bō-vuhn
big, large/small	groot/klein	khrōt/klyn
deep/shallow	diep/ondiep	deep/on-deep
empty/full	leeg/vol	laykh/vol
fat/lean	dik, vet/mager	dik, vet/mā-khuhr
heavy/light	zwaar/licht	zwār/likht
high/low	hoog/laag	hōkh/lākh
long, tall/short	lang/kort	lang/kort
narrow/wide	nauw/wijd	now/wyt
thick/thin	dik/dun	dik/duhn
least/most	minst/meest	minst/mayst
many/few	veel/weinig	vayl/wy-nuhkh
more/less	meer/minder	mayr/min-duhr
much/little	veel/weinig	vayl/wy-nuhkh
beautiful/ugly	mooi/lelijk	mōee/lay-luhk
better/worse	beter/slechter	bay-t'r/slekh-t'r
cheap/dear	goedkoop/duur	khoot-kōp/dür

clean/dirty	**schoon/vuil**	skhōn/vuil
cold/hot, warm	**koud/heet, warm**	kowt/hayt, warm
easy/difficult	**makkelijk/moeilijk**	mak-kuh-luhk/ mooee-luhk
fresh/stale	**vers/oudbakken**	vers/owt-ba-kuhn
good/bad	**goed/slecht**	khoot/slekht
new, young/old	**nieuw, jong/oud**	neew, yong/owt
nice/nasty	**aardig/akelig**	ār-duhkh/ā-kuh-luhkh
right/wrong	**goed/verkeerd**	khoot/vuhr-kayrt
free/taken	**vrij/bezet**	vry/buh-zet
open/closed, shut	**open/gesloten, dicht**	ō-puhn/khuh-slō-tuhn, dikht
quick/slow	**vlug/langzaam**	vluhkh/lang-zām
quiet/noisy	**rustig/lawaaiig**	ruhs-tuhkh/la-wā-yuhkh
sharp/blunt	**scherp/bot**	skherp/bot

SIGNS & PUBLIC NOTICES[1]

Alleen staanplaatsen	standing room only
Bellen s.v.p.	please ring
Bezet	engaged/occupied
Binnen zonder kloppen	enter without knocking
Dames	ladies
Duwen	push
Geen drinkwater	not drinking water
Geen toegang	no entry
Geopend van ... tot ...	open from ... to ...
Gereserveerd	reserved
Gesloten	closed
Gevaar	danger
Heren	gentlemen
Ingang	entrance
Inlichtingen	information
Kamers te huur	rooms to let
Kassa	cashier

1. See also SIGNS TO LOOK FOR AT STATIONS (p. 23) and ROAD SIGNS (p. 42).

Kloppen a.u.b.	please knock
Lift	lift/elevator
Men wordt verzocht niet te ...	you are requested not to ...
Niet (roken)	do not (smoke)
Niet aanraken	do not touch
Nooduitgang	emergency exit
Open	open
Openbaar vervoer	public transport
Openbare bibliotheek	public library
Politiebureau	police station
Postkantoor	post office
Tapvergunning	fully licensed
Te huur	to let/for hire
Te koop	for sale
Toegang verboden	no entry
Toegang vrij	admission free
Toilet/WC	lavatory/toilet
Trekken	pull
Uitgang	exit
Uitverkocht	sold out/house full (*cinema, etc.*)
Uitverkoop	sale
Verboden te ...	do not ...
Verboden te roken/Niet roken	no smoking
Verboden toegang	private/no trespassing
Verboden toegang voor onbevoegden	authorized personnel only
Voetgangers	pedestrians
Vol	no vacancies
Voorzichtig	caution
Vrij	vacant/free/unoccupied

ABBREVIATIONS

alg.	algemeen	general
A.N.P.	Algemeen Nederlands Persbureau	largest news agency
A.N.W.B.	Algemene Nederlandse Wielrijdersbond	Dutch Automobile Association
A.O.W.	Algemene Ouderdoms Wet	old age pension
a.u.b.	alstublieft	please
		broadcasting companies
A.V.R.O.		liberal
E.O.		evangelical
IKON		eucumenical
K.R.O		roman catholic
N.C.R.V.		protestant
V.A.R.A.		labour
V.O.O.		commercial
V.P.R.O.		reformed church
bijv./b.v.	bijvoorbeeld	e.g.
B.T.W.	Belasting toegevoegde waarde	value added tax (V.A.T.)
B.V.	Besloten Vennootschap	limited company

C.D.A.	**Christelijk Democratisch Appèl**	protestant–catholic coalition party
cm	**centimeter**	centimetre
CS	**centraal station**	main (railway) station
ct	**cent**	cent
dag.	**dagelijks**	daily
d.w.z.	**dat wil zeggen**	i.e.
e.a.	**en andere(n)**	a.o.
e.d.	**en dergelijke(n)**	and other similar
E.E.G.	**Europese Economische Gemeenschap**	E.E.C.
E.H.B.O.	**eerste hulp bij ongelukken**	first aid
enz.	**enzovoort**	etc.
Fa	**firma**	company
(H)fl	**gulden**	(Dutch) guilders
K.N.A.C.	**Koninklijke Nederlandse Automobiel Club**	Royal Dutch Automobile Club
K.N.M.I.	**Koninklijk Nederlands Meteorologisch Instituut**	weather centre

l	**liter**	litre
m	**meter**	metre
mej.	**mejuffrouw**	Miss
mevr.	**mevrouw**	Mrs
mm	**millimeter**	millimetre
n.Chr.	**na Christus**	A.D.
N.O.S.	**Nederlandse Omroep Stichting**	national broadcasting authority
N.S.	**Nederlandse Spoorwegen**	Dutch railways
N.T.S.	**Nederlandse Televisie Stichting**	national television authority
N.V.	**naamloze vennootschap**	limited company
P.T.T.	**Post, telefoon, telegraaf**	State post and telecommunications service
P.v.d.A.	**Partij van de Arbeid**	Labour Party
R.K.	**Rooms Katholiek**	Roman Catholic
s.v.p.	**s'il vous plaît**	please
T.R.O.S.	**Televisie & Radio Omroep Stichting**	national broadcasting authority
t.z.t.	**te zijner tijd**	in due course
v.Chr.	**voor Christus**	B.C.

V.V.D	**Volkspartij voor Vrijheid en Democratie**	Liberal Party
V.V.V.	**Vereniging voor Vreemdelin- genverkeer**	tourist information office
W.W.	**Wegenwacht**	mobile units of the A.N.W.B.
z.o.z.	**zie ommezijde**	p.t.o.

MONEY[1]

Is there a bank/an exchange bureau near here?	**Is hier een bank/wisselkantoor in de buurt?**	is heer uhn bank/wis-suhl-kan-tōr in duh bürt
Do you change travellers' cheques?	**Accepteert u reis cheques?**	ak-sep-tayrt ü rys sheks
Where can I change travellers' cheques?	**Waar kan ik reischeques wisselen?**	wār kan ik rys sheks wis-suh-luh
Can I change private bank cheques here?	**Accepteert u Eurocheques?**	ak-sep-tayrt ü œ-rō-sheks
Do you have any identification/a banker's card?	***Hebt u een legitimatie bewijs/betaalpas?**	hebt ü uhn lay-khee-tee-mā-tsee buh-wys/buh-tāl-pas

1. In Holland, banks are usually open from 9.00 until 16.00, Monday through Friday. Exchange offices in tourist centres and at main railway stations are usually open until 20.00, some even later.

In Belgium, banking hours are 9.00 to 12 noon and 14.00 to 16.00. In the larger towns many banks stay open at midday.

I want to change some pounds/dollars	Ik wil Engels/Amerikaans geld wisselen	ik wil eng-uhls/a-may-ree-kāns khelt wis-suh-luh
How much do I get for a pound/dollar?	Hoeveel krijg ik voor een pond/dollar?	hoo-vayl krykh ik vōr uhn pont/dol-lar
What is the current rate of exchange?	Wat is de wisselkoers vandaag?	wat is duh wis-suhl-koors van-dākh
Where do I sign?	Waar moet ik tekenen?	wār moot ik tay-kuh-nuhn
Sign here, please	*Wilt u hier even tekenen?	wilt ü heer ay-vuh tay-kuh-nuhn
Go to the cashier	*Gaat u maar naar de kassa	khāt ü mār nār duh kas-sā
Can you give me some small change?	Kunt u me wat kleingeld geven?	kuhnt ü muh wat klyn-khelt gay-vuhn
I arranged for money to be transferred from England; has it arrived yet?	Ik heb geld laten overmaken uit Engeland; is het al aangekomen?	ik heb khelt lā-t'n ō-vuhr-mā-kuhn uit eng-uh-lant; is uht al ān-khuh-kō-muhn
I want to open an account	Ik wil een rekening openen	ik wil uhn ray-kuh-ning ō-puh-nuhn
Please credit this to my account	Wilt u dit op mijn rekening bijschrijven?	wilt ü dit op myn ray-kuh-ning by-skhry-vuhn

Can I get cash on my credit card?	**Kan ik met mijn creditcard contant geld opnemen?**	kan ik met myn kre-dit-kärt kon-tant khelt op-nay-muhn
Current account	**Rekening courant**	ray-kuh-ning koo-rant
Deposit account	**Spaar-rekening**	spär-ray-kuh-ning
Statement	**Dagafschrift**	dakh-af-skhrift
Balance	**Saldo**	sal-dō
Banker's card	**Betaalpas**	buh-tāl-pas[1]
Giro bank	**Postbank**	post-bank
Savings bank	**Spaarbank**	spär-bank

CURRENCY

HOLLAND

fl 1 (one Dutch guilder) = **100 cent**

COINS:[2]

5 cent – 'een stuiver' (uhn **stui**-vuhr)
10 cent – 'een dubbeltje' (uhn **duh**-buhl-tyuh)
25 cent – 'een kwartje' (uhn **kwar**-tyuh)
fl 1 – 'een gulden' (uhn **khul**-duhn)
fl 2.50 – 'een rijksdaalder' (uhn ryks-**dāl**-duhr)
fl 5

BANKNOTES:

fl 10 – 'een tientje' (uhn **teen**-tyuh)
fl 25 – 50 – 100 – 250 – 1000

1. To go with blue Europcheques (maximum fl 300), green bank cheques (maximum fl 200) or with a Girobank card (**giro betaalkaart** – maximum fl 100).
2. Since the 1 cent coin was discontinued, prices in cents are rounded off to the nearest 5.

BELGIUM
fr 1 (one Belgian franc) = **100 centimes**

COINS:[3]
50 centimes – 1, 5, 20 and 50 francs

BANKNOTES:
50, 100, 500, 1000 and 5000 francs

---

3. The 50 franc note is being phased out in favour of the 50 franc coin.

TRAVEL

ARRIVAL

PASSPORTS

Passport control	*Pascontrole	pas-kon-tro-luh
Your passport, please	*Uw pas, alstublieft	üw pas, als-tü-bleeft
Are you together?	*Hoort u bij elkaar?	hōrt ü by muh-kār
I'm travelling alone	Ik reis alleen	ik rys al-layn
I'm travelling with my wife/a friend	Ik reis met mijn vrouw/een vriend(in)	ik rys met myn vrow/uhn vreent (vreen-din)
I'm here on business/on holiday	Ik ben hier voor zaken/op vakantie	ik ben heer vōr zā-kuhn/op va-kan-tsee
What is your address in Amsterdam?	*Wat is uw adres in Amsterdam?	wat is üw a-dres in Am-stuhr-dam

How long are you staying here?	*Hoe lang blijft u hier?	hoo lang blyft ü heer
How much money have you got?	*Hoeveel geld hebt u bij u?	hoo-vayl khelt hebt ü by ü
I have ... pounds/dollars	Ik heb ... pond/dollar	ik heb ... pont/dol-lar

CUSTOMS

Customs	*Douane	doo-wā-nuh
Nothing to declare	Niets aan te geven	neets ān tuh khay-vuhn
Which is your luggage?	*Wat is uw bagage?	wat is üw ba-khā-zhuh
Do you have any more luggage?	*Hebt u nog meer bagage?	hebt ü nokh mayr ba-khā-zhuh
This is (all) my luggage	Dit is (al) mijn bagage	dit is (al) myn ba-khā-zhuh
Have you anything to declare?	*Hebt u iets aan te geven?	hebt ü eets ān tuh khay-vuhn
I have only my personal things in it	Er zitten alleen gebruiksartikelen in	d'r zi-tuhn al-layn khuh-bruiks-ar-tee-kuh-luhn in
I have a carton of cigarettes and bottle of gin/wine	Ik heb een slof sigaretten en een fles gin/wijn	ik heb uhn slof see-khā-re-tuhn en uhn fles dzyin/wyn
Open this bag/suitcase, please	*Maakt u deze tas/koffer even open?	mākt ü day-zuh kof-fuhr ay-vuhn ō-puhn

You will have to pay duty on this	*Hierop moet u invoerrechten betalen	heer-op moot ü in-voor-rekh-tuhn buh-tā-luhn
Can I shut my case now?	Kan ik mijn koffer weer dicht doen?	kan ik myn kof-fuhr wayr dikht doon
May I go?	Kan ik gaan?	kan ik khān

LUGGAGE

Porter!	Kruier!	krui-yuhr
My luggage has not arrived	Mijn bagage is niet aangekomen	myn ba-khā-zhuh is neet ān-khuh-kō-muhn
My suitcase is damaged	Mijn koffer is beschadigd	myn kof-fuhr is bu-skhā-duhkht
One bag is missing	Er ontbreekt een tas	d'r ont-braykt uhn tas
Are there any luggage trolleys?	Zijn er ergens karretjes	zyn uhr er-khuhns kar-ruh-tyuhs
Where is the left-luggage office	Waar is het bagage depot	wār is uht ba-khā-zhuh day-pō
Luggage lockers	Bagagekluizen	ba-khā-zhuh-klui-zuhn

MOVING ON

| Where is the information bureau, please? | Waar is het inlichtingen bureau? | wār is uht in-likht-ting-uhn-bü-rō |
| Would you take these bags to a taxi/to the bus? | Wilt u deze koffers naar een taxi/de bus brengen? | wilt ü day-zuh kof-fuhrs nār uhn tak-see/duh buhs breng-uhn |

What's the price for each piece of luggage?	**Wat is het tarief?**	wat is uht ta-**reef**
I shall take this myself	**Dit draag ik zelf**	dit drākh ik zel-luhf
That's not mine	**Dat is niet van mij**	dat is neet van my
Would you call a taxi?	**Wilt u een taxi voor me roepen?**	wilt ü uhn **tak**-see vōr muh **roo**-puhn
How much do I owe you?	**Hoeveel krijgt u van mij?**	hoo-vayl krykht ü van muh
Is there a bus/train into the town?	**Is er een bus/trein naar de binnenstad?**	is uhr uhn bus/trayn nār duh **bi**-nuh-stat
How can I get to ...?	**Hoe kom ik naar ...?**	hoo kom ik nār

SIGNS TO LOOK FOR AT AIRPORTS AND STATIONS

Arrivals	**Aankomst**	**ān**-komst
Booking office/Tickets	**Plaatskaarten**	**plāts**-kār-tuhn
Buses	**(Auto)bus**	(ō-tō)-buhs
Car rental	**Auto verhuur**	ō-tō-vuhr-hür
Connections	**Aansluitingen/ Verbindingen**	**ān**-slui-ting-uhn/ vuhr-**bin**-ding-uhn
Departures	**Vertrek**	vuhr-**trek**
Exchange	**Wisselkantoor**	wis-suhl-kan-tōr

Gentlemen	**Heren**	hay-ruhn
Hotel reservations	**Hotel reservering**	hō-tel ray-ser-vay-ring
Information	**Inlichtingen**	in-likh-ting-uhn
Ladies' room	**Dames**	dā-muhs
Left luggage	**Bagage depot**	ba-khā-zhuh day-pō
Lockers	**Bagagekluizen**	ba-khā-zhuh-klui-zuhn
Lost property	**Gevonden voorwerpen**	khuh-von-duh vōr-wer-puhn
News stand	**(Kranten) kiosk**	(kran-tuh)-kee-yosk
No smoking	**Niet roken**	neet rō-kuhn
Platform/Track	**Perron/Spoor**	per-ron/spōr
Refreshments	**Restauratie/Buffet**	res-tō-rā-tsee/bü-fet
Reservations	**Plaatsbespreking**	plāts-buh-spray-king
Smokers	**Roken**	rō-kuhn
Taxi (rank)	**Taxi (standplaats)**	tak-see(stant-plāts)
Tourist office	**V.V.V. (kantoor)**	vay-vay-vay (kan-tōr)
Underground	**Metro**	may-trō
Waiting room	**Wachtkamer**	wakht-kā-muhr

BUYING A TICKET

Where's the nearest travel agency?	**Is hier een reisbureau in de buurt?**	is uhr uhn rys-bü-rō in duh bürt

Have you a timetable, please?	**Hebt u een dienstregeling voor me?**	hebt ü uhn **deenst-ray-khuh-ling** vōr muh
What's the return fare to …?	**Wat kost een retour naar …?**	wat kost uhn ruh-**toor** nār
A first-/second-class single to …	**Een enkele reis eerste/tweede klas naar …**	uhn **eng-kuh-luh** rys **ayr-stuh/tway-duh** klas nār
May I have a multiple ticket?[1]	**Mag ik een strippenkaart?**	makh ik uhn **stri-puhn-kārt**
Can I use this on the tram/bus/underground as well?	**Kan ik dit ook voor de tram/bus/metro gebruiken?**	kan ik dit ōk vōr de trem/buhs/**may-trō** khuh-**brui**-kuhn

BY TRAIN[2]

RESERVATIONS AND INQUIRIES

Where's the (main) railway station?	**Waar is het (centraal) station?**	wār is uht (sen-**trāl**) stat-syon
Where is the ticket office?	**Waar is het kaartjesloket?**	wār is uht kār-tyuhs-**lō**-ket
Three singles to …	**Drie enkele (reis) naar …**	dree en-kuh-luh (rys) nār

1. Used nationwide on public transport other than trains; several sections may be cancelled depending on distance travelled.
2. For help in understanding the answers to these and similar questions see TIME AND DATES (p. 198), NUMBERS (p. 204), DIRECTIONS (p. 37).

A (weekend) return	**Een (weekend) retourtje**	uhn week-ent ruh-toor-tyuh
Is there a day trip to ...	**Is er een dagtocht naar ...**	is uhr uhn **dakh**-tokht nār (train price will include entrance to destination park, museum, etc.)
Two evening returns to ...	**Twee avondretours naar ...**	tway ā-vont-ruh-toors nār
Two seats on the ... (*time*) to	**Twee plaatsen in de trein van ... naar ...**	tway **plāt**-suhn in duh tryn van ... nār ...
I want a window seat	**Ik wou een plaats bij het raam**	ik wow uhn plāts by uht rām
a corner seat	**een hoekplaats**	uhn **hook**-plāts
a seat in a non-smoking compartment	**een plaats in een niet-roken afdeling**	uhn plāts in uhn **neet-rō**-kuhn av-day-ling
Is there a supplementary charge?	**Moet ik ook toeslag betalen?**	moot ik ōk **too**-slakh buh-**tā**-luhn
I want to reserve a sleeper[1]	**Kan ik een slaapplaats reserveren?**	kan ik uhn **slāp**-plāts ray-ser-**vay**-ruhn
How much does a couchette cost?	**Wat kost een couchette?**	wat kost uhn koo-**shet**
I want to register this luggage through to ...	**Kan ik deze bagage rechtstreeks naar ... sturen?**	kan ik day-zuh ba-khā-zhuh **rekht**-strayks nār ... **stü**-ruhn

1. Sleepers and couchettes can be reserved through travel bureaux but not at the stations.

Is it an express or a local train?[2]	Is dit een sneltrein of een stoptrein?	is dit uhn **snel**-tryn ov uhn **stop**-tryn
Is there an earlier/later train?	Is er een vroegere/latere trein?	is uhr uhn **vroo**-khuh-ruh/**lā**-tuh-ruh tryn
Is there a restaurant car on this train?	Is er een restauratie-wagen in deze trein?	is uhr uhn res-tō-**rā**-tsee **wā**-khuhn in **day**-zuh tryn
When is the next train to …?	Wanneer gaat de volgende trein naar …?	wan-nayr khāt duh **vol**-luh-khuhn-duh tryn nār
Is there a reduced rate for families?	Is er een groepstarief?	is uhr uhn **khroops**-ta-reef
Can the children have cheap tickets?	Kunnen de kinderen op railrunners reizen?	**kuh**-nuh duh **kin**-duh-ruh op **rayl**-ruh-nuhrs **ry**-zuhn
How old is he/she?	*Hoe oud is hij/zij?	hoo owt is hy/zy
Are there reductions for pensioners?	Is er een speciaal tarief voor 65-plussers?	is uhr uhn spay-see-**yāl** ta-reef vōr vyf-en-zes-tuhkh-**pluhs**-suhrs
I'd like to make a motorail reservation to …	Ik wil een autoslaaptrein reserveren naar …	ik wil uhn ō-tō-**slāp**-tryn ray-ser-vay-ruhn nār

1. Trains are classified as follows: **stoptrein**: stops at all stations; **sneltrein**: stops at selected stations only; **D-trein**: international train which stops at main stations only (supplementary charge); **TEE**: Trans-Europ Express, luxury international trains stopping at a few main stations only, limited access.

| Where is the motorail loading platform for ...? | **Waar is het laadperron voor de autoslaaptrein naar ...?** | wār is uht lāt-per-ron vōr duh ō-tō-slāp-tryn nār |

CHANGING

Is there a through train to ...?	**Is er een doorgaande trein naar ...?**	is uhr uhn dōr-khān-duh tryn nār
Do I have to change?	**Moet ik overstappen?**	moot ik ō-vuhr-sta-puhn
Where do I change?	**Waar moet ik overstappen?**	war moot ik ō-vuhr-sta-puhn
Change at ... and take the local train	***In ... overstappen en de stoptrein nemen**	in ... ō-vuhr-sta-puhn en duh stop-tryn nay-muhn
What time is there a connection to ...?	**Wanneer is er een aansluiting naar ...?**	wan-nayr is uhr uhn ān-slui-ting nār

DEPARTURE

When does the train leave?	**Hoe laat gaat de trein?**	hoo lāt khāt duh tryn
Which platform does the train to ... leave from?	**Van welk spoor/perron gaat de trein naar ...?**	van wel-luhk spōr/per-ron khāt de tryn nār
Is this the train for ...?	**Is dit de trein naar ...?**	is dit duh tryn nār
There will be a delay of ... minutes/hours	***Er is ... minuten/uur vertraging**	uhr is ... mee-nü-tuhn/ür vuhr-trā-khing

ARRIVAL

When does it get to …?	**Wanneer komt hij in … aan?**	wan-**nayr** komt hy in … ān
Does this train stop at …?	**Stopt deze trein in …?**	stopt **day**-zuh tryn in …
How long do we stop here?	**Hoe lang stoppen we hier?**	hoo lang **sto**-puhn wuh heer
Is the train late?	**Heeft de trein vertraging?**	hayft duh tryn vuhr-**trā**-khing
When does the train from … get in?	**Wanneer komt de trein uit … aan?**	wan-**nayr** komt duh tryn uit … ān
At which platform?	**Op welk perron?**	op **wel**-luhk per-**ron**

ON THE TRAIN

Is this smoking or no smoking?	**Is dit roken of niet roken?**	is dit **rō**-kuhn ov **neet rō**-kuhn
We have reserved seats	**Wij hebben gereserveerde plaatsen**	wuh **he**-buhn khuh-**ray**-ser-vayr-duh **plāt**-suhn
Is this seat free?	**Is deze plaats vrij?**	is **day**-zuh plāts vry
This seat is taken	***Deze plaats is bezet**	**day**-zuh plāts is buh-**zet**
Where is the sleeping car?	**Waar is de slaapwagen?**	wār is duh **slāp**-wā-khuhn
Which is my berth?	**Waar is mijn couchette?**	wār is myn koo-**shet**
The heating is too high/low	**De verwarming staat te hoog/laag**	duh vuhr-**war**-ming stāt tuh hōkh/lākh

I can't open/close the window	**Ik kan het raam niet open/dicht krijgen**	ik kan uht rām neet ō-puhn/dikht kry-khuhn
Dining car	**Restauratiewagen**	res-tō-rā-tsee-wā-khuhn
Two tickets for lunch, please	**Twee plaatsen voor lunch, alstublieft**	tway plāt-suhn vōr luhnsh, als-tü-bleeft
Conductor	**Conducteur**	kon-duhk-**toer**
Your tickets, please	***Plaatskaarten alstublieft**	plāts-kār-tuhn, als-tü-bleeft
What station is this?	**Welk station is dit?**	wel-luhk stat-syon is dit
How long do we stop here?	**Hoe lang stoppen we hier?**	hoo lang sto-puhn wuh heer

BY AIR

Where's the ... office?	**Waar is het kantoor van de ...?**	wār is uht kan-tōr van duh ...
I have an open ticket	**Ik heb een open ticket**	ik heb uhn ō-puhn ti-kuht
Can I change my ticket?	**Kan ik mijn ticket veranderen?**	kan ik myn ti-kuht vuhr-an-duh-ruhn
Will it cost more?	**Kost dat meer?**	kost dat mayr
I'd like to book two seats on the plane to ...	**Ik wil graag twee plaatsen boeken naar ...**	ik wil khrākh tway plāt-suhn boo-k'n nār ...

Is there a flight to …?	**Is er een vlucht naar …?**	is uhr uhn vlukht nãr
What is the flight number?	**Wat is het nummer van de vlucht?**	wat is uht **nuhm-muhr** van duh vluhkht
When does the plane leave/arrive?	**Wanneer vertrekt/landt het toestel?**	wan-nayr **vuhr-trekt/lant** uht **too-stel**
When does the next plane to … leave?	**Wanneer is de volgende vlucht naar …?**	wan-nayr is duh **vol-luh-khuhn-duh** vluhkht nãr
Is there a coach to the airport/town?	**Is er een bus naar het vliegveld/de stad?**	is uhr uhn buhs nãr uht **vleekh-velt/duh** stat
When must I check in?	**Wat is de check-in tijd?**	wat is duh shek-in tyt
I'd like to change/cancel my reservation	**Ik wil mijn boeking veranderen/ annuleren**	ik wil myn **boo-king vuhr-an-duh-ruhn/ an-nü-lay-ruhn**

BY BOAT

Is there a boat/(car) ferry from here to …?	**Is er een boot/(auto) veer van hier naar …?**	is uhr uhn bõt/(õ-tõ-)vayr van heer nãr
How long does it take to get to …?	**Hoe lang duurt het om naar … te komen?**	hoo lang dürt uht om nãr … tuh kõ-muhn

How often do the boats leave?	Hoe vaak gaat er een boot?	hoo vāk khāt uhr uhn bōt
Where does the boat put in?	Welke plaatsen doet de boot aan?	wel-kuh plāt-suhn doot duh bōt ān
Does it call at ...?	Doet de boot ... aan?	doot duh bōt ... ān
When does the next boat leave?	Wanneer vertrekt de volgende boot?	wan-nayr vuhr-trekt duh vol-luh-khuhn-duh bōt
Can I book a single-berth cabin?	Kan ik een enkele hut reserveren?	kan ik uhn en-kuh-luh huht ray-ser-vay-ruhn
How many berths are there in that cabin?	Hoeveel plaatsen zijn er in die hut?	hoo-vayl plāt-suhn zyn uhr in dee huht
When must we go on board?	Wanneer moeten we aan boord zijn?	wan-nayr moo-tuhn wuh ān bōrt zyn
When do we dock?	Hoe laat leggen we aan?	hoo lāt le-khun wuh ān
How long do we stay in port?	Hoe lang blijven we in de haven?	hoo lang bly-vuhn wuh in duh hā-vuhn
Can we do a sightseeing tour?	Kunnen we een rondvaart maken?	kuh-nuh wuh uhn ront-vārt mā-kuhn
Hovercraft	Hovercraft	ho-vuhr-krāft
Hydrofoil	Vleugelboot	vlœ-khuhl-bōt
Lifebelt	Reddingsgordel	re-dings-khor-duhl
Life jacket	Zwemvest	zwem-vest
Lifeboat	Reddingsboot	re-dings-bōt

| How do we get on to the deck? | Hoe komen we op het dek? | hoo kō-muh wuh op uht dek |

BY BUS, TRAM OR UNDERGROUND

Where is the bus/underground station?	Waar is het bus/metro station?	wār is uht buhs/may-trō stat-syon
Bus/tram stop	Bushalte/tramhalte	buhs-hal-tuh/ trem-hal-tuh
Request stop	Halte op verzoek	hal-tuh op vuhr-zook
Which tram/metro goes to ...?	Welke lijn gaat naar ...?	wel-kuh lyn khāt nār
Do I have to change?	Moet ik overstappen?	moot ik ō-vuhr-sta-puhn
Is this the right stop for ...?	Is dit de goede halte voor ...?	is dit duh khoo-yuh hal-tuh vōr
I want to get off at ...	Ik moet er bij ... uit	ik moot uhr by ... uit
When does the coach/tram leave?	Wanneer gaat de bus/tram?	wan-nayr khāt duh buhs/trem
What time do we get to ...?	Wanneer komen we in ... aan?	wan-nayr kō-muh wuh in ... ān
What stops does the bus/tram/ underground make?	Waar stopt de bus/tram/metro allemaal?	wār stopt duh buhs/trem/may-trō al-luh-māl
Is it a long journey?	Is het een lange rit?	is uht uhn lang-uh rit

We want to do a sightseeing tour of the city	We willen een stadstoer maken	wuh wil-luhn uhn stats-toor mā-kuhn
Is there a sightseeing tour?	Is er een rondrit (*coach*)/rondvaart (*boat*)?	is uhr uhn ront-rit/ront-vārt
What is the fare?	Wat kost het?	wat kost uht
Does the bus/coach stop at our hotel?	Stopt de bus bij ons hotel?	stopt duh buhs by ons hō-tel
Is there an excursion to ... tomorrow?	Is er morgen een excursie naar ...?	is uhr mor-khuhn uhn eks-kuhr-zee nār
What time is the next tram?	Wanneer gaat de volgende tram?	wan-nayr khāt duh vol-luh-khuhn-duh trem
How often does the ... run?	Hoe vaak gaat de ...?	hoo vāk khāt duh
Has the last bus gone?	Is de laatste bus al weg?	is duh lāt-stuh buhs al wekh
Does this bus go to the centre/the beach/the station?	Gaat deze bus naar het centrum/ het strand/het station?	khāt day-zuh buhs nār uht sen-truhm/uht strant/uht stat-syon
Does this bus go near ...?	Komt deze bus in de buurt van ...?	komt day-zuh buhs in duh bürt van
Where can I get a bus to ...?	Waar kan ik een bus naar ... krijgen?	wār kan ik uhn buhs nār ... kry-khuhn
I want to go to ...	Ik wil naar ...	ik wil nār

Where do I get off?	**Waar moet ik uitstappen?**	wār moot ik uit-sta-puhn
The bus/tram to ... stops over there	***De bus/tram naar ... stopt daar**	duh buhs/trem nār ... stopt dār
You must take a number ...	***U moet met de ... gaan**	ü moot met duh ... khān
You get off at the next stop	***U moet er bij de volgende halte uit**	ü moot 'r by duh vol-luh-khuhn-duh hal-tuh uit
This bus runs every ten minutes/every (half) hour	***Deze bus gaat iedere tien minuten/ieder (half) uur**	day-zuh buhs khāt ee-duh-ruh teen mee-nü-tuhn/ee-duhr (hal-luhf) ür

BY TAXI

Please get me a taxi	**Wilt u een taxi voor me roepen?**	wilt ü uhn tak-see vōr muh roo-p'n
Where can I find a taxi?	**Waar kan ik een taxi vinden?**	wār kan ik uhn tak-see vin-duhn
Are you free?	**Bent u vrij?**	bent ü vry
Please take me to the Central Hotel/the station/this address	**Ik wil naar het Centraal Hotel/het station/dit adres**	ik wil nār uht sen-trāl hō-tel/uht stat-syon/dit a-dres
Can you hurry, I'm late?	**Zo vlug mogelijk, alstublieft, ik ben laat**	zō vluhkh mō-khuh-luhk, als-tü-bleeft, ik ben lāt

I want to go through the centre	**Ik wil door het centrum gaan**	ik wil dōr uht sen-truhm khān
Turn right/left at the next corner	**Bij de volgende hoek rechts/links af**	by duh vol-luh-khuhn-duh hook rekhts/links af
Straight on	**Rechtdoor**	rekht-dōr
Please wait here for me	**Wacht hier op mij, alstublieft**	wakht heer op muh, als-tü-bleeft
Stop here (a moment)	**Kunt u hier (even) stoppen?**	kuhnt ü heer (ay-vuhn) sto-p'n
Is it far?	**Is dat ver?**	is dat ver
How far is it to ...?	**Hoe ver is het naar ...?**	hoo ver is uht nār
How much do you charge by the hour/for the day?	**Wat rekent u per uur/per dag?**	wat ray-kuhnt ü per ür/per dakh
I'd like to go to ... How much would you charge?	**Ik wil naar ... Hoeveel kost dat?**	ik wil nār ... hoo-vayl kost dat
That's all right/too much	**Dat is goed/te veel**	dat is khoot/tuh vayl
I am not prepared to spend that much	**Dat is mij te veel**	dat is my tuh vayl
How much is it?	**Wat krijgt u van me?**	wat krykht ü van muh

DIRECTIONS

Excuse me – may I ask you something?	**Mag ik u even wat vragen?**	makh ik ü ay-vuhn wat vrā-khuhn
Could you tell me . . .	**Kunt u me zeggen . . .**	kuhnt ü muh **zekh**-khuhn
Where is . . . ?	**Waar is . . . ?**	wār is
Is this the way to . . . ?	**Is dit de goede weg naar . . . ?**	is dit duh **khoo**-yuh wekh nār
Which is the road for . . . ?	**Wat is de weg naar . . . ?**	wat is duh wekh nār
How far is it to . . . ?	**Hoe ver is het naar . . . ?**	hoo ver is uht nār
How far is the next village/petrol station?	**Hoe ver is het naar het volgende dorp/benzine station?**	hoo ver is uht nār uht vol-luh-khuhn-duh do-ruhp/ben-zee-nuh stat-syon
How many kilometres?	**Hoeveel kilometer?**	hoo-vayl kee-lō-may-t'r

How do we get on to the motorway to ...?	Hoe komen we op de rijksweg naar ...?	hoo kō-muh wuh op duh ryks-wekh nār
Which is the best road to ...?	Wat is de beste weg naar ...?	wat is duh bes-tuh wekh nār
Is there a scenic route to ...?	Is er een toeristenroute naar ...?	is uhr uhn too-ris-tuh-roo-tuh nār
Where does this road lead to?	Waar gaat deze weg heen?	wār khāt day-zuh wekh hayn
Is it a good road?	Is dat een goede weg?	is dat uhn khoo-yuh wekh
Will we get to ... by evening?	Kunnen we voor donker in ... komen?	kun-nuh wuh vōr dong-kuhr in ... kō-muhn
Where are we now?	Waar zijn we nu?	war zyn wuh nü
What is the name of this place?	Hoe heet deze plaats?	hoo hayt day-zuh plāts
Please show me on the map	Kunt u het op de kaart aanwijzen?	kunt ü uht op duh kārt ān-wy-zuhn
You are going the wrong way	*U gaat de verkeerde kant op	ü khāt duh vuhr-kayr-duh kant op
It's that way	*(Het is) die kant op	(uht is) dee kant op
It isn't far	*Het is niet ver	uht is neet ver
Follow this road for 5 kilometres	*Volg deze weg vijf kilometer	vol-luhk day-zuh wekh vyf kee-lō-may-t'r

Follow the signs for ...	*Volg de borden naar ...	vol-lukh duh **bor**-duhn nār
Keep straight on	*Blijf rechtuit gaan	blyf rekht-uit khān
Turn right/left at the crossroads	*Bij het kruispunt gaat u rechtsaf/linksaf	by uht **kruis**-puhnt khāt ü **rekhts**-av/**links**-av
Take the second road on the left	*Neem de tweede straat links	naym duh **tway**-duh strāt links
Turn right at the traffic-lights	*Bij het stoplicht rechtsaf	by uht **stop**-likht **rekhts**-av
Turn left after the bridge	*Over de brug linksaf	ō-vuhr duh bruhkh **links**-av
The best road is ...	*De beste weg is ...	duh **bes**-tuh wekh is
Take this road as far as ... and ask again	*Volg deze weg tot ... en vraag dan verder	vol-lukh **day**-zuh wekh tot ... en vrākh dan **ver**-duhr
One-way system	**Eenrichtingsverkeer**	**ayn**-**rikh**-tings-vuhr-kayr
North	**Noord**	nōrt
East	**Oost**	ōst
South	**Zuid**	zuit
West	**West**	west

DRIVING

GENERAL

Have you a road map, please?	**Hebt u een wegenkaart voor me?**	hebt ü uhn way-khuhn-kärt võr muh
Where is the nearest car park/garage?	**Waar is de dichtstbijzijnde parkeerplaats/ garage?**	wär is duh dikhtst-by-zyn-duh par-kayr-pläts/ kha-rä-zhuh
(How long) can I park here?	**(Hoe lang) kan ik hier parkeren?**	(hoo lang) kan ik heer par-kay-ruhn
Have you any change for the meter?	**Hebt u misschien kleingeld voor de meter?**	hebt ü muh-skheen klyn-khelt võr duh may-t'r
Speed limit	**Maximum snelheid**	mak-see-muhm snel-hyt
Pedestrian precinct	**Voetgangersdomein**	voot-khang-uhrs-dõ-myn
Is this your car?	***Is dit uw auto?**	is dit uw õ-tõ

May I see your licence/ logbook, please?	***Uw rijbewijs/ autopapieren, alstublieft**	üw ry-buh-wys/ō-tō-pa-pee- ruhn, als-tü-bleeft
How far is the next petrol station?	**Hoe ver is het volgende benzinestation?**	hoo ver is uht vol-luh-khuhn-duh ben-zee-nuh-stat-syon

CAR HIRE

Where can I hire a car?	**Waar kan ik een auto huren?**	wār kan ik uhn ō-tō hü-ruhn
I want to hire a small/large car	**Ik wil een kleine/grote auto huren**	ik wil uhn kly-nuh/khrō-tuh ō-tō hü-ruhn
I want to hire an automatic	**Ik wil een automat huren**	ik wil uhn ō-tō-māt hü-ruhn
I need it for two days/a week	**Ik heb hem twee dagen/een week nodig**	ik heb uhm tway dā-khuhn/uhn wayk nō-duhkh
How much is it by the hour/day/week?	**Wat kost het per uur/dag/week?**	wat kost uht perür/dakh/wayk
Is there a weekend/ midweek rate?	**Is er een weekend/ midweek tarief?**	is uhr uhn week-ent/ mid-wayk ta-reef
Does that include mileage?	**Is de kilometerprijs inbegrepen?**	is duh kee-lō-may-t'r-prys in-buh-khray-puhn
The charge per kilometre is ...	***De prijs per kilometer is ...**	duh prys per kee-lō-may-t'r is

Do you want full insurance?	*Wilt u een volledige verzekering?	wilt ü uhn vol-**lay**-duh-khuh vuhr-**zay**-kuh-ring
Do you want a deposit?	Wilt u een borgsom?	wilt ü uhn **borkh**-som
I will pay by credit card	Ik betaal met mijn creditcard	ik buh-**tāl** met myn **kre**-dit-kārt
May I see your driving licence?	*Mag ik uw rijbewijs zien?	makh ik üw **ry**-buh-wys zeen
Would you sign here, please?	*Wilt u hier even tekenen?	wilt ü heer **ay**-vuhn **tay**-kuh-nuhn
Can I return it in ...?	Kan ik hem terugbrengen in ...?	kan ik uhm **truhkh**-breng-uhn in
Could you show me the controls/lights?	Kunt u me wijzen hoe het werkt/hoe het licht werkt?	kuhnt ü muh **wy**-zuhn hoo uht werkt/hoo uht likht werkt

ROAD SIGNS

Betaald parkeren	Parking with ticket machine
Bij nat wegdek	When wet
Bromfietsers	Moped riders
Bus	Bus lane
Centrum	Town centre
Doodlopende weg	Dead end
Doorgaand verkeer (gestremd)	Through traffic (diverted)
Douane	Customs

Eenrichtings-verkeer	One way traffic
Einde parkeerverbod	End of no parking zone
Eigen weg	Private road
(Alleen) Fietsers	Cyclists (only)
Fietspad	Cycle path
Gemeente ...	... city limits
Gereserveerd voor (arts/invaliden)	Reserved for (doctor/handicapped)
Gevaar	Danger
Gevaarlijke (bocht/stoffen)	Dangerous (curve/goods)
Grens	Frontier
Groot licht	Use headlights
Indien verkeerslichten branden	When traffic lights are in operation
Inhalen (*picture*) toegestaan	Overtaking ... permitted
Inhalen verboden	No overtaking
Invoegen	Get in lane
Langzaam (verkeer)	Slow (traffic)
Let op	Beware
Licht aan	Lights on
Maximum snelheid	Speed limit[1]
Motor afzetten	Switch off engine
Omleiding	Diversion
Onbewaakte overweg	Unguarded level crossing
Ontsteek uw lichten	Lights on
Oprijden tot stopstreep	Stop at the white line
Parkeerautomaat	Parking ticket machine
Parkeerplaats	Parking

---

1. 120 km/h (75 mph) on motorways and main roads; 80 km/h (50 mph) on minor (B) roads; 50 km/h (30 mph) within city limits.

Parkeervak	Parking space
Parkeren verboden	No parking
Pas op	Caution
Rechtshouden	Keep right
Rijwielpad	Cycle path
Ruiterpad	Bridle path
Slecht wegdek	Bad road surface
Slipgevaar	Danger of skidding
Stadsverkeer	Local traffic
Steenslag	Grit
Stijle helling	Steep hill
Tegenliggers	Oncoming traffic
Toegang verboden	No entry
Uitgezonderd ...	Except ...
Uitsluitend werkverkeer	Works traffic only
Uitrit	Exit (for lorries)
Uitrit vrijlaten	Do not block exit
Verboden toegang	No entry/Private
Verkeerslichten	Traffic lights
Voetgangers	Pedestrians
Voorsorteren	Get in lane
Voorzichtig	Drive with care
Vrachtverkeer	Heavy vehicles
WACHT tot het rode licht gedoofd is	Wait until the red light is off
Weg afgesloten	Road closed
Wegomlegging	Diversion
Werk in uitvoering	Road works
Wisselautomaat	Machine giving change
Ijzelvorming	Icy surface

AT THE GARAGE OR PETROL STATION

… litres of 2-star/4-star, please	… liter benzine/super, alstublieft	… lee-t'r ben-zee-nuh/sü-puhr, als-tü-bleeft
… litres of diesel/leadfree	… liter diesel/loodvrije benzine	… lee-t'r dee-zuhl/lōt-vry-yuh ben-zee-nuh
… (money's worth) of petrol, please	Voor … gulden benzine, alstublieft	vōr … khuhl-duhn ben-zee-nuh, als-tü-bleeft
What is the price per litre?	Wat kost benzine per liter?	wat kost ben-zee-nuh per lee-t'r
Fill it up, please	Vol, alstublieft	vol, als-tü-bleeft
Please check the oil and water	Wilt u olie en water nakijken?	wilt ü ō-lee en wā-tuhr nā-ky-kuhn
The oil needs changing	De olie moet ververst worden	de ō-lee moot vuhr-verst wor-duh
Check the tyre pressure/battery, please	Wilt u mijn banden/accu nakijken, alstublieft?	wilt ü myn ban-duhn/ak-kü na-ky-k'n, als-tü-bleeft
Please wash the car	Kunt u mijn auto wassen?	kuhnt ü myn ō-tō was-suhn
Would you clean the windscreen?	Wilt u de voorruit schoonmaken?	wilt ü duh vōr-ruit skhōn-mā-k'n

Can I garage the car here?	**Kan mijn auto hier in de garage?**	kan myn ō-tō heer in duh kha-rā-zhuh
What time does the garage close?	**Wanneer sluit de garage?**	wan-nayr sluit duh kha-rā-zhuh
Where are the toilets?	**Waar is het toilet?**	wār is uht twa-let

REPAIRS

My car has broken down	**Mijn auto is kapot**	myn ō-tō is ka-pot
Can you give me a lift to a telephone?	**Kunt u me een lift geven naar een telefoon?**	kuhnt ü muh uhn lift khay-vuhn nār uhn tay-luh-fōn
Please tell the next garage to send help	**Wilt u de dichtstbijzijnde garage vragen om hulp te sturen?**	wilt ü duh dikhtst-by-zyn-duh kha-rā-zhuh vrā-khuhn om hul-luhp tuh stü-ruhn
May I use your phone?	**Mag ik uw telefoon gebruiken?**	makh ik üw tay-luh-fōn khuh-**brui**-kuhn
Where is there a ... agency?	**Is hier ergens een ... garage?**	is heer er-ruh-khuhns uhn ... kha-rā-zhuh
Have you a breakdown service?	**Hebt u een sleepwagen?**	hebt ü uhn slayp-wā-khuhn
Is there a mechanic?	**Is er een monteur**	is uhr uhn mon-tœr
Can you send someone to look at it/tow it away?	**Kunt u iemand sturen om er naar te kijken/hem weg te slepen?**	kuhnt ü ee-mant stü-ruhn om uhr nār tuh ky-k'n/uhm wekh tuh slay-puhn

It is an automatic and cannot be towed	**Het is een automaat, hij kan niet gesleept worden**	uht is uhn ō-tō-māt, hy kan neet khuh-**slaypt** wor-duhn
Where are you?	***Waar bent u?**	wār bent ü
Where is your car?	***Waar is uw auto?**	wār is üw ō-tō
I am on the road from ... to ... near kilometre post ...	**Ik ben op de weg van ... naar ... bij kilometerpaal ...**	ik ben op duh wekh van ... nār ... by kee-lō-may-t'r-pāl
When will you be here?	**Wanneer kunt u hier zijn?**	wan-nayr kuhnt ü heer zyn
The battery is flat, it needs charging	**De accu is leeg, hij moet opgeladen worden**	duh ak-kü is laykh, hy moot op-khuh-lā-duh wor-duhn
The exhaust is broken	**De uitlaat is kapot**	duh uit-lāt is ka-pot
The windscreen wipers do not work	**De ruitenwissers doen het niet**	duh rui-tuh-wis-suhrs doon uht neet
The tyre is flat, can you mend it?	**Mijn band is lek, kunt u hem maken?**	myn bant is lek, kuhnt ü uhm mā-k'n
The valve/radiator is leaking	**Het ventiel/De radiator lekt**	uht ven-teel/duh ra-dee-yā-tor lekt
I've lost my car key	**Ik heb mijn auto-sleuteltje verloren**	ik heb muhn ō-tō-slœ-tuhl-tyuh vuhr-lō-ruhn
The lock is broken/jammed	**Het slot is kapot/zit vast**	uht slot is ka-pot/zit vast
My car won't start	**Mijn auto wil niet starten**	muhn ō-tō wil neet star-t'n

It's not running properly	**Hij loopt niet goed**	hy lōpt neet khoot
The engine is overheating	**De motor loopt warm**	duh mō-t'r lōpt wa-ruhm
Can you change the plugs?	**Kunt u de bougies verwisselen?**	kuhnt ü duh boo-zhees vuhr-wis-suh-luhn
There's a petrol/oil leak	**Ik verlies benzine/olie**	ik vuhr-lees ben-zee-nuh/ō-lee
There's a smell of petrol/rubber	**Het ruikt naar benzine/rubber**	uht ruikt nār ben-zee-nuh/ruh-buhr
Something is wrong with my car	**Er is iets mis met mijn auto**	d'r is eets mis met muhn ō-to
There's a squeak/whine/rumble/rattle	**Het piept/giert/bromt/ratelt**	uht peept/kheert/bromt/rā-tuhlt
It's a high/low noise	**Het is een piep/brom geluid**	uht is uhn peep/brom khuh-luit
It's intermittent/continuous	**Het is afgebroken/onafgebroken**	uht is af-khuh-brō-kuhn/on-af-khuh-brō-kuhn
The carburettor needs adjusting	**De carburateur moet bijgesteld worden**	duh kar-bü-rā-tœr moot by-khuh-stelt wor-duhn
Can you repair it?	**Kunt u het repareren?**	kuhnt ü uht ray-pa-ray-ruhn
How long will it take to repair?	**Hoe lang duurt het repareren?**	hoo lang dürt uht ray-pa-ray-ruhn
What will it cost?	**Wat gaat het kosten?**	wat khāt uht kos-t'n

When can I pick the car up?	**Wanneer kan ik de auto halen?**	wan-nayr kan ik duh ō-tō hā-luhn
I need it as soon as possible	**Ik heb hem zo gauw mogelijk weer nodig**	ik heb uhm zō khow mō-khuh-luhk wayr nō-duhkh
I need it in three hours/ tomorrow morning	**Ik moet hem over drie uur/ morgenochtend weer hebben**	ik moot uhm ō-vuhr dree ür/ mor-khuhn-okh-tuhnt wayr he-buhn
It will take two days	***Het duurt twee dagen**	uht dürt tway dā-khuhn
We can repair it temporarily	***We kunnen het tijdelijk repareren**	wuh kuhn-nuhn uht ty-duh-luhk ray-pa-ray-ruhn
We haven't the right spares	***We hebben de goede onderdelen niet**	wuh he-buhn duh khoo-yuh on-duhr-day-luh neet
We have to send for the spares	***We moeten de onderdelen laten komen**	wuh moo-t'n duh on-duhr-day-luh lā-tuh kō-muhn
You will need a new …	***U hebt een nieuwe … nodig**	ü hebt uhn nee-wuh … nō-duhkh
Could I have an itemized bill?	**Kan ik een gespecificeerde rekening krijgen?**	kan ik uhn khuh-spay-see-fee-sayr-duh ray-kuh-ning kry-khuhn

PARTS OF A CAR AND OTHER USEFUL WORDS

accelerate (to)	gas geven	khas khay-vuhn
accelerator	gaspedaal (n)	khas-puh-dāl
adjust (to)	bijstellen	by-stel-luhn
airpump	luchtpomp	luhkht-pomp
anti-freeze	antivries	an-tee-vrees
automatic transmission	automatische versnelling	ō-tō-mā-tee-suh vuhr-snel-ling
axle (front, rear)	as (voor, achter)	as (vōr, akh-tuhr)
battery	accu	ak-kü
beam	lichtbundel	likht-buhn-duhl
big end	drijfstangkop	dryf-stang-kop
blow (to)	doorslaan	dōr-slān
blown *gasket or fuse*	doorgeslagen	dōr-khuh-slā-khuhn
blown *tyre*	gesprongen	khuh-sprong-uhn
bolt	bout	bowt
bonnet/hood	motorkap	mō-t'r-kap
boot/trunk	kofferruimte	kof-fuhr-ruim-tuh
brake	rem	rem
disc brakes	schijfrem	skhyv-rem
drum brakes	trommelrem	trom-muhl-rem
footbrake	voetrem	voot-rem
handbrake	handrem	hant-rem
brake fluid	remvloeistof	rem-vlooee-stof
brake light	remlicht (n)	rem-likht
brake lining	remvoering	rem-voo-ring

breakdown	pech	pekh
bulb	lampje	lam-pyuh
bumper	bumper	buhm-puhr
camshaft	nokkenas	no-kuhn-as
carburettor	carburateur	kar-bü-rā-tœr
choke	choke	shōk
clean (to)	schoonmaken	skhōn-mā-k'n
clutch	koppeling	ko-puh-ling
clutch plate	koppelingsplaat	ko-puh-lings-plāt
coil	bobine	bo-bee-nuh
condenser	condensator	kon-den-sā-tor
connecting rod	drijfstang	dryf-stang
cooling system	koelsysteem	kool-see-staym
crank case	carter (n)	kār-tuhr
crankshaft	krukas	kruhk-as
cylinder (head)	cilinder (kop)	see-lin-duhr-(kop)
differential gear	differentiëel	dif-fuh-ren-tsyayl
dip stick	(olie)peilstok	(ō-lee-)pyl-stok
distilled water	gedistilleerd water	khuh-dis-til-layrt wā-t'r
distributor	verdeler	vuhr-day-luhr
distributor cap	verdeelkap	vuhr-dayl-kap
door	deur	dœr
doorhandle	deurknop	dœr-knop
drive (to)	rijden	ry-duhn
driver	bestuurder	buh-stür-duhr
dynamo	dynamo	dee-nā-mō
electrical trouble	elekrische storing	ay-lek-tree-suh stō-ring
engine	motor	mō-t'r
exhaust pipe	uitlaatpijp	uit-lāt-pyp
fan	ventilator	ven-tee-lā-tor

fanbelt	drijfriem	dryv-reem
(oil) filter	(olie) filter (*n*)	(ō-lee) fil-tuhr
flywheel	vliegwiel (*n*)	vleekh-weel
foglamp	mistlamp	mist-lamp
fuse	zekering	zay-kuh-ring
gasket	pakking	pa-king
gauge	meter	may-t'r
gear	versnelling	vuhr-snel-ling
gear box	versnellingsbak	vuhr-snel-lings-bak
gear lever	versnellingshandle	vuhr-snel-lings-hen-duhl
grease (to)	doorsmeren	dōr-smay-ruhn
head gasket	koppakking	kop-pa-king
headlights	koplampen	kop-lam-puhn
heater	verwarming	vuhr-war-ming
horn	toeter/claxon	too-t'r/klak-son
hose	slang	slang
hub	naaf	nāf
ignition	ontsteking	ont-stay-king
ignition key	contactsleutel	kon-takt-slœ-tuhl
indicator	richtingaanwijzer	rikh-ting-ān-wy-zuhr
inner tube	binnenband	bin-nuh-bant
jack	krik	krik
lightbulb	lampje	lam-pyuh
lights		
head	koplampen	kop-lam-puhn
side	zijlichten	zy-likh-tuhn
rear	achterlichten	akh-tuhr-likh-tuhn
lead *electr*.	draad/leiding	drāt/ly-ding
lock/ catch	slot (*n*)	slot
mirror	spiegel	spee-khuhl

number plate	nummerplaat	nuhm-muhr-plat
nut	moer	moor
oil	olie	ō-lee
oil pressure	oliedruk	ō-lee-druhk
overdrive	overdrive	ō-vuhr-dryf
parking lights	parkeerlichten	par-kayr-likh-tuhn
petrol	benzine	ben-zee-nuh
petrol can/pump/tank	benzineblik/pomp/ tank	ben-zee-nuh-blik/pomp/ tenk
piston	zuiger	zui-khuhr
piston ring	zuigerveer	zui-khuhr-vayr
(sparking) plug	bougie	boo-zhee
plug lead	bougiekabel	boo-zhee-kā-buhl
points	onderbrekerpunten	on-duhr-bray-khur- puhn-tuhn
propeller shaft	cardan as	kar-dan as
(fuel) pump	(benzine) pomp	(ben-zee-nuh) pomp
puncture	lekke band	le-kuh bant
radial ply tyre	radiaalband	rā-dee-yāl-bant
radiator	radiator	ra-dee-yā-tor
reverse (to)	achteruit rijden	akh-tuhr-uit ry-duhn
reverse	achteruit	akh-tuhr-uit
reversing lights	achteruitrijlicht	akh-tuhr-uit-ry-likht
(sliding) roof	(schuif) dak	skhuiv-dak
screwdriver	schroevendraaier	skhroo-vuh-drā-yuhr
seat	zitting	zi-ting
shaft	as	as
shock absorber	schokbreker	skhok-bray-kuhr
short circuit	kortsluiting	kort-slui-ting
silencer	knalpot/knaldemper	knal-pot/knal-dem-puhr

(plug) spanner	**(bougie) sleutel**	(boo-zhee) slœ-tuhl
spares	**reserve-onderdelen**	ruh-ser-vuh on-duhr-day-luhn
spare wheel	**reserve wiel (*n*)**	ruh-ser-vuh weel
speed	**snelheid**	snel-hyt
speedometer	**snelheidsmeter**	snel-hyts-may-t'r
spring	**veer**	vayr
stall (to)	**afslaan**	af-slān
starter motor	**startmotor**	start-mō-t'r
steering	**besturing**	buh-stü-ring
steering wheel	**stuurwiel (*n*)**	stür-weel
sunroof	**schuifdak (*n*)**	skhuiv-dak
suspension	**vering**	vay-ring
switch	**schakelaar**	skhā-kuh-lār
switch on/off (to)	**in/uit schakelen**	in/uit skhā-kuh-luhn
tank	**(benzine) tank**	ben-zee-nuh-tenk
tappets	**kleplichters**	klep-likh-tuhrs
terminal	**aansluitklem**	ān-sluit-klem
timing chain	**distributieketting**	dis-tree-bü-tsee ke-ting
tools	**gereedschap (*n*)**	khuh-rayt-skhap
trailer	**aanhangwagen**	ān-hang-wā-khuhn
transmission	**transmissie**	trans-mis-see
tube	**buis**	buis
tube (*in tyre*)	**binnenband**	bin-nuh-bant
tyre	**band**	bant
tyre pressure	**spanning van de banden**	span-ning van duh ban-duhn
valve	**klep**	klep
washer	**sluitring**	sluit-ring
(distilled) water	**(gedistilleerd) water**	khuh-dis-til-layrt wā-t'r

water circulation	**wateromloop**	wā–t'r-om-lōp
water pump	**waterpomp**	wā–t'r-pomp
wheel (front, back, spare)	**wiel (*n*) (voor, achter, reserve)**	weel (vōr, akh-tuhr, ruh-ser-vuh)
window	**raam (*n*)/ruit**	rām/ruit
windscreen	**voorruit**	vōr-ruit
windscreen washers	**ruitensproeiers**	rui-tuh-sproo-yuhrs
windscreen wipers	**ruitenwissers**	rui-tuh-wis-suhrs

CYCLING

Is there a bicycle park near here?	Is er een fietsenstalling/ rijwielstalling in de buurt?	is uhr uhn **feet-sen-stal-ling/ry-weel-stal-ling** in duh bürt
Can I park my bike here?	Kan ik hier mijn fiets neerzetten?	kan ik heer muhn feets **nayr-ze-t'n**
Where can I hire a bicycle/moped?	Waar kan ik een fiets/bromfiets huren?	wār kan ik uhn feets/**brom-feets** hü-ruhn
Do you have a bicycle with gears?	Hebt u een fiets met versnellingen?	hebt ü uhn feets met vuhr-**snel-ling-uhn**
The saddle is too high/low	Het zadel is te hoog/laag	uht zā-duhl is tuh hōkh/lākh
Where is the cycle shop?	Waar is de fietsenwinkel/ rijwielhandel?	wār is duh **feet-suh-wing-kuhl/ry-weel-han-duhl**

Do you repair bicycles?	**Repareerts u fietsen?**	ray-pa-**rayrt** ü **feet**-suhn
The brake isn't working	**De rem doet het niet**	duh rem doot uht neet
Could you tighten/loosen the brake cable?	**Kunt u de remkabel vaster/losser zetten?**	kuhnt ü duh **rem-kā**-buhl vas-tuhr/**los**-suhr ze-t'n
A spoke is broken	**Er is een spaak gebroken**	d'r is uhn spāk kuh-**brō**-kuhn
The tyre is punctured	**De band is lek**	duh bant is lek
The gears need adjusting	**De versnelling moet bijgesteld worden**	duh vuhr-**snel**-ling moot by-khuh-stelt wor-duh
Could you straighten the wheel?	**Kunt u het wiel richten?**	kuhnt ü uht weel **rikh**-t'n
The handlebars are loose	**De handvaten zitten los**	duh hant-vā-t'n zi-t'n los
Could you please lend me a spanner/tyre lever?	**Hebt u misschien een (moer)sleutel/ bandenlichter voor me?**	hebt ü muh-**skheen** uhn (moor)-**slœ**-tuhl/ **ban**-duh-likh-tuhr võr muh

PARTS OF A BICYCLE

axle	**as**	as
bell	**bel**	bel
brake (front, rear)	**rem (voor, achter)**	rem (võr, **akh**-tuhr)

brake cable	**remkabel**	rem-kā-buhl
brake lever	**remhendel**	rem-hen-duhl
bulb	**lampje**	lam-pyuh
chain	**ketting**	ke-ting
chain casing	**kettingkast**	ke-ting-kast
dynamo	**dynamo**	dee-nā-mŏ
frame	**frame**	fraym
gear lever	**versnellingshendel**	vuhr-snel-lings-hen-duhl
gears	**versnellingen**	vuhr-snel-ling-uhn
handlebars	**handvaten/stuur**	hant-vā-t'n/stür
inner tube	**binnenband**	bin-nuh-bant
light – front	**koplamp**	kop-lamp
– rear	**achterlicht**	akh-tuhr-likht
mudguard	**spatbord**	spat-bort
panniers	**mandje**	man-tyuh
pedal	**pedaal/trapper**	puh-dāl/tra-puhr
pump	**pomp**	pomp
reflector	**reflector**	ruh-flek-tor
rim	**velg**	vel-luhkh
saddle(bag)	**zadel(tas)**	zā-duhl(-tas)
spoke	**spaak**	spāk
tyre	**band**	bant
valve	**ventiel**	ven-teel
wheel	**wiel**	weel
wheelguard	**jasbeschermer**	yas-buh-skher-muhr

HOTELS & GUEST HOUSES

BOOKING A ROOM

Rooms to let/vacancies	***Kamers te huur**	kā-muhrs tuh hür
No vacancies	***Vol**	vol
Reception	**Receptie**	ruh-**sep**-see
Receptionist	**Receptionist(e)**	ruh-sep-shō-**nist**(uh)
Have you a room for the night?	**Hebt u een kamer voor één nacht?**	hebt ü uhn kā-muhr vōr ayn nakht
I've reserved a room; my name is …	**Ik heb een kamer gereserveerd; mijn naam is …**	ik heb uhn kā-muhr khuh-ray-ser-vayrt; myn nām is …
Can you suggest another hotel near here?	**Is er een ander hotel hier dichtbij?**	is uhr uhn an-duhr hō-tel heer dikht-**by**
I want a single room with a shower/bath	**Een éénpersoonskamer met douche/bad**	uhn ayn-per-sōns-kā-muhr met doosh/bat

We want a room with a double bed and a bathroom	**Wij zoeken een kamer met een dubbel bed en een badkamer**	wuh zoo-kuhn uhn kā-muhr met uhn duh-b'l bet en uhn bat-kā-muhr
a private toilet	**een eigen toilet**	uhn y-khuhn twa-let
Have you a room with twin beds?	**Hebt u een kamer met twee bedden?**	hebt ü uhn kā-muhr met tway be-duhn
How long will you be staying?	***Hoe lang blijft u?**	hoo lang blyft ü
Is it for one night only?	***Is het maar voor één nacht?**	is uht mār vōr ayn nakht
I want a room for two or three days/for a week/until Friday	**Een kamer voor twee of drie dagen/een week/tot vrijdag**	uhn kā-muhr vōr tway ov dree dā-khuhn/vōr uhn wayk/tot vry-dakh
What floor is the room on?	**Op welke verdieping is de kamer?**	op wel-kuh vuhr-dee-ping is duh kā-muhr
Is there a lift/elevator?	**Is er een lift?**	is uhr uhn lift
Are there facilities for the disabled?	**Zijn er voorzieningen voor invaliden?**	zyn uhr vōr-zee-ning-uhn vōr in-va-lee-duhn
Have you a room on the first floor?	**Hebt u een kamer op de eerste verdieping?**	hebt ü uhn kā-muhr op duh ayr-stuh ver-dee-ping
May I see the room?	**Kan ik de kamer eerst zien?**	kan ik duh kā-muhr ayrst zeen

I like this room, I'll take it	**Ja, dat is goed, deze kamer neem ik**	yā, dat is khoot, day-zuh kā-muhr naym ik
I don't like this room	**Deze kamer bevalt me niet**	day-zuh kā-muhr buh-valt muh neet
Have you another one?	**Hebt u een andere kamer?**	hebt ü uhn an-duh-ruh kā-muhr
I want a quiet/bigger room	**Ik wil een rustige/grotere kamer**	ik wil uhn ruhs-tuh-khuh/khrō-tuh-ruh kā-muhr
There's too much noise	**Hier is teveel lawaai**	heer is tuh-vayl la-wāee
I'd like a room with a balcony	**Ik wil een kamer met een balkon**	ik wil uhn kā-muhr met uhn bal-kon
Have you a room looking on to the sea/street?	**Hebt u een kamer die op zee/op straat uitkijkt?**	hebt ü uhn kā-muhr dee op zay/op strāt uit-kykt
Is there a telephone/radio/television in the room?	**Is er telefoon/radio/televisie op de kamer?**	is uhr tay-luh-fōn/rā-dee-yō/tay-luh-vee-zee op duh kā-muhr
We've only a double room	***We hebben alleen een tweepersoonskamer**	wuh he-buhn al-layn uhn tway-per-sōns-kā-muhr
This is the only room vacant	***Dit is de enige kamer die vrij is**	dit is duh ay-nuh-khuh kā-muhr dee vry is
We shall have another room tomorrow	***Morgen komt er een andere kamer vrij**	mor-khuhn komt uhr uhn an-duh-ruh kā-muhr vry

The room is only available tonight	*De kamer is maar voor één nacht vrij	duh kā-muhr is mār vōr ayn nakht vry
How much is the room per night?	Wat kost deze kamer per dag?	wat kost day-zuh kā-muhr per dakh
It's too expensive	Dat is te duur	dat is tuh dür
Have you nothing cheaper?	Hebt u niets voor een lagere prijs?	hebt ü neets vōr uhn lā-khuh-ruh prys
What do we pay for the child(ren)?	Hoeveel betalen we voor het kind (de kinderen)?	hoo-vayl buh-tā-luh wuh vōr uht kint/duh kin-duh-ruhn
Could you put a cot/extra bed in the room?	Kunt u een kinder bedje/extra bed in de kamer zetten?	kuhnt ü uhn kin-duhr-bed-yuh/ek-strā bet in duh kā-muhr ze-t'n
How much is the room without meals?	Wat kost de kamer zonder maaltijden?	wat kost duh kā-muhr zon-duhr māl-ty-duhn
How much is full board/half board?	Wat kost vol pension/ half pension?	wat kost vol pen-syon/hal-luhf pen-syon
Is breakfast included in the price?	Is ontbijt in de prijs inbegrepen?	is ont-byt in duh prys in-buh-khray-puh
Do you have a weekly rate?	Hebt u een speciaal week-tarief?	hebt ü uhn spay-see-yāl wayk-ta-reef
Would you fill in the registration form, please?	*Wilt u het registratie-formulier invullen, alstublieft?	wilt ü uht ray-khis-trā-tsee for-mü-leer in-vuhl-luhn, als-tü-bleeft

IN YOUR ROOM

Could we have breakfast in our room, please?	Kunnen we op de kamer ontbijten?	kun-nuh wuh op de kā-muhr ont-by-t'n
Please wake me at 8.30	Kunt u mij om half negen wekken?	kunt ü muh om hal-luhf nay-khuhn we-k'n
There's no ashtray in my room	Er is geen asbak op mijn kamer	d'r is khayn as-bak op myn kā-muhr
Can I have more hangers, please?	Hebt u nog een paar kleerhangers voor me?	hebt ü nokh uhn pār klayr-hang-uhrs vōr muh
Is there a point for an electric razor?[1]	Is er een stopcontact voor een scheerapparaat?	is uhr uhn stop-kon-takt vōr uhn skhayr-a-pā-rāt
Where is the bathroom/the lavatory?	Waar is de badkamer/het toilet?	wār is de bat-kā-muhr/uht twa-let
Is there a shower?	Is er een douche?	is uhr uhn doosh
There is no towel/soap/water in my room	Er is geen handdoek/zeep/water op mijn kamer	d'r is khayn han-dook/zayp/wā-t'r op myn kā-muhr
There's no plug in my washbasin	Er is geen stop in mijn wasbak	d'r is khayn stop in myn was-bak

1. Voltage is the same throughout Holland: 240 V at 50 cycles. In Belgium it is 220 V. Plugs are continental two-pin (round) in both countries.

There's no toilet paper	**Er is geen toilet papier**	d'r is khayn twa-let pa-peer
The lavatory won't flush	**De WC spoelt niet door**	duh way-say spoolt neet dōr
The bidet leaks	**Het bidet lekt**	uht bee-de lekt
May I have the key to the bathroom, please?	**Mag ik de sleutel van de badkamer hebben, alstublieft?**	makh ik duh sloe-tuhl van duh bat-kā-muhr he-buhn, als-tü-bleeft
May I have another blanket/pillow?	**Hebt u nog een deken/ kussen voor me?**	hebt ü nokh uhn day-k'n/ kuhs-suhn vōr muh
These sheets are dirty	**Deze lakens zijn vuil**	day-zuh lā-kuhns zyn vuil
I can't open my window	**Ik kan mijn raam niet open krijgen**	ik kan myn rām neet ō-puh kry-khuhn
It's too hot/cold	**Het is te heet/koud**	uht is tuh hayt/kowt
Can the heating be turned up/down/off?	**Kan de verwarming hoger/lager/uit-gedraaid worden?**	kan duh vuhr-war-ming hō-khur/lā-khur/uit-khuh-drāeet wor-duhn
The light doesn't work	**Het licht doet het niet**	uht likht doot uht neet
The lamp is broken	**De lamp is stuk**	duh lamp is stuhk
The blind is stuck	**Het rolgordijn zit vast**	uht rol-khor-dyn zit vast

The curtains won't close	De gordijnen sluiten niet	duh khor-dy-nuh slui-t'n neet
Come in!	Binnen!	bin-nuh
Put it on the table, please	Wilt u het op tafel zetten?	wilt ü uht op tā-fuhl ze-t'n
I'd like some ice cubes	Ik wou graag wat ijs	ik wow khrākh wat ys
Can I have these shoes cleaned?	Kan ik mijn schoenen gepoetst krijgen?	kan ik muh skhoo-nuh khuh-pootst kry-khuhn
Can I have a dress cleaned?	Kan ik een jurk laten stomen?	kan ik uhn juhrk lā-tuh stō-muhn
Can I have this suit pressed?	Kan ik dit pak laten persen?	kan ik dit pak lā-tuh per-suhn
How long will the laundry take?	Hoe lang duurt het voor de was klaar is?	hoo lang dürt uht vōr duh was klār is
Have you a needle and thread?	Hebt u een naald en draad?	hebt ü uhn nālt en drāt

OTHER SERVICES

Porter	Portier	por-teer
Page	Picolo	pee-kō-lō
Manager	Manager	me-nuh-dzur
Telephonist	Telefonist(e)	tay-luh-fō-nist(uh)

The key for no. ...., please	**Sleutel voor nummer ... alstublieft**	slœ-tuhl vōr nuhm-muhr ... als-tü-bleeft
Have you a map of the town/an amusement guide?	**Hebt u een stadsplan/een theatergids?**	hebt ü uhn stats-plan/uhn tay-yā-t'r-khits
Could you put this in the safe?	**Wilt u dit in de kluis bewaren?**	wilt ü dit in duh kluis buh-wā-ruhn
Are there any letters for me?	**Is er post voor mij?**	is uhr post vōr my
Is there a telex/fax?	**Is er een telex/fax?**	is uhr uhn tay-leks/faks
Please post this	**Wilt u dit op de post doen?**	wilt ü dit op duh post doon
Are there any messages for me?	**Zijn er boodschappen voor mij?**	zyn uhr bōt-skha-puh vōr muh
Can I dial direct to England/America?	**Kan ik Engeland/Amerika rechtstreeks bellen?**	kan ik eng-uh-lant/a-may-ree-kā rekht-strayks bel-luhn
If anyone phones, tell them I'll be back at 5.30	**Als iemand opbelt, wilt u dan zeggen dat ik om half zes terug ben?**	als ee-mant op-belt, wilt ü dan ze-khun dat ik om hal-luhf zes truhkh ben
Someone/No one telephoned	***Iemand/Niemand heeft opgebeld**	ee-mant/nee-mant hayft op-khuh-belt
There's a lady/gentleman to see you	***Er is een dame/heer voor u**	d'r is uhn dā-muh/hayr vor ü

Please ask her/him to come up	**Wilt u haar/hem vragen naar boven te komen?**	wilt ü hār/uhm vrā-khuh nār bō-vuh tuh kō-muh
I'm coming down	**Ik kom naar beneden**	ik kom nār buh-**nay**-duh
Have you any writing paper/envelopes/ stamps?	**Hebt u schrijfpapier/ enveloppen/ postzegels?**	hebt ü skhryf-pā-peer/ an-vuh-lo-puhn/pos-say-khuhls
Can I borrow/hire a typewriter?	**Kan ik een schrijfmachine lenen/huren?**	kan ik uhn skhryf-mā-shee-nuh lay-nuhn/hü-ruhn
Can you get me a babysitter, please?	**Kunt u een babysitter voor me vinden?**	kuhnt ü uhn bay-bee-si-t'r vōr muh vin-duh
Please send the chambermaid/waiter	**Wilt u het kamermeisje/de kelner sturen?**	wilt ü uht kā-muhr-my-syuh/duh kel-nuhr stü-ruhn
I need a guide/an interpreter	**Ik heb een gids/tolk nodig**	ik heb uhn khits/tolk nō-duhkh
Where is the dining room?	**Waar is de eetkamer?**	wār is duh ayt-kā-muhr
Where is the toilet/ the cloakroom?	**Waar is het toilet/de garderobe?**	wār is uht twa-**let**/duh khar-duh-ro-buh
What time is breakfast/lunch/ dinner?	**Hoe laat is ontbijt/lunch/ diner?**	hoo lāt is ont-**byt**/lunsh/ dee-nay

Where can I park the car?	**Waar kan ik parkeren?**	wār kan ik par-kay-ruhn
Is there a garage?	**Is er een garage?**	is uhr uhn kha-rā-zhuh
Is the hotel open all night?	**Is het hotel de hele nacht open?**	is uht hō-tel duh hay-luh nakht ō-puhn
What time does it close?	**Hoe laat sluit u?**	hoo lāt sluit ü

DEPARTURE

I have to leave tomorrow	**Ik vertrek morgen**	ik vuhr-trek mo-ruh-khuhn
Can we check out at …?	**Kunnen we om … vertrekken?**	kuhn-nuh wuh om … vuhr-tre-k'n
Can you have my bill ready?	**Wilt u mijn rekening klaarmaken?**	wilt ü myn ray-kuh-ning klār-mā-k'n
Do you accept credit cards?	**Accepteert u credit cards?**	ak-sep-tayrt ü kre-dit kārts
There is a mistake on the bill	**Er zit een fout in de rekening**	d'r zit uhn fowt in duh ray-kuh-ning
I shall be coming back on Thursday/the 14th; can I book a room for that date?	**Ik kom donderdag/de veertiende terug; kan ik voor die dag een kamer reserveren?**	ik kom don-duhr-dakh/duh vayr-teen-duh truhkh; kan ik vōr dee dakh uhn kā-muhr ray-ser-vay-ruhn

Could you have my luggage brought down?	**Kunt u mijn bagage naar beneden laten brengen?**	kuhnt ü myn ba-khā-zhuh när buh-nay-duh lā-tuh breng-uh
Please store the luggage, we will be back at ...	**Wilt u onze bagage ergens bewaren? Wij zijn om ... uur terug**	wilt ü on-zuh ba-khā-zhuh er-ruh-khuhns buh-wā-ruhn; wy zyn om ... ür truhkh
Please call/phone a taxi for me	**Kunt u een taxi voor me roepen/bellen?**	kuhnt ü uhn tak-see vōr me roo-p'n/bel-luhn
Thank you for all your trouble	**Hartelijk dank voor al uw moeite**	har-tuh-luhk dank vōr al üw mooee-tuh

CAMPING

Is there a camp site nearby?	Is er een camping in de buurt?	is uhr uhn kem-ping in duh bürt
May we	Mogen we	mō-khuh wuh
camp here?	hier kamperen?	heer kam-pay-ruhn
camp in your field?	in uw weiland kamperen?	in üw wy-lant kam-pay-ruhn
camp on the beach?	op het strand kamperen?	op uht strant kam-pay-ruhn
Where should we put our tent/caravan?	Waar moeten we onze tent/caravan neerzetten?	wār moo-tuh wuh on-zuh tent/ke-ruh-ven nayr-ze-t'n
Can I park next to the tent?	Kan ik naast de tent parkeren?	kan ik nāst duh tent par-kay-ruhn
Can we hire a tent?	Kunnen we een tent huren?	kuh-nuh wuh uhn tent hü-ruhn

Is there drinking water/electricity/a shower/a toilet?	**Is er stromend water/electriciteit/ een douche/een toilet?**	is uhr strō-muhnt wā-t'r/ay-lek-tree-see-tyt/uhn doosh/uhn twa-let
What does it cost per night/week/head?	**Wat kost dat per nacht/week/ persoon?**	wat kost dat per nakht/wayk/per-sōn
Is there a shop on the site?	**Is er een kampwinkel?**	is uhr uhn kamp-wing-kuhl
Is there a swimming pool/playground/restaurant/launderette?	**Is er een zwembad/ speeltuin/ restaurant/ wasserette?**	is uhr uhn zwem-bat/ spayl-tuin/res-tō-ran/was-suh-ret
Can I get ice?	**Kan ik ijs krijgen?**	kan ik ys kry-khuhn
Where can I get paraffin/butane gas?	**Waar kan ik petroleum/ butagas krijgen?**	wār kan ik pay-trō-lee-yuhm/ bü-tā-khas kry-khuhn
Where do I put rubbish?	**Waar laat ik het afval?**	wār lāt ik uht af-fal
Where can I wash up/ wash clothes?	**Waar kan ik afwassen/ kleren wassen?**	wār kan ik af-was-suhn/ klay-ruh was-suhn
Is there somewhere to dry clothes/ equipment?	**Kan ik ergens kleren/ kampeerspullen drogen?**	kan ik er-ruh-khuhns klay-ruh/kam-payr-spuh- luh drō-khuhn
My camping gas has run out	**Mijn butagas is op**	myn bü-tā-khas is op

The toilet is blocked	De WC is verstopt	duh way-say is vuhr-stopt
The shower doesn't work	De douche doet het niet	duh doosh doot uht neet
The washing space is flooded	De wasplaats staat blank	duh was-plāts stāt blank
May we light a fire?	Mogen we een vuur stoken?	mo-khuh wuh uhn vür stō-k'n
We are leaving today	We gaan vandaag weg	wuh khān van-dākh wekh
Please prepare our bill	Wilt u onze rekening opmaken?	wilt ü on-zuh ray-kuh-ning op-mā-k'n
How long do you want to stay?	*Hoe lang wilt u blijven?	hoo lang wilt ü bly-vuhn
What is your car registration number?	*Wat is het kenteken van uw auto?	wat is uht ken-tay-kuhn van üw ō-tō
I'm sorry, the camp site is full	*Het spijt me, de camping is vol	uht spyt muh, duh kem-ping is vol
No camping	Kamperen verboden	kam-pay-ruhn vuhr-bō-duhn

YOUTH HOSTELLING

How long is the walk to the youth hostel?	Hoe lang is het lopen naar de jeugdherberg?	hoo lang is uht lō-puh nār duh yœkht-her-be-ruhkh
Is there a youth hostel here?	Is er hier een jeugdherberg?	is uhr heer uhn yœkht-her-be-ruhkh
Have you a room/bed for the night?	Hebt u een kamer/bed voor vannacht?	hebt ü uhn kā-muhr/bet vōr van-nakht
How many days can we stay?	Hoeveel dagen kunnen we blijven?	hoo-vayl dā-khuhn kuhn-nuh wuh bly-vuhn
Here is my membership card	Hier is mijn lidmaatschaps-kaart	heer is myn lit-māt-skhaps-kārt
Do you serve meals?	Verzorgt u ook maaltijden?	vuhr-zor-ruhkht ü ōk māl-ty-duhn
Can I use the kitchen?	Mag ik de keuken gebruiken?	makh ik duh kœ-kuh khuh-brui-kuhn

Is there somewhere cheap to eat nearby?	**Is er een goedkope eet-gelegenheid in de buurt?**	is uhr uhn khoot-kō-puh ayt-khuh-lay-khuhn-hyt in duh bürt
I want to rent a sheet for my sleeping bag	**Ik wou een laken huren voor mijn slaapzak**	ik wow uhn lā-kuh hü-ruhn vōr muh slāp-zak

RENTING A HOUSE OR OWNING A PLACE

We have rented an apartment/villa/ bungalow	We hebben een appartement/ villa/ bungalow gehuurd	wuh he-buhn uhn a-par-tuh-ment/vee-lā/ buhn-ga-lō khuh-hürt
Here is our reservation	Hier is onze reservering	heer is on-zuh ray-ser-vay-ring
Please show us around	Kunt u ons rondleiden	kuhnt ü ons ront-ly-duhn
Is the cost of electricity/gas/gas cylinder/the maid included in the price?	Is electriciteit/ gas/butagas/de werkster in de prijs inbegrepen?	is ay-lek-tree-see-tyt/ khas/bü-tā-khas/duh we-rukh-stuhr in duh prys in-buh-khray-puhn

Where is the mains switch?	Waar is de hoofd-schakelaar?	wār is duh hōft-skhā-kuh-lār
the gas/water mains stopcock?	de hoofdkraan van het gas/water?	duh hōft-krān van uht khas/wā-t'r
the fuse box?	de stoppenkast?	duh sto-puhn-kast
Where is the light switch/power point?	Waar is het lichtknopje/stopcontact?	wār is uht likht-knop-yuh/stop-kon-takt
How does the heating/hot water work?	Hoe werkt de verwarming/het warme water?	hoo we-ruhkt duh vuhr-war-ming/uht wa-ruh-muh wā-t'r
Is there a spare gas cylinder?	Is er een reserve gasfles?	is uhr uhn ruh-ser-vuh khas-fles
Do gas cylinders get delivered?	Worden gasflessen bezorgd?	wor-duh khas-fles-suhn buh-zo-rukht
Please tell me how this works	Kunt u me uitleggen hoe dit werkt?	kuhnt ü muh uit-le-khuhn hoo dit we-ruhkt
Which day does the maid come?	Op welke dag komt de werkster?	op wel-kuh dakh komt duh we-ruhk-stuhr
For how long?	Hoe lang?	hoo lang?
Is there a fly-screen?	Is er een hor?	is uhr uhn hor
When is rubbish collected?	Wanneer wordt het vuil opgehaald?	wan-nayr wort uht vuil op-khuh-hālt

Where can we get logs for the fire?	Waar kunnen we brandhout krijgen?	wār kun-nuh wuh brant-howt kry-khuhn
Is there a barbecue?	Is er een barbecue?	is uhr uhn bār-buh-kyoo
Could I have another set of keys?	Mag ik nog een stel sleutels?	makh ik nokh uhn stel slœ-tuhls
We have replaced the broken ...	We hebben de/het kapotte ... vervangen	wuh he-buhn duh/uht ka-po-tuh ... vuhr-vang-uhn
Here is the bill	Hier is de rekening	heer is de ray-kuh-ning
Can I have my deposit back?	Mag ik mijn borgsom terug?	makh ik muh borkh-som truhkh

PROBLEMS

The drain/sink is blocked	De afvoer/gootsteen is verstopt	duh af-foor/khōt-stayn is vuhr-stopt
The toilet doesn't flush	De WC spoelt niet door	duh way-say spoolt neet dōr
There is no water	Er is geen water	d'r is khayn wā-t'r
We can't turn the tap off	We kunnen de kraan niet dichtkrijgen	wuh kuh-nuh duh krān neet dikht kry-khuhn
We can't turn the shower on	We kunnen de douche niet open krijgen	wuh kuh-nuh duh doosh neet ō-puh kry-khuhn

There is a leak	**Het lekt**	uht lekt
There is a window broken	**Er is een ruit kapot**	d'r is uhn ruit ka-pot
The shutters won't close	**De luiken gaan niet dicht**	duh lui-kuhn khān neet dikht
The window won't open	**Het raam gaat niet open**	uht rām khāt neet ō-puh
The electricity has gone off	**De electriciteit is uitgevallen**	duh ay-lek-tree-see-tyt is uit-khuh-val-luhn
The heating/ the cooker/the refrigerator/ the water heater doesn't work	**De verwarming/het fornuis/de koelkast/ de geyser doet het niet**	duh vuhr-war-ming/uht for-nuis/duh kool-kast/ duh khy-suhr doot uht neet
The lock is stuck	**Het slot zit vast**	uht slot zit vast
This is broken	**Dit is kapot**	dit is ka-pot
This needs repairing	**Dit moet gerepareerd worden**	dit moot khuh-ray-pa-rayrt wor-duhn
The apartment/villa has been burgled	**Er is ingebroken**	d'r is in-khuh-brō-kuhn

MEETING PEOPLE

How are you/things?	**Hoe maakt u het?/Hoe gaat het?**	hoo mākt ü uht/hoo khāt uht
Fine, thanks; and you?	**Goed, dank u; en u?**	khoot, dank ü; en ü
May I introduce myself?	**Mag ik mij even voorstellen?**	makh ik my ay-vuh vōr-stel-luhn
My name is ...	**Mijn naam is ...**	myn nām is
May I introduce ...	**Mag ik even voorstellen? Dit is ...**	makh ik ay-vuh vōr-stel-luhn? dit is
Have you met ...?	**Kent u ...?**	kent ü
Glad to meet you	**Hoe maakt u het?**	hoo mākt ü uht
Am I disturbing you?	**Stoor ik?**	stōr ik
Leave me alone	**Laat me met rust**	lāt muh met ruhst
Sorry to have troubled you	**Het spijt me als ik u lastig viel**	uht spyt muh als ik ü las-tuhkh veel

MAKING FRIENDS

Do you live/Are you staying here?	**Woont/Logeert u hier?**	wōnt/lō-zhayrt ü heer
We've been here a week	**Wij zijn hier al een week**	wy zyn heer al uhn wayk
Is this your first time here?	**Bent u hier voor het eerst?**	bent ü heer vōr uht ayrst
Do you like it here?	**Bevalt het u/je hier?**	buh-valt uht ü/yuh heer
Do you travel a lot?	**Reist u veel?**	ryst ü vayl
Are you on your own?	**Bent u/Ben je alleen?**	bent ü/ben yuh al-layn
I am with my husband/wife	**Ik ben met mijn man/vrouw**	ik ben met muhn man/vrow
my parents	**mijn ouders**	muhn ow-duhrs
my family	**mijn familie**	muhn fa-mee-lee
a (girl)friend	**een vriend(in)**	uhn vreent/vreen-din
I am travelling alone	**Ik reis alleen**	ik rys al-layn
Where do you come from?	**Waar komt u vandaan?**	wār komt ü van-dān
I come from ...	**Ik kom uit ...**	ik kom uit
What do you do?	**Wat voor werk doet u?**	wat vōr werk doot ü
What are you studying?	**Wat studeer je?**	wat stü-dayr yuh

I'm on holiday/a (business) trip	**Ik ben op vacantie/(zaken)reis**	ik ben op va-kan-tsee/(zā-kuh)-rys
Are you married?	**Bent u getrouwd?**	bent ü khuh-**trowt**
No, I am single	**Nee, ik ben vrijgezel/alleen**	nay, ik ben vry-khuh-zel/al-**layn**
Do you have children?	**Hebt u kinderen?**	hebt ü **kin**-duh-ruhn
Have you been to England/America?	**Bent u ooit in Engeland/Amerika geweest?**	bent ü ōeet in Eng-uh-lant/A-**may**-ree-kā khuh-**wayst**
I hope to see you again	**Hopelijk tot ziens**	hō-puh-luhk tot zeens
Give my regards to ...	**De groeten aan ...**	de khroo-t'n ān
Do you smoke?	**Rookt u/Rook je?**	rōkt ü/rōk yuh
No, I don't, thanks	**Nee, dank u/je wel**	nay, dank ü/yuh wel
Help yourself	**Helpt uzelf/Ga je gang**	hel-luhpt ü-zelf/khā yuh khang
Can I get you a drink?	**Wilt u iets drinken?**	wilt ü eets **dring**-k'n
I'd like a ..., please	**Graag een ...**	khrākh uhn

INVITATIONS

| Are you waiting for someone? | **Wacht u/je op iemand?** | wakht ü/yuh op **ee**-mant |
| Are you doing anything tonight/tomorrow afternoon? | **Doet u/Doe je iets vanavond/morgen middag?** | doot ü/doo yuh eets van-ā-vont/mor-khuhn mi-dakh |

Would you like to have lunch with me tomorrow?	Wilt u morgen met me lunchen?	wilt ü mor-khuhn met muh luhn-shuhn
Could we have a coffee/a drink somewhere?	Zullen we ergens koffie/een glaasje drinken?	zuhl-luh wuh er-ruh-khuhns kof-fee/uhn khlās-yuh dring-kuhn
Would you go out with me?	Kan ik u/je mee uit nemen?	kan ik ü/yuh may uit nay-muhn
I'm sorry, I can't come	Het spijt me, ik kan niet komen	uht spyt muh, ik kan neet kō-muhn
I'd love to come	Ik kom graag	ik kom khrākh
Shall we go to the cinema/theatre/beach?	Zullen we naar de bioscoop/een theater/ het strand gaan?	zuhl-luh wuh nār de bee-yos-kōp/uhn tay-yā-tuhr/uht strant khān
Would you like to go dancing or go for a drive?	Zullen we gaan dansen of een ritje maken?	zuhl-luh wuh khān dan-suh ov uhn ri-tyuh mā-kuh
Do you know a good disco/a good restaurant?	Weet u/je een goede disco/een goed restaurant?	wayt ü/yuh uhn khoo-yuh dis-kō/uhn khoot res-tō-ran
Can you come to dinner?	Kunt u komen eten?	kuhnt ü kō-muh ay-tuh
Could you come for a drink?	Komt u een borrel drinken?	komt ü uhn bo-ruhl dring-kuhn
Do you mind if I smoke?	Hebt u er bezwaar tegen als ik rook?	hebt ü uhr buh-zwār tay-khuhn als ik rōk

We're giving/There is a party; would you like to come?	We geven/Er is een feestje; hebt u/heb je zin om te komen?	wuh khay-vuhn/d'r is uhn fays-yuh; hebt ü/heb yuh zin om tuh kō-muhn
Can I bring a (girl) friend?	Mag ik een vriend(in) meebrengen?	makh ik uhn vreent/ vreen-**din** may-breng-uh
Thanks for the invitation	Bedankt voor de uitnodiging	buh-dankt vōr duh uit-nō-duh-khing
Where shall we meet?	Waar zullen we elkaar treffen?	wār zul-luh wuh muh-kār tref-fuhn
What time shall I/we come?	Hoe laat zal ik/zullen we komen?	hoo lāt zal ik/zul-luh wuh kō-muhn
I could pick you up at ...	Ik kan u/je om (*time*) bij (*place*) oppikken	ik kan ü/yuh om ... by ... op-pi-kuhn
Could you meet me at (*time*) near (*place*)?	Kunt u/Kun je me om ... bij ... ontmoeten?	kuhnt ü/kuhn yuh muh om ... by ... ont-**moo**-tuhn
What time do you have to be back?	Hoe laat moet u/je terug zijn?	hoo lāt moot ü/yuh truhkh zyn
May I see you home?	Kan ik u/je thuisbrengen?	kan ik ü/yuh tuis breng-uhn
Can we give you a lift?	Kunnen we u/je een lift geven?	kuhn-nuh wuh ü/yuh uhn lift khay-vuhn
Can I see you again?	Kunnen we elkaar weer zien?	kuhn-nuh wuh muh-kār wayr zeen

Where do you live?	**Waar woont u/Waar woon je?**	wār wōnt ü/wār wōn yuh
What is your telephone number?	**Wat is uw/je telefoonnummer?**	wat is üw/yuh tay-luh-fōn-nuhm-muhr
Do you live alone?	**Woont u/woon je alleen?**	wōnt ü/wōn yuh al-layn
Thanks for the pleasant evening/ drink/ride	**Bedankt voor de gezellige avond/ borrel/rit**	buh-**dankt** vor duh khuh-**zel**-luh-khuh ā-vont/**bo**-ruhl/rit
It was lovely	**Het was heel fijn**	uht was hayl fyn
Hope to see you again soon	**Ik hoop u/je gauw weer te zien**	ik hōp ü/yuh khow wayr tuh zeen
See you soon/ later/tomorrow	**Tot gauw/ straks/morgen**	tot khow/straks/**mor**-ruh-khuhn

GOING TO A RESTAURANT

Can you suggest a good/cheap/vegetarian restaurant?	**Kunt u me een goed/ goedkoop/ vegetarisch restaurant aanbevelen?**	kuhnt ü muh uhn khoot/khoot-kōp/vay-khuh-tā-rees res-tō-ran ān-buh-vay-luhn
I'd like to book a table for four at 1 o'clock	**Kan ik een tafel reserveren voor vier personen om één uur?**	kan ik uhn tā-fuhl ray-ser-vay-ruhn vōr veer per-sō-nuhn om ayn ür
I've reserved a table; my name is ...	**Ik heb een tafel gereserveerd; mijn naam is ...**	ik heb uhn tā-fuhl khuh-ray-ser-vayrt; myn nām is
We did not make a reservation	**We hebben niet gereserveerd**	wuh he-buh neet khuh-ray-ser-vayrt
Have you a table for three?	**Hebt u een tafel voor drie?**	hebt ü uhn tā-fuhl vōr dree

Is there a table on the terrace/by the window/in a corner?	**Is er een tafel op het terras/bij het raam/in een hoek?**	is uhr uhn tā-fuhl op uht tuh-**ras**/by uht rām/in uhn hook
You would have to wait about . . . minutes	***U zult een minuut of . . . moeten wachten**	ü zuhlt uhn mee-**nüt** ov . . . moo-tuh wakh-tuhn
We shall have a table free in half an hour	***Over een half uur hebben we een tafel voor u**	ō-vuhr uhn **hal**-luhf ür **heb**-buh wuh uhn tā-fuhl vōr ü
Is there a non-smoking area?	**Is er een gedeelte voor niet-rokers?**	is uhr uhn khuh-**dayl**-tuh vōr **neet**-rō-kuhrs
This way, please	***Deze kant op, alstublieft**	**day**-zuh kant op, als-tü-bleeft
We don't serve lunch until 12.30	***Wij zijn pas om half één open voor lunch**	wuh zyn pas om **hal**-luhf ayn ō-puh vōr lunsh
We don't serve dinner until 8 o'clock	***Wij zijn 's avonds pas om acht uur open**	wuh zyn sā-vonts pas om akht ür ō-puh
Sorry the kitchen is closed	***Het spijt me, de keuken is gesloten**	uht spyt muh, duh koe-kuh is khuh-**slō**-tuhn
Where is the cloakroom/toilet?	**Waar is de garderobe/het toilet?**	wār is duh **khar**-duh-ro-buh/uht twa-**let**
It is downstairs/upstairs	***Beneden/boven**	buh-**nay**-duh/bō-vuh

ORDERING

Service charge	*Bediening(sgeld)	buh-**dee**-ning(s-khelt)
Service and V.A.T. (not) included	*Bediening en B.T.W. (niet) inbegrepen	buh-**dee**-ning en bay-tay-way (neet) in-buh-khray-puhn
Cover charge	*Bestek	buh-**stek**
Waiter/Waitress *to call*	Ober/Juffrouw	ō-buhr/yuhf-frow
May I see the menu/the wine list, please?	Mag ik het menu/de wijnkaart zien, alstublieft?	makh ik uht muh-**nü**/duh wyn-kārt zeen, als-tü-bleeft
Is there a set menu for lunch?	Hebt u een dagkaart?	hebt ü uhn **dakh**-kārt
I want something light	Ik wil graag iets lichts	ik wil khrākh eets likhts
Do you have children's helpings?	Hebt u ook kinderporties?	hebt ü ōk **kin**-duhr-por-sees
What is your dish of the day?	Wat is de dagschotel?	wat is duh **dakh**-skhō-t'l
We are in a hurry	We hebben haast	wuh **heb**-buh hāst
Do you serve snacks?	Hebt u iets dat vlug klaar is?	hebt ü eets dat vluhkh klār is
Do you have any vegetarian dishes?	Hebt u ook vegetarische schotels?	hebt ü ōk vay-khuh-tā-ree-suh **skhō**-t'ls

What do you recommend?	**Wat kunt u aanbevelen?**	wat kuhnt ü ān-buh-vay-luh
Can you tell me what this is?	**Kunt u me zeggen wat dit is?**	kunt ü muh zekh-khuh wat dit is
What are the specialities of this restaurant?	**Wat zijn de specialiteiten van dit restaurant?**	wat zyn duh spay-see-yā-lee-ty-tuhn van dit res-tō-ran
You might like to try ...	***Probeert u ... eens**	pro-bayrt ü ... uhs
There's no more ...	***Er is/zijn geen ... meer**	d'r is/zyn khayn ... mayr
I'd like ...	**Ik wil graag ...**	ik wil khrāk
Is it hot or cold?	**Is dat warm of koud?**	is dat warm ov kowt

COMPLAINTS

Where are our drinks?	**Waar blijft ons bier/onze wijn?**	wār blyft ons beer/on-zuh wyn
Why is the food taking so long?	**Waarom laat het eten zo lang op zich wachten?**	wār-om lāt uht ay-tuhn zo lang op zikh wakh-tuhn
That isn't what I ordered	**Dit heb ik niet besteld**	dit heb ik neet buh-stelt
I asked for ...	**Ik heb om ... gevraagd**	ik heb om ... khuh-vrākht
This isn't fresh	**Dit is niet vers**	dit is neet vers

This is bad/stale	**Dit is bedorven/oud**	dit is buh-**dor**-ruh-vuhn/owt
This is undercooked/overcooked	**Dit is niet gaar/te gaar**	dit is neet khār/tuh khār
This is too cold/salty	**Dit is te koud/zout**	dit is tuh kowt/zowt
This plate/knife/glass is not clean	**Dit bord/mes/glas is niet schoon**	dit bort/mes/khlas is neet skhōn
This fork/spoon is dirty	**Deze vork/lepel is vuil**	day-zuh vo-ruhk/lay-p'l is vuil
I'd like to see the headwaiter	**Ik wil de chef/gerant spreken**	ik wil duh shef/zhay-rant spray-k'n

PAYING

The bill, please	**De rekening, alstublieft**	duh ray-kuh-ning, als-tü-bleeft
Does it include service?	**Is bediening inbegrepen?**	is buh-**dee**-ning in-buh-khray-puhn
Please check the bill – I don't think it's correct	**Wilt u de rekening even nakijken, hij klopt niet, geloof ik**	wilt ü duh ray-kuh-ning nā-ky-k'n; hy klopt neet, khlōf ik
What is this amount for?	**Waar is dit bedrag voor?**	wār is dit buh-**drakh** vōr
I didn't have soup	**Ik heb geen soep gehad**	ik heb khayn soop khuh-hat

I had chicken, not steak	**ik had kip, geen biefstuk**	ik hat kip, khayn beef-stuhk
May we have separate bills?	**Mogen we aparte rekeningen, alstublieft?**	mō-khuh wuh a-par-tuh ray-kuh-ning-uhn, als-tü-bleeft
Do you take credit cards/travellers' cheques?	**Accepteert u credit cards/reischeques?**	ak-sep-tayrt ü kre-dit kārts/rys-sheks
Keep the change	**Laat maar/Zo is het goed**	lāt mār/zō is uht khoot
It was very good	**Dat was erg goed**	dat was e-ruhkh khoot
We enjoyed it, thank you	**We hebben er van genoten, dank u wel**	wuh he-buhn uhr van khuh-nō-tuhn, dank ü wel

BREAKFAST[1] AND TEA

Breakfast	**Ontbijt**	ont-byt
What time is breakfast served?	**Hoe laat is ontbijt?**	hoo lāt is ont-byt
Help yourself at the buffet	**Het is zelfbediening**	uht is zelf-buh-dee-ning

1. Dutch breakfast usually includes several kinds of bread and egg-rusk (**beschuit**), and a selection of cheese and cold meats as well as butter, jam, and coffee or tea. It is a much more elaborate affair than the average 'continental breakfast'.

A large white coffee, please	**Koffie met melk, alstublieft**	kof-fee met **mel**-luhk, als-tü-bleeft
A black coffee	**Een zwarte koffie**	uhn zwar-tuh kof-fee
I would like decaffeinated coffee	**I wou graag caffeïnevrije koffie**	ik wow khrākh kaf-fay-ee-nuh-vry-yuh kof-fee
A cup/pot of tea, please	**Een kop/potje thee, alstublieft**	uhn kop/pot-yuh tay, als-tü-bleeft
I would like a herb tea	**Ik wil graag een kruiden-thee**	ik wil khrākh uhn krui-duhn-tay
May we have some sugar?	**Mogen we een beetje suiker?**	mō-khuh wuh uhn bay-tyuh sui-kuhr
Do you have artificial sweeteners?	**Hebt u zoetjes?**	hebt ü **zoot**-yuhs
Hot/cold milk	**Hete/koude melk**	hay-tuh/kow-uh **mel**-luhk
I'd like tea with milk/lemon	**Thee met melk/citroen, graag**	tay met **mel**-luhk/see-troon, khrākn
A roll and butter	**Een broodje met boter**	uhn brōt-yuh met bō-t'r
We'd like more butter, please	**Nog wat boter, alstublieft**	nokh wat bō-t'r, als-tü-bleeft
Have you some jam/marmalade?	**Hebt u jam/marmelade?**	hebt ü zyem/mar-muh-lā-duh
I would like a hard-boiled/soft-boiled egg	**Mag ik een hard/zacht gekookt eitje?**	makh ik uhn hart/zakht khuh-kōkt y-tyuh

What fruit juices do you have?	**Wat voor vruchtensap hebt u?**	wat vōr **vrukh-tuh-sap** hebt ü
Orange/grapefruit/ tomato juice	**Sinaasappel/ grapefruit/ tomaten sap**	**see-nas-a-puhl/krayp-froot**/tō-mā-tuh sap
Is there any fresh fruit?	**Is er ook vers fruit?**	is uhr ōk vers fruit
White/brown/ wholemeal bread	**Wit/bruin/volkoren brood**	wit/bruin/vol-kō-ruhn brōt
Pumpernickel, dark rye bread	**Roggebrood**	ro-khuh-brōt
Honey cake	**Ontbijtkoek**	ont-byt-kook
Cheese[1]	**Kaas**	kās
Chocolate vermicelli	**Hagelslag**	hā-khuhl-slakh
Drinking chocolate	**Chocolade(melk)**	shō-kō-lā-duh(-mel-luhk)
Yoghurt	**Yoghurt**	yo-khuhrt
Honey	**Honing**	hō-ning
Pastry[2]	**Gebak**	khuh-bak
Peanut butter	**Pindakaas**	pin-dā kās

1. Dutch cheese comes in four main varieties: **Gouda** and **Maaslander** are both round and flat; **Edam** is spherical and often red-coated; **Leiden** has cumin seeds and **Boeren-Leidse** is spiced more subtly. All Dutch cheeses are sold in at least three age-groups (which make a remarkable difference to texture and taste): **jong, belegen** and **oud**, meaning young, mature and old. Processed cheese is often called **korstloze kaas** (rindless cheese) and cheese spread is **smeerkaas**.
2. For names of cakes and pastry, see pp. 107-8.

Porridge	**Havermout**	hā-vuhr-mowt
Egg rusk	**Beschuit**	buh-**skhuit**
(Apple)syrup	**(Appel)stroop**	(a-puhl)-strōp

SNACKS AND PICNICS

Can I have a ... sandwich, please?	**Een broodje met ... alstublief** (*see list, pp.* 94–5)	uhn brō-tyuh met ... als-tü-bleeft
What are those things over there?	**Wat zijn dat voor dingen?**	wat zyn dat vōr **ding-**uhn
What is in them?	**Wat zit er in?**	wat zit uhr in
I'll have one of these, please	**Een van deze, alstublieft**	ayn van **day-**zuh, als-tü-bleeft
It's to take away	**Om mee te nemen**	om may tuh **nay-**muh
Almond bun	**Amandelbroodje**	a-**man-**duhl-brō-tyuh
Beefburger	**Hamburger**	**ham-**buhr-khuhr
Biscuits	**Biscuit/Koekjes**	buhs-**kwee**/**kook-**yuhs
Bread	**Brood**	brōt
Butter	**Boter**	**bō-**t'r
Cheese	**Kaas**	kās
Chips	**Patates (frites)/ Patat/Friet(en)**	puh-**tat** (freet)/(puh-tat/freet-(uh)
Chocolate bar	**Chocoladereep**	shō-kō-lā-duh-rayp

Cold cuts	**Koud vlees**	kowt vlays
Crisps	**Chips**	tsyips
Egg(s)	**Ei(eren)**	y-(yuh-ruh)
French bread	**Stokbrood**	stok-brōt
Ham	**Ham**	ham
Ice-cream	**Ijs**	ys
Pancakes (plain/with jam/apple/preserved ginger/thick bacon)	**Pannekoeken (naturel/ confiture/appel/ gember/spek)**	pan-nuh-koo-kuhn (na-tü-**rel**/ kon-fee-**tür**/a-puhl/ **khem**-buhr/spek)
Dollar pancakes	**Poffertjes**	pof-fuhr-tyuhs
Pastries	**Gebak**	khuh-bak
Pickles	**Zuur**	zür
Roast chicken	**Gebraden kip**	khuh-bra-duh kip
Roll (with)	**Broodje[1] (met)**	brō-tyuh (met)
deep-fried croquette (with fillings of meat/cheese/ shrimps/fish)	**croquet (vlees/kaas/ garnalen/vis)**	krō-ket (vlays/kās/khar-nā-luh/vis)
roast pork	**fricandeau**	free-kan-dō
(cold) meat ball	**gehakt**	khuh-hakt

---

1. The sandwich-shop (**broodjeswinkel**), which sells a large variety of fresh rolls with generous helpings of cooked meats and sausages, is a great favourite for lunchtime eating. They also sell soup, coffee and soft drinks, no alcoholic beverages. Gradually the rolls are being replaced with **stokbrood** (French bread).

smoked sausage	**gelderse worst**	khel-duhr-suh worst
salt beef and larded cooked liver	**halfom**	hal-luhf-om
boiled larded liver	**lever**	lay-vuhr
liver sausage	**leverworst**	lay-vuhr-worst
soft white cheese	**meikaas**	my-kās
smoked eel	**paling**	pā-ling
salt beef/silverside	**pekelvlees**	pay-kuhl-vlays
raw minced steak with/without chopped onion	**tartaar met/zonder uitjes**	tar-tār met/zon-duhr ui-tyuhs
hot sausage	**warme worst**	war-ruh-muh worst
Salad	**Sla**	slā
Sausage	**Worst**	worst
Sausage roll	**Saucijzebroodje**	sō-sy-zuh-brō-tyuh
Snack	**Hapje**	hap-yuh
Snack bar	**Snack bar**	snek bār
Soft drink	**Frisdrank**	fris-drank
Soup	**Soep**	soop
Tomato	**Tomaat**	tō-māt
Waffles	**Wafels**	wā-fuhls

DRINKS[1]

Pub	Café[2]	ka-fay
What will you have to drink?	Wat wilt u drinken?	wat wilt ü dring-kuhn
Do you serve wine by the glass?	Hebt u open wijn/schenkwijn?	hebt ü ō-puh wyn/skhenk-wyn
Carafe/glass	Karaf/glas	ka-raf/khlas
Bottle/half bottle	Fles/halve fles	fles/**hal**-luh-vuh fles
Two glasses of lager/dark ale	Twee glazen pils/donker bier	tway khlā-zuh pils/**dong**-kuhr beer
Large/small beer	Grote/kleine pils	khrō-tuh/**kly**-nuh pils
Two more beers	Nog twee pils	nokh tway pils
Do you serve cocktails?	Hebt u ook cocktails?	hebt ü ōk kok-tayls
An aged/young Dutch gin	Een oude/jonge (jenever)	uhn ow-wuh/yong-uh (yuh-**nay**-vuhr)
Neat	Puur/zonder iets	pür/**zon**-duhr eets
On the rocks	Met ijs	met ys
With (soda) water	Met (soda) water	met (sō-dā) wā-t'r

1. For the names of beverages see pp. 109–110.
2. The Dutch café is both pub and coffee house; opening times are anything between 10.00 and midnight (market areas open earlier, the bigger towns often close later on Saturdays).

Mineral water (with/without gas)	Mineraal water (wel/ niet mousserend)	mee-nuh-rāl-wā-t'r (wel/neet moo-say-ruhnt)
Cheers!	Proost!	prōst
Your very good health!	Op uw/je gezondheid!	op üw/yuh khuh-zont-hyt
Small deep-fried meat croquettes	Bitterballen	bi-tuhr-bal-luhn
Selection of bar snacks	Bittergarnituur	bi-tuhr-khar-nee-tür
I'd like a soft drink	Ik wou graag een frisdrank	ik wow khrāhk uhn fris-drank
Fruit/apple/orange juice	Vruchten/appel/ sinaasappel sap	vruhkh-tuh/a-puhl/see-nas-a-puhl sap
A milk shake	Een milk shake	uhn mil-luhk shayk
Hot chocolate	Warme chocola	war-muh shō-kō-lā
Indian tea/China tea	Thee/Chinese thee	tay/shee-nay-suh tay
Iced tea	Ijsthee	ys-tay
Tea with milk/lemon	Thee met melk/citroen	tay met mel-luhk/see-troon
I'd like a glass of water, please	Mag ik een glas water, alstublieft?	makh ik uhn khlas wā-t'r, als-tü-bleeft
The same again, please	Nog eens, alstublieft	nokh uhs, als-tü-bleeft
Three black coffees and one with milk/cream	Drie zwarte koffie en één met melk/room	dree zwar-tuh kof-fee en ayn met mel-luhk/rōm

Warm milk with a little coffee	**Koffie verkeerd**	kof-fee vuhr-kayrt
May we have an ashtray?	**Hebt u een asbak voor ons?**	hebt ü uhn **as**-bak vōr ons

RESTAURANT VOCABULARY

artificial sweeteners	**zoetjes**	zoo-tyuhs
ashtray	**asbak**	as-bak
bill	**rekening**	ray-kuh-ning
bowl	**kom**	kom
bread	**brood** (*n*)	brōt
butter	**boter**	bō-t'r
cigarettes	**sigaretten**	see-khā-re-tuhn
cloakroom	**garderobe**	khar-duh-rō-buh
course *dish*	**gang**	khang
cream/whipped cream	**room/slagroom**	rōm/slakh-rōm
cup	**kop**	kop
fork	**vork**	vo-ruhk
glass	**glas** (*n*)	khlas
hungry (to be)	**honger hebben**	hong-uhr he-buhn
knife	**mes** (*n*)	mes
matches	**lucifers**	lü-see-fers
menu	**menu** (*n*)	muh-nü
mustard	**mosterd**	mos-tuhrt
napkin	**servet**	ser-vet
oil	**olie**	ō-lee
pepper	**peper**	pay-puhr

plate	**bord** (*n*)	bort
salt	**zout** (*n*)	zowt
sauce	**saus**	sows
saucer	**schotel**	skhō-t'l
service	**bediening**	buh-**dee**-ning
spoon	**lepel**	lay-p'l
table	**tafel**	tā-fuhl
tablecloth	**tafellaken** (*n*)	tā-fuhl-lā-kuhn
terrace	**terras** (*n*)	tuh-ras
thirsty (to be)	**dorst hebben**	dorst he-buhn
tip	**fooi**	fōee
toothpick	**tandenstoker**	tan-duh-stō-kuhr
vegetarian	**vegetarisch**	vay-khuh-tā-rees
vinegar	**azijn**	a-zyn
waiter	**kelner**	kel-nuhr
waiter *to call*	**ober**	ō-buhr
waitress	**dienster**	deen-stuhr
waitress *to call*	**juffrouw**	yuhf-frow
water	**water** (*n*)	wā-t'r

THE MENU

VOORGERECHTEN

champignons (op toast)	fried mushrooms (on toast)
garnalen/krab/kreeften cocktail	shrimp/crab/lobster cocktail
gerookte paling/zalm/forel	smoked eel/salmon/trout
haringsla	herring fillet with apple and potato salad, hard-boiled egg, pickled onions and mayonnaise
huzarensalade	salad of cold meat, apple, potato and hard-boiled egg
kalfs(vlees) pasteitje	vol-au-vent with veal ragoût
(gemengd) koud vlees	cold meat platter
oesters	oysters
russische eieren	hard-boiled eggs with anchovy, capers and mayonnaise
zalmschelp	tinned salmon in mayonnaise with chopped carrots, aspic, peas

SOEP

aspergesoep	asparagus
bouillon	stock/broth
champignonsoep	mushroom
erwtensoep met worst/kluif	green pea with smoked sausage/meat
gebonden soep	thick or cream soup
groentesoep	vegetable
heldere soep	clear soup
juliennesoep	vegetable
kippesoep	chicken broth
koninginnesoep	chicken soup bound with egg yolk and cream
ossestaartsoep	oxtail
schildpadsoep	turtle
soep van de dag	soup of the day
tomatensoep	tomato
vermicellisoep	chicken broth with vermicelli

VIS

baars	bass (usually freshwater)
bokking	bloater
(tar)bot	turbot
forel	trout
garnalen	shrimps/prawns

nieuwe/zoute haring	raw/salted herring
kabeljauw	cod
karper	carp
koolvis	coley
kreeft	lobster
makreel	mackerel
mosselen	mussels
paling	eel
schar	flounder
schelvis	haddock
schol	plaice
snoek	pike
spiering	whitebait
tong	sole
wijting	whiting
zalm	salmon

VLEES (GERECHTEN)

biefstuk (hollandse)	steak
(duitse)	hamburger
blinde vinken	escalopes stuffed with minced meat
bloedworst	black pudding
fricandeau	knuckle or leg cut
gehakt	minced meat
gehaktballen	meatballs
haché	chopped meat cooked with onions and flour in stock and vinegar
hersenen	brains

hoofdkaas	brawn
jachtschotel	mash of meat, potato, onions, apple, cooked in the oven
kalfsbiefstuk	veal steak
kalfslapje	fillet of veal
kalfsoesters	eye of the veal fillet
kalfsvlees	veal
karbonade	chop
klapstuk	flank
kotelet	cutlet
lam(svlees)	lamb
lende	loin
lever	liver
nieren	kidneys
ossehaas	fillet of beef
riblap	cut from the loin
rollade	rolled roast
rookworst	smoked sausage/boiling ring
runderlap	rump steak
spek	fat kind of bacon
(osse) tong	(ox) tongue
varkenskarbonade	pork chop/cutlet
varkenshaas	pork fillet
varkensvlees	pork

WILD EN GEVOGELTE

eend	duck
fazant	pheasant

gans	goose
haan	cock
haas	hare
hazepeper	jugged hare
kalkoen	turkey
kip	chicken
(duin) konijn	(wild) rabbit
patrijs	partridge
piepkuiken	spring chicken
ree bout/rug	venison steak/saddle

GROENTE EN SALADE

aardappelen	potatoes
andijvie	a sort of endive
augurk	gherkin
biet	beetroot
bloemkool	cauliflower
boerenkool	curly kale
bruine/witte bonen	brown/white beans
cantharellen	chanterelle (a sort of mushroom)
capucijners	brown peas
champignons	mushrooms
doperwten	petits pois
erwten	green peas
(patates) frites	chips
hete bliksem	mash of potatoes and small red cooking apples

hutspot	mash of potato, carrot and onion
knoflook	garlic
komkommer	cucumber
groene/rode/witte/spits kool	green/red/white/Chinese cabbage
(brussels) lof	chicory
noedels	noodles
peterselie	parsley
peultjes	sugar peas, mange-tout
peulvruchten	any beans or peas
prei	leek
radijs	radish
rijst	rice
schorseneren	salsify
bleek/knol/blad selderij	celery/celeriac/celery herb
sla	lettuce
slabonen	French beans
snijbonen	runner beans
sperciebonen	French/green beans
spinazie	spinach
spruitjes	(Brussels) sprouts
stamppot	any mash of potato and a vegetable
stoofsla	lettuce (cooked in butter or water)
tomaten	tomatoes
tuinbonen	broad beans
uien	onions
venkel	fennel
wortelen	carrots
zuurkool	sauerkraut

EIEREN

gebakken	fried
gekookt	boiled
hard/zacht	hard/soft
gepocheerd	poached
omelet	omelette
boerenomelet	Spanish omelette
omelet champignons	mushrooms
ham	ham
kaas	cheese
naturel	plain
roer-ei(eren)	scrambled eggs
uitsmijter ham	ham and eggs (usually two fried eggs on a large slice of ham, with pickles)
ros	roast beef and eggs
spek	bacon and eggs
zak-ei	poached egg

NAGERECHTEN

appelbeignets	apple fritters
drie in de pan	small pancakes
flensjes	thin pancakes/crêpes
kaas	cheese
pannekoeken	pancakes

boerepannekoek	pancake with onion, bacon, sometimes vegetables
spekpannekoek	pancake with fat bacon cooked in it
poffertjes	a kind of dollar pancakes served with butter and powdered sugar
griesmeel/chocolade pudding	semolina/chocolate milk pudding (cold, set in form)
(slag)room	(whipped) cream
vla	milk pudding
vruchtensla	fruit salad
wafels	waffles
wentelteefjes	French toast

GEBAK

amandelbroodje	almond bun
appelbol	apple cake
appelgebak	strudel
beignet	fritter
boterkoek	a sort of shortbread
gemberkoek	ginger cake
gevulde koek	round cake with ground-almond filling
koekjes	biscuits
krentenbol/brood	raisin bun/loaf
mokkapunt	mocca-flavoured cream cake
roomhoren/soes	cream-filled horn/bun
roomtaart	cream cake
tompoes	mille-feuille

vlaai	shallow open fruit pastry
vruchtengebak	fruit tart
ijstaart	ice-cream gâteau

FRUIT EN NOTEN

aardbei	strawberry
abrikoos	apricot
amandelen	almonds
ananas	pineapple
appel	apple
banaan	banana
rode/witte/zwarte bessen	red/white/black currants
bosbessen	blueberries
bramen	blackberries
citroen	lemon
dadel	date
druif	grape
framboos	raspberry
gember	ginger
hazelnoot	hazelnut
kastanje	chestnut
kers	cherry
kokosnoot	coconut
krent	currant
kruisbes	gooseberry
mandarijn	tangerine
morel	morello cherry
peer	pear

perzik	peach
pinda	peanut
pruim	plum/prune
rabarber	rhubarb
Reine-Claude	greengage
rozijn	raisin
sinaasappel	orange
vijg	fig
vossebes	cranberry
walnoten	walnuts

DRANKEN

bier[1]	beer
flesje/blikje	bottle/can
(van de) tap	draught
donker (bier)	dark beer, like brown ale
boerenjongens	raisins in 'brandewijn'
borrel	generic term for a drink, but most commonly referring to 'jenever'
brandewijn	clear spirit
chocola(demelk)	hot cocoa
citroenjenever	gin flavoured with lemon
cognac	brandy
frisdranken	non-alcoholic beverages, soft drinks

1. Dutch beer is different from the more common varieties of English beer. The basic kind is pils, known in England as lager; donker (bier) comes close to brown ale; oud bruin is darker and bokbier is very dark and quite sweet. Stouts can now be had in many places too.

oude/jonge jenever	mature/young grain spirit, commonly known as 'Dutch gin' but to be drunk strictly on its own, never mixed in a long drink
karnemelk	buttermilk
koffie	coffee (with milk)
zwarte koffie	black coffee
koffie met (slag) room	coffee with (whipped) cream
limonade	generic term for fruit squash
melk	milk
met ijs	with ice/on the rocks
zonder iets/puur	neat
mineraalwater	mineral water
pils	lager
sap	juice
appel/druiven/grapefruit/ sinaasappel/tomaten sap	apple/grape/grapefruit/orange/ tomato juice
spiritualiën	alcoholic beverages
thee met citroen/melk	tea with lemon/milk
Chinese/kamillen/lindebloesem/ munt thee	China/camomile/lime/ mint tea
vruchtensap	fruit juice
warme dranken	hot drinks
water	water
wijn	wine
wit/rood/rosé	white/red/rosé
droog/zoet	dry/sweet
bitterballen	deep-fried ragoût balls
kaasstokjes	cheese-flavoured biscuits
zoutjes	salt biscuits

RIJSTTAFEL[1]

ajam	chicken
asam	tamarind
asin	salty
atjar	pickle
babi	pork
ba(h)mi	noodles with meat or chicken and vegetables
bawang	onion
bumbu	spices
dadar	omelet
daging	beef
dendeng	spiced dried meat
djahé	ginger
djintan	cumin
gado gado	vegetables in a thin peanut sauce
garam	salt
goreng	fried
(h)ati	liver
ikan	fish
katjang	peanut
katjang idjo	green mung beans
kemiri	(macadamia) nut
kering	dried
ketan	sticky rice

1. 'Rice table', an enormous Indonesian feast of 12 to 25 separate small dishes (all served at once) eaten with plain boiled rice; jasmin or other Chinese tea goes well with it, so does lager.

ketimun	cucumber
ketjap	soy sauce
ketumbar	coriander
klappa/klapper	coconut
krupuk (udang)	(prawn) crackers
laos	a gingery root (galangel)
lumpia	spring roll
manis	sweet
mi(e)	Chinese noodles
nasi	(boiled) rice
nasi djawa	'Javanese rice', a miniature 'rijsttafel'
nasi goreng	fried rice with meat or chicken and vegetables
nasi kuning	'yellow rice', another miniature 'rijsttafel'
nasi rames	one-plate 'rijsttafel'
panggang	roast
pedis	hot/very spicy
petis	shrimp or fish paste (condiment)
pisang	banana
sajur	a vegetable 'soup' which is the base of many other dishes
sambal	a condiment made of hot red peppers – the straight crushed kind is red and known as oelek (oo-lek); others are mixed with a variety of fried spices, nuts and onions: the most common ones are badjak (bat-yak), kemiri (kuh-mee-ree), manis (ma-nis) and trassi (tras-see)

santen	creamed coconut
saté	meat grilled on small skewers (as kebab)
semur	stewed
serundeng	shredded coconut, spiced and fried
taogé	bean sprouts
telur	egg
terasi/trassi	pungent paste of sun-dried shrimp
udang	shrimp, prawn

SOME COOKING METHODS AND SAUCES

blauw gekookt	au bleu
(in de oven) gebakken	baked
gekookt	boiled
gesmoord	braised
gedroogd	dried
(in diep vet) gebakken	(deep) fried
geraspt	grated
gegrilld	grilled
gemarineerd	marinated
vlees – rood	meat – rare
half doorbakken	medium
doorbakken	well-done
gemarineerd/ingelegd	pickled (fish/vegetable)
gepocheerd	poached

puree van ...	puréed/creamed ...
rauw	raw
gebraden	roast
gerookt	smoked
gestoomd	steamed
gestoofd	stewed
gevuld	stuffed
in gelei	in aspic
warm/koud	hot/cold
zure saus	white sauce with egg and vinegar
roomsaus	plain white sauce made with cream
hollandse saus	butter-and-egg sauce
mousseline	extra rich 'hollandse saus'

SHOPPING[1] & SERVICES

WHERE TO GO

Which is the best ...?	**Wat is de/het beste ...?**	wat is duh/uht bes-tuh
Where is the market?	**Waar is de markt?**	wār is duh ma-ruhkt
Is there a market every day?	**Is er iedere dag markt?**	is uhr ee-duh-ruh dakh ma-ruhkt
Where's the nearest ...?	**Is hier ergens een ...?**	is heer e-ruh-khuhns uhn
Can you recommend a good ...?	**Weet u misschien een goede ...?**	wayt ü muh-skheen uhn khoo-yuh
Where can I buy ...?	**Waar kan ik ... kopen?**	wār kan ik ... kō-p'n

1. Shops are usually open Monday to Saturday 9.00–18.00; in small towns they may close for lunch 13.00–14.00. Each town has a half-day early closing which varies from place to place. Most towns have one late-night shopping day each week.

| When do the shops open/close?[1] | Hoe laat gaan de winkels open/dicht? | hoo lāt khān duh wing-kuhls ō-puh/dikht |

SHOPS AND SERVICES

Antique shop	Antiekwinkel	an-teek-wing-kuhl
Antiques fair (country)	Braderie	brā-duh-ree
Baker	(Warme) bakker	(wa-ruh-muh) ba-kuhr
Bank	Bank	bank
Barber (see p. 134)	(Heren)kapper	(hay-ruh)-ka-puhr
Bookshop (see p. 140)	Boekhandel	book-han-duhl
Builder	Aannemer	ān-nay-muhr
Butcher (see p. 132)	Slager	slā-khuhr
Cake shop (see p. 107)	Banketbakker	ban-ket-ba-kuhr
Camera shop (see p. 143)	Fotohandel	fō-tō-han-duhl
Camping equipment	Kampeeruitrusting	kam-payr-uit-ruhs-ting
Chemist[1] (see p. 126)	Apotheek/Drogist	a-pō-tayk/drō-khist
Confectioner (see p. 107)	Banketbakker	ban-ket-ba-kuhr
Dairy	Melkhandel	mel-luhk-han-duhl
Decorator	Behanger	buh-hang-uhr

1. A **drogist** sells toilet goods, etc.; an **apotheek** is usually a dispensing chemist only.

Dentist (see p. 192)	**Tandarts**	tant-arts
Department store (see p. 119 and 129)	**Warenhuis**	wā-ruhn-huis
Doctor (see p. 181)	**Dokter**	dok-t'r
Dry cleaner (see p. 138)	**Chemische wasserij/Stomerij**	khay-mee-suh was-suh-ry/stō-muh-ry
Electrician	**Electricien**	ay-lek-tree-shen
Electrical appliances	**Huishoudelijke apparaten**	huis-how-duh-luh-kuh a-pa-rā-tuhn
Fishmonger (see p. 133)	**Vishandel**	vis-han-duhl
Flea market	**Vlooienmarkt**	vlō-yuh-ma-ruhkt
Florist	**Bloemenwinkel**	bloo-muh-wing-kuhl
Greengrocer (see p. 133)	**Groentewinkel**	khroon-tuh-wing-kuhl
Grocer (see p. 132)	**Kruidenier**	krui-duh-neer
Hairdresser (see p. 134)	**(Dames)kapper**	(dā-muhs)-ka-puhr
Hardware store/ Ironmonger (see p. 136)	**Ijzerhandel**	y-zuhr-han-duhl
Jeweller	**Juwelier**	yü-wuh-leer
Launderette	**Wasserette**	was-suh-ret
Laundry (see p. 138)	**Wasserij**	was-suh-ry
Liquor store (see p. 109)	**Wijnhandel**	wyn-han-duhl
Market	**Markt**	ma-ruhkt
Newsagent (see p. 140)	**Krantenwinkel**	kran-tuh-wing-kuhl
Notary	**Notaris**	nō-tā-ruhs

Optician (see p. 142)	**Opticien**	op-tee-shen
Photographer	**Fotograaf**	fō-tō-khrāf
Plumber	**Loodgieter**	lōt-khee-t'r
Police (station)	**Politie (bureau)**	pō-lee-tsee (bü-rō)
Post office (see p. 149)	**Postkantoor**	pos-kan-tōr
Shoemaker	**Schoenmaker**	skhoo-mā-kuhr
Shoe shop (see p. 130)	**Schoenenwinkel**	skhoo-nuh-wing-kuhl
Sports shop	**Sporthuis**	sport-huis
Stationer	**Kantoorboekhandel**	kan-tōr-book-han-duhl
Supermarket	**Supermarkt**	sü-puhr-ma-ruhkt
Sweet shop	**Snoepwinkel**	snoop-wing-kuhl
Tobacconist (see p. 146)	**Sigarenwinkel**	see-khā-ruh-wing-kuhl
Toy shop	**Speelgoedwinkel**	spayl-khoot-wing-kuhl
Travel agent	**Reisbureau**	rys-bü-rō
Wine merchant	**Wijnhandel**	wyn-han-duhl

IN THE SHOP

Self service	*Zelfbediening	zel-luhf-buh-dee-ning
Sale (clearance)	*Opruiming/ Uitverkoop	op-rui-ming/uit-vuhr-kōp
Cash desk	*Kassa	kas-sā
Shop assistant	Verkoper/ Verkoopster	vuhr-kō-puhr/ vuhr-kōp-stuhr
Manager	Chef	shef
Can I help you?	*Kan ik u helpen/Wat mag het zijn?	kan ik ü hel-p'n/wat makh uht zyn
I want to buy ...	Ik zoek ...	ik zook
Do you sell ...?	Hebt u ...?/Verkoopt u ...?	hebt ü/vuhr-kōpt ü
I just want to look around	Ik kijk alleen maar	ik kyk al-layn mār
I don't want to buy anything now	Ik zoek niets bepaalds op het ogenblik	ik zook neets buh-pālts op uht ō-khuhn-blik
Could you show me ...?	Kunt u me ... laten zien?	kuhnt ü muh ... lā-t'n zeen
We do not have that	*Dat hebben we niet	dat he-buh wuh neet
You'll find them at that counter	*Die vindt u aan die toonbank	dee vint ü ān dee tōn-bank

We've sold out	*Op het moment hebben we dat niet	op uht mō-**ment** he-buh wuh dat neet
We'll have more tomorrow/next week	*We krijgen het morgen/volgende week weer	wuh kry-khuhn uht mo-ruh-khuh/vol-luh-khuhn-duh wayk wayr
I (don't) like this	Dit bevalt me (niet)	dit buh-valt muh (neet)
I'll have this	Ik neem dit	ik naym dit
Anything else?	*Anders nog iets?	an-duhrs nokh eets
That will be all	Dat is alles	dat is al-luhs
Will you take it with you?	*Wilt u het meenemen?	wilt ü uht may-nay-muh
I will take it with me	Ik neem het gelijk mee	ik naym uht khlyk may
Please send them to this address/hotel ...	Wilt u het sturen naar dit adres/naar hotel ...	wilt ü uht stü-ruhn nār dit a-**dres**/nār hō-**tel**

CHOOSING

I want something in leather/green	Ik zoek iets in leer/groen	ik zook eets in layr/khroon
I need it to match this	Het moet hier bij passen	uht moot heer by pas-suhn
I like the one in the window	Die in de etalage leek me goed	dee in duh ay-ta-lā-zhuh layk muh khoot

Could I see that one, please?	**Mag ik die even zien, abstublieft?**	makh ik dee ay-vuh zeen, als-tü-**bleeft**
I like the colour but not the style	**De kleur bevalt me wel, maar de snit niet**	de klœr buh-**valt** muh wel mār duh snit neet
I want a darker/lighter shade	**Ik wil een donkerder/ lichtere kleur**	ik wil uhn **dong-kuhr-**duhr/**likh-**tuh-ruh klœr
I need something warmer/thinner	**Ik zoek iets warmers/dunners**	ik zook eets **war-**muhrs/**duh-**nuhrs
Do you have one in another colour/size?	**Hebt u dit in een andere kleur/maat?**	hebt ü dit in uhn **an-**duh-ruh klœr/māt
Have you anything better/cheaper?	**Hebt u niet iets beters/goedkopers?**	hebt ü neet eets **bay-**tuhrs/khoot-**kō-**puhrs
How much is this?	**Wat kost dit?**	wat kost dit
That is too much for me	**Dat is mij te duur**	dat is my tuh dür
What kind of material is this?	**Wat voor materiaal is dit?**	wat vōr ma-tuh-ree-**yāl** is dit
What is this made of?	**Waar is dit van gemaakt?**	wār is dit van khuh-**mākt**
What size is this?	**Welke maat is dit?**	**wel-**kuh māt is dit
Have you a larger/smaller one?	**Hebt u een grotere/kleinere?**	hebt ü uhn **khrō-**tuh-ruh/**kly-**nuh-ruh

I take size[1] ...	Ik draag maat ...	ik drākh māt
The English/American size is ...	De engelse/ amerikaanse maat is ...	duh eng-uhl-suh/a-may-ree-kān-suh māt is
My collar size is ...	Mijn boordmaat is ...	myn bōrt-māt is
My chest measurement is ...	Mijn borstwijdte is ...	myn borst-wy-tuh is
My waist/hip measurement is ...	Mijn taille/ heupwijdte is ...	myn ta-yuh/hœp-wy-tuh is
Can I try it on?	Kan ik het passen?	kan ik uht pas-suhn
It's too short/ long/tight/loose	Het is te kort/ lang/nauw/wijd	uht is tuh kort/ lang/now/wyt
Is there a mirror?	Is er een spiegel?	is uhr uhn spee-khuhl
Is it colourfast?	Is het kleurecht?	is uht klœr-ekht
Is it machine washable?	Kan het met de machine gewassen worden?	kan uht met duh ma-shee-nuh khuh-was-suhn wor-duhn
Will it shrink?	Krimpt het?	krimpt uht
Is it handmade?	Is het met de hand gemaakt?	is uht met duh hant khuh-mākt

---

1. See p. 131 for continental sizes.

MATERIALS

cotton	**katoen**	ka-toon
lace	**kant**	kant
leather	**leer**	layr
linen	**linnen**	lin-nuhn
plastic	**plastic**	ples-tik
silk	**zij(de)**	zy(-duh)
suede	**suède**	sü-wè-duh
synthetic	**synthetisch**	sin-tay-tees
wool	**wol**	wol

COLOURS

beige	**beige**	bè-zhuh
black	**zwart**	zwart
blue	**blauw**	blow
brown	**bruin**	bruin
gold	**goud(kleurig)**	khowt(-klœ-ruhkh)
green	**groen**	khroon
grey	**grijs**	khrys
mauve	**lila**	lee-lā
orange	**oranje**	ō-ran-yuh
pink	**roze**	ro-zuh
purple	**paars**	pārs
red	**rood**	rōt
silver	**zilver(kleurig)**	zil-vuhr(-klœ-ruhkh)

| white | **wit** | wit |
| yellow | **geel** | khayl |

COMPLAINTS

I want to see the manager	**Kan ik de chef spreken?**	kan ik duh shef **spray-k'n**
I bought this yesterday	**Ik heb dit gisteren gekocht**	ik heb dit **khis-tuh-ruh khuh-kokht**
It doesn't work/fit	**Het werkt/past niet**	uht werkt/past neet
This is dirty/stained/torn/broken/bad	**Het is vuil/gevlekt/gescheurd/kapot/slecht**	uht is vuil/**khuh-vlekt**/**khuh-skhœrt**/ka-pot/slekht
Will you change it please?	**Kan ik het ruilen?**	kan ik uht **rui-luhn**
I want to return this	**Ik wou dit teruggeven**	ik wow dit tuh-**rukh-khay-vuhn**
Will you refund my money?	**Kunt u me mijn geld teruggeven?**	kunt ü muh muh khelt tuh-**rukh-khay-vuhn**
Here is the receipt	**Hier is de bon**	heer is duh bon

PAYING

| How much do I owe you? | **Wat krijgt u van me?** | wat krykht ü van muh |

That's 10 guilders, please	*Dat is tien gulden, alstublieft	dat is teen khuhl-duhn, als-tü-bleeft
They are 80 cents each	*Die kosten tachtig cent per stuk	dee kos-t'n takh-tuhkh sent per stuhk
How much does that come to?	Hoeveel is dat bij elkaar?	hoo-vayl is dat by muh-kār
That will be ...	*Dat is dan ...	dat is dan
Can I pay with English/American currency?	Kan ik met engels/amerikaans geld betalen?	kan ik met eng-uhls/ā-may-ree-kāns khelt buh-tā-luhn
Do you take credit cards/ travellers' cheques?	Neemt u credit cards/ reischeques?	naymt ü kre-dit kārts/rys-sheks
Do I have to pay VAT?	Moet ik ook BTW betalen?	moot ik ōk bay-tay-way buh-tā-luh
May I have a VAT invoice?	Mag ik een rekening met de BTW?	makh ik uhn ray-kuh-ning met duh bay-tay-way
Please pay the cashier	*Wilt u aan de kassa betalen, alstublieft?	wilt ü ān de kas-sā buh-tā-luhn, als-tü-bleeft
May I have a receipt, please?	Mag ik de rekening/een bonnetje hebben?	makh ik duh ray-kuh-ning/uhn bon-nuh-tyuh he-buhn
You've given me too little/too much change	*U hebt me te weinig/te veel teruggegeven	ü hebt muh tuh wy-nuhkh/ tuh vayl tuh-ruhkh-khuh-khay-vuhn

CHEMIST[1]

Can you prepare this prescription for me, please?	**Kunt u dit recept voor me maken, alstublieft?**	kuhnt ü dit re-sept võr muh mā-k'n, als-tü-bleeft
Have you a small first-aid kit?	**Hebt u een klein verbandtrommeltje?**	hebt ü uhn klyn vuhr-bant-trom-muhl-tyuh
I want some aspirin/ sun cream (for children)	**Ik zoek aspirine/ zonnebrand-crème (voor kinderen)**	ik zook as-pee-ree-nuh/ zon-nuh-brant-krèm (võr kin-duh-ruhn)
A roll/packet of plaster	**Een rolletje pleister/ pakje Hansaplast**	uhn rol-luh-tyuh plys-tuhr/ pak-yuh han-sā-plast
Can you suggest something for indigestion constipation diarrhoea?	**Hebt u iets tegen** **indigestie verstopping diarree?**	hebt ü eets tay-khuhn in-dee-khes-tee vuhr-sto-ping dee-a-ray
Can you give me something for sunburn?	**Hebt u een zonnebrandolie?**	hebt ü uhn zon-nuh-brant-ō-lee

1. You go to an **apotheek** for prescriptions, to a **drogist** for toilet requisites and most patent medicines.

I want	Ik wou	ik wow
an antiseptic cream	een ontsmettende crème	uhn ont-**sme**-tuhn-duh krèm
a disinfectant	een desinfecteer-middel	uhn des-in-fek-**tayr**-mi-duhl
a mouthwash	een mondspoeling	mont-**spoo**-ling

I want some	Ik zoek	ik zook
throat lozenges	keeltabletten	kayl-ta-ble-tuhn
stomach pills	maagtabletten	**mākh**-ta-ble-tuhn
nose drops	neusdruppels	**nœs**-druh-puhls

Do you have	Hebt u	hebt ü
sanitary towels	maandverband	**mānt**-vuhr-bant
tampons	tampons	tam-pons
cotton wool	watten	**wa**-tuhn
panty liners?	inlegkruisjes?	in-lekh-**kruis**-yuhs

I need something for	Ik zoek iets tegen	ik zook eets tay-**khuhn**
insect bites	insectenbeten	in-**sek**-tuh-bay-tuhn
a hangover	een kater	uhn **kā**-tuhr
travel sickness	reisziekte	**rys**-zeek-tuh

Do you sell	Hebt u ook	hebt ü ōk an-tee-kon-
contraceptives/	anticonceptie	sep-see mi-duh-
condoms?	middelen/	luhn/kon-**dōms**
	condooms?	

TOILET ARTICLES

| A packet of razor blades, please | Een pakje scheermesjes, alstublieft | uhn **pak**-yuh **skhayr**-mes-yuhs, als-tü-**bleeft** |

Have you got ... after-shave lotion?	**Hebt u after-shave van ...?**	hebt ü āf-tuhr-shayv van
How much is this lotion?	**Wat kost deze lotion?**	wat kost day-zuh lōt-syon
A tube of toothpaste, please	**Een tube tandpasta, alstublieft**	uhn tü-buh tam-pas-tā, als-tü-bleeft
Can I have a box of tissues?	**Mag ik een doos tissues?**	makh ik uhn dōs ti-shoos
I want some eau-de-cologne/perfume	**Ik zoek eau-de-cologne/ parfum**	ik zook ō duh kō-lon-yuh/ par-fuhm
What kinds of soap have you?	**Wat voor soorten zeep hebt u?**	wat vōr sōr-tuhn zayp hebt ü
A bottle/tube of shampoo, please, for dry/greasy hair	**Een flesje/tube shampoo, alstublieft, voor droog/vettig haar**	uhn fles-yuh/tü-buh syam-poo, als-tü-bleeft, vōr drōkh/ve-tuhkh hār
I'd like some hair conditioner	**Ik wou graag een haar-versteviger**	ik wow khrākh uhn hār-vuhr-stay-vuh-khuhr
hand cream moisturizer	**handcrème vochtinbrengende crème**	hant-krèm vokht-in-breng-uhn-duh krèm
Do you have any suntan oil/cream?	**Hebt u zonnebrand olie/crème?**	hebt ü zon-nuh-brant ō-lee/krèm

CLOTHES AND SHOES[1]

I want a hat/sunhat	Ik zoek een hoed/ zonnehoed	ik zook uhn hoot/zon-nuh-hoot
I'd like a pair of gloves shoes sandals	Ik zoek een paar handschoenen schoenen sandalen	ik zook uhn pār hant-skhoo-nuhn skhoo-nuhn san-dā-luhn
Where can I find some dresses/ trousers, please?	Waar vind ik jurken/broeken?	wār vind ik yuhr-kuhn/broo-kuhn
Where is the underwear/ haberdashery/coats department?	Waar is de afdeling ondergoed/ fournituren/ jassen?	wār is duh av-day-ling on-duhr-khoot/ foor-nee-tü-ruh/ yas-suhn
Where are beach clothes?	Waar vind ik badkleding?	wār vint ik bat-klay-ding
The men's department is on the first/second floor	*De heren-afdeling is op de eerste/tweede verdieping	duh hay-ruhn-av-day- ling is op duh ayr-stuh/tway-duh vuhr-dee-ping
I want a short/long sleeved shirt, collar size . . .	Ik zoek een overhemd met korte/lange mouwen, boordmaat . . .	ik zook uhn ō-vuhr-hemt met kor-tuh/lang-uh mow-wuhn, bōrt-mat . . .

---

1. See p. 131 for continental sizes.

I don't know the Dutch size	Ik weet de nederlandse maat niet	ik wayt duh nay-duhr-lant-suh māt neet
Can you measure me?	Kunt u mij de maat nemen?	kuhnt ü muh duh māt nay-muh
It's for a 3-year old	Het is voor een kind van drie	tis vor uhn kint van dree
Where can I find socks/ stockings?	Waar vind ik sokken/ kousen?	wār vint ik so-k'n/kow-suhn
I am looking for a blouse bra dress jumper	Ik zoek een blouse b.h. jurk jumper	ik zook uhn bloo-suh bay-hā yuh-ruhk yuhm-puhr
I need a coat raincoat jacket	Ik zoek een jas regenjas jasje	ik zook uhn yas ray-khuhn-yas yas-yuh
Do you sell buttons elastic zips?	Hebt u knopen elastiek ritsen?	hebt ü knō-puh ay-las-teek rit-suhn
I need a pair of walking shoes sandals black shoes	Ik zoek een paar wandelschoenen sandalen zwarte schoenen	ik zook uhn pār wan-duhl-skhoo-nuhn san-dā-luhn zwar-tuh skhoo-nuhn
These heels are too high/too low	Deze hakken zijn te hoog/te laag	day-zuh ha-k'n zyn tuh hōkh/tuh lākh
This doesn't fit	Dit past niet	dit past neet

CLOTHING SIZES

WOMEN'S DRESSES, ETC.

British	10	12	14	16	18	20
American	8	10	12	14	16	18
Italian	42	44	46	48	50	52

MEN'S SUITS

British and American	36	38	40	42	44	46
Continental	46	48	50	52	54	56

MEN'S SHIRTS

British and American	14	$14\frac{1}{2}$	15	$15\frac{1}{2}$	16	$16\frac{1}{2}$	17
Continental	36	37	38	39	41	42	43

STOCKINGS

British and American	8	$8\frac{1}{2}$	9	$9\frac{1}{2}$	10	$10\frac{1}{2}$	11
Continental	0	1	2	3	4	5	6

SOCKS

British and American	$9\frac{1}{2}$	10	$10\frac{1}{2}$	11	$11\frac{1}{2}$
Continental	38–39	39–40	40–41	41–42	42–43

WAIST, CHEST/BUST AND HIPS

Inches	24	26	28	30	32	34	36	38
Centimetres	61	66	71	76	81	87	92	97
Inches	40	42	44	46	48	50	52	54
Centimetres	102	107	112	117	122	127	132	137

SHOES

British	1	2	3	4	5	6	7	8	9	10	11	12
American	$2\frac{1}{2}$	$3\frac{1}{2}$	$4\frac{1}{2}$	$5\frac{1}{2}$	$6\frac{1}{2}$	$7\frac{1}{2}$	$8\frac{1}{2}$	$9\frac{1}{2}$	$10\frac{1}{2}$	$11\frac{1}{2}$	$12\frac{1}{2}$	$13\frac{1}{2}$
Continental	33	34–5	36	37	38	39–40	41	42	43	44	45	46

FOOD[1]

Give me a kilo/half a kilo of . . ., please	Een kilo/Een halve kilo . . ., alstublieft	uhn kee-lō/uhn hal-luh-vuh kee-lō . . ., als-tü-bleeft
Can I have a quarter of . . .	Mag ik honderd gram . . .	makh ik hon-duhrt khram
I want some sweets/chocolate	Ik wou wat snoepjes/chocola	ik wow wat snoop-yuhs/shō-kō-lā
A bottle of milk beer wine fruit juice	Een fles melk bier wijn vruchtensap	uhn fles mel-luhk beer wyn vruhkh-tuh-sap
Is there anything back on the bottle?	Is er statiegeld op de fles?	is uhr stā-tsee-khelt op duh fles
. . . slices of ham	. . . plakjes ham	. . . plak-yuhs ham
Is it fresh or frozen?	Is dit vers of diepvries?	is dit vers ov deep-vrees

1. See also the various MENU sections (p. 100 onwards) and WEIGHTS AND MEASURES (p. 207).

Will you mince it? bone it?	**Kunt u het malen? uitbenen?**	kuhnt ü uht **mā-luh uit-bay-nuh**
Will you clean the fish?	**Wilt u de vis schoonmaken?**	wilt ü duh vis **skhōn-mā-kuh**
Leave/take off the head	**Kop er aan/af, alstublieft**	kop d'r ān/af, als-tü-**bleeft**
Please fillet the fish	**Wilt u de vis fileren?**	wilt ü duh vis fee-lay-ruh
I'll take the bones	**Ik neem de graat mee**	ik naym duh khrāt may
Is there any shellfish?	**Zijn er ook schaaldieren?**	zyn uhr ōk **skhāl-dee-ruhn**
Can I help myself?	**Mag ik zelf pakken?**	makh ik zel-luhf pa-kuh
I want a jar/tin/packet of ...	**Hebt u een fles/blik/doos ...**	hebt ü uhn fles/blik/dōs
Do you sell frozen foods?	**Verkoopt u ook diepvries?**	vuhr-kōpt ü ōk **deep-vrees**
These pears are too hard/soft	**Deze peren zijn te hard/zacht**	day-zuh pay-ruh zyn tuh hart/zakht
Is it fresh?	**Is het vers?**	is uht vers
Are they ripe?	**Zijn ze rijp?**	zyn zuh ryp
This is bad/stale	**Dit is bedorven/oud**	dit is buh-**dor**-ruh-vuh/owt

| A loaf of white/ brown/wholemeal bread | **Een wit/bruin/volkoren brood** | uhn wit/bruin/vol-kō-ruh brōt |
| How much a kilo a litre a piece? | **Wat kost dit per kilo liter stuk?** | wat kost dit per kee-lō lee-t'r stuhk |

HAIRDRESSER AND BARBER

May I make an appointment for tomorrow/ this afternoon?	**Kan ik een afspraak maken voor morgen/vanmiddag?**	kan ik uhn af-sprāk mā-kuh vōr mor-ruh-khuh/van-mi-dakh
What time?	***Hoe laat?**	hoo lāt
I want my hair cut/ trimmed	**Ik wil mijn haar laten knippen/een beetje laten bijknippen**	ik wil myn hār lā-tuh kni-puh/uhn bay-tyuh lā-tuh by-kni-puh
Not too short at the sides	**Niet te kort opzij**	neet tuh kort op-zy
I'll have it shorter at the back, please	**Wat korter van achteren, alstublieft**	wat kor-tuhr van akh-tuh-ruhn, als-tü-bleeft
Short(er) on top	**Kort(er) van boven**	kort/(kor-tuhr) van bō-vuh
Not shorter	**Niet korter**	neet kor-tuhr

I want my hair washed, styled and blow-dried	Wassen, knippen en föhnen, alstublieft	was-suh, kni-puhn en fœ-nuh, als-tü-bleeft
Please set it	Zet u het alstublieft	zet ü uht als-tü-bleeft
without rollers	zonder krulspelden	zon-duhr kruhl-spel-duh
on large rollers	op grote rollen	op khrō-tuh rol-luh
on small rollers	op kleine rollen	op kly-nuh rol-luh
Please do not use any hairspray	Wilt u alstublieft geen haarlak gebruiken?	wilt ü als-tü-bleeft khayn hār-lak khuh-brui-kuh
I want a dark/light rinse	Ik wou graag een donkere/lichte spoeling	ik wow khrākh uhn don-kuh-ruh/likh-tuh spoo-ling
Please use conditioner	Wilt u een versteviger gebruiken?	wilt ü uhn vuhr-stay-vuh-khuhr khuh-brui-kuh
I want a perm	Ik wou een permanent	ik wow uhn per-mā-nent
I'd like it set this way, please	Kunt u het alstublieft zó doen?	kunt ü uht als-tü-bleeft zō doon
The water is too cold/hot	Het water is te koud/heet	uht wā-t'r is tuh kowt/hayt
The dryer is too hot	De droger is te heet	duh drō-khuhr is tuh hayt
Thank you, I like it very much	Zo is het heel goed, dank u wel	zō is uht hayl khoot, dank ü wel

| I want a shave/manicure | Scheren/manicure, alstublieft | skhay-ruhn/ma-nee-kür, als-tü-bleeft |
| Please trim my beard/ moustache | Wilt u mijn baard/snor knippen? | wilt ü muhn bärt/snor kni-puh |

HARDWARE

Where is the camping equipment?	Waar is de kampeerafdeling?	wār is duh kam-payr-av-day-ling
Do you have a battery for this?	Hebt u hier een batterij voor?	hebt ü heer uhn ba-tuh-ry vōr
Where can I get butane gas/paraffin?	Waar kan ik butagas/petroleum krijgen?	wār kan ik bü-tā-khas/pay-trō-lee-yuhm kry-khuh
I need a bottle opener tin opener corkscrew	Ik had graag een flesopener blikopener kurketrekker	ik hat khrākh uhn fles-ō-puh-nuhr blik-ō-puh-nuhr kuh-ruh-kuh-tre-kuhr
A small/large screwdriver	Een kleine/grote schroevendraaier	uhn kly-nuh/khrō-tuh skhroo-vuh-drā-yuhr
I'd like some candles/ matches	Ik wou graag wat kaarsen/lucifers	ik wow khrākh wat kār-suhn/lü-see-fers
I want a flashlight (pen)knife pair of scissors	Ik zoek een zaklantaarn (zak)mes schaar	ik zook uhn zak-lan-tā-ruhn (zak)-mes skhār

Do you sell any string/ rope?	**Hebt u touw?**	hebt ü tow
Where can I find washing-up liquid scouring powder soap pads?	**Waar vind ik afwasmiddelen schuurpoeder pannesponzen?**	wār vint ik af-was-mi-duh-luh skhür-poo-yuhr pan-nuh-spon-zuh
Do you have a dishcloth/ brush?	**Hebt u een theedoek/ borstel?**	hebt ü uhn tay-dook/bor-stuhl
I need a groundsheet bucket frying pan	**Ik zoek een grondzeil emmer koekepan**	ik zook uhn gront-zyl em-muhr koo-kuh-pan
I want to buy a barbecue	**Ik wil een barbecue kopen**	ik wil uhn bār-buh-kyoo kō-p'n
Do you sell charcoal/fire lighters?	**Verkoopt u houtskool/ aanmakers?**	vuhr-kōpt ü howts-kōl/ān-mā-kuhrs
Adapter	**Driewegstekker**	dree-wekh-ste-kuhr
Basket	**Mandje**	man-tyuh
Duster	**Stofdoek**	stov-dook
Electrical flex	**Snoer**	snoor
Extension lead	**Verlengsnoer**	vuhr-leng-snoor
Fuse *in apparatus*	**Stop/Zekering**	stop/zay-kuh-ring
Insulating tape	**Isolatieband**	ee-so-lā-tsee-bant
Lightbulb	**(Gloei)lamp**	(khlooee)-lamp
(Pen)knife	**(Zak)mes**	(zak)-mes

Plug – bath	**Stop**	stop
– electrical	**Stekker**	ste-kuhr
– wall	**Stopcontact**	stop-kon-takt

LAUNDRY AND DRY CLEANING

Where is the nearest launderette/dry cleaner?	**Is er een wasserette/ chemische wasserij in de buurt?**	is uhr uhn was-suh-ret/khay-mee-suh was-suh-ry in duh bürt
I want to have these things washed/cleaned	**Ik wil deze dingen laten wassen/ chemisch laten reinigen**	ik wil day-zuh ding-uh lā-tuh was-suh/khay-mees lā-tuh ry-nuh-khuh
These stains won't come out	**Ik krijg deze vlekken er niet uit**	ik krykh day-zuh vle-kuhn uhr neet uit
Can you get this stain out?	**Kunt u deze vlek er uit krijgen?**	kuhnt ü day-zuh vlek d'r-uit kry-khuh
Is it coffee/wine/grease	**Het is koffie/wijn/vet**	uht is kof-fee/wyn/vet
It only needs to be pressed/ironed	**Dit hoeft alleen maar geperst/ gestreken te worden**	dit hooft al-layn mār khuh-perst/khuh-stray- kuh tuh wor-duh
This is torn; can you mend it?	**Dit is gescheurd; kunt u het maken?**	dit is khuh-skhœrt, kuhnt ü uht mā-k'n

Do you do invisible mending?	**Kunt u ook onzichtbaar stoppen?**	kunt ü ōk on-**zikht**-bār **sto**-p'n
There's a button missing	**Hier is een knoop af**	heer is uhn knōp av
Can you sew on a button here, please?	**Kunt u hier een knoop aanzetten, alstublieft?**	kuhnt ü heer uhn knōp **ān**-ze-t'n, als-tū-bleeft
Can you put in a new zip, please?	**Kunt u hier een nieuwe rits inzetten?**	kuhnt ü heer uhn **nee**-wuh rits **in**-ze-t'n
When will it be ready?	**Wanneer is het klaar?**	wan-nayr is uht klār
I need this by this evening/tomorrow	**Ik heb dit vanavond/ morgen nodig**	ik heb dit van-**ā**-vont/**mor**-ruh-khuh **nō**-duhkh
Call back at/after 5 o'clock	***U kunt het om/na vijf uur halen**	ü kuhnt uht om/nā vyf ür **hā**-luh
We can do it by Tuesday	***Het kan dinsdag klaar zijn**	uht kan **dins**-dakh klār zyn
It will take three days/ two hours	***Dat duurt drie dagen/ twee uur**	dat dürt dree **dā**-khuhn/tway ür
This isn't mine	**Dit is niet van mij**	dit is neet van my
I've lost my ticket	**Ik ben mijn bon kwijt**	ik ben muh bon kwyt
Bath towel	**Badhanddoek**	bat-**han**-dook
Blanket	**Deken**	**day**-k'n

Napkin	**Servet**	ser-vet
Pillow case	**(Kussen)sloop**	(kuhs-suhn)-slōp
Sheet	**Laken**	lā-k'n
Tea towel	**Theedoek**	tay-dook

NEWSPAPERS, BOOKS AND WRITING MATERIALS

Do you sell English/ American newspapers/ magazines?	**Hebt u engelse/ amerikaanse kranten/ tijdschriften?**	hebt ü eng-uhl-suh/a-may-ree-kān-suh kran-tuh/ tyt-skhrif-tuh
Can you get me the magazine called ...?	**Kunt u me aan het tijdschrift ... helpen?**	kuhnt ü muh ān uht tyt-skhrift ... hel-luh-puh
Where can I get the ...?	**Waar kan ik ... krijgen?**	wār kan ik ... kry-khuh
I want a map of the city/a road map	**Ik zoek een plattegrond van de stad/een wegenkaart**	ik zook uhn pla-tuh-khront van duh stat/uhn way-khuhn-kārt
Do you have any English books?	**Hebt u ook engelse boeken?**	hebt ü ōk eng-uhl-suh boo-k'n
Have you any novels by ...?	**Hebt u misschien boeken van ...?**	hebt ü muh-skheen boo-k'n van
I want some coloured postcards	**Ik zoek gekleurde prentbriefkaarten**	ik zook khuh-klœr-duh prent-breef-kār-tuhn

I want some plain postcards/letter paper	Ik zoek briefkaarten/ postpapier	ik zook breef-kār- tuhn/pos-pa-peer
Do you sell souvenirs/ toys?	Verkoopt u ook souveniers/ speelgoed?	vuhr-kōpt ü ōk soo-vuh- neers/spayl-khoot
Ballpoint	Balpen	bal-pen
Calculator	Rekenmachine	ray-kuhn-ma-shee-nuh
Pocket calculator	Zakjapanner	zak-ja-pan-nuhr
Card	Kaart	kārt
Dictionary	Woordenboek	wor-duh-book
Drawing paper	Tekenpapier	tay-kuhn-pa-peer
Drawing pin	Punaise	pü-nè-zuh
Elastic band	Elastiekje	ay-las-teek-yuh
Envelope	Envelop	an-vuh-lop
Felt-tip pen	Viltstift	vilt-stivt
Glue	Lijm	lym
Guide book	Gids	khits
Ink	Inkt	ing-k't
Notebook	Notitieblok	nō-tee-tsee-blok
Pen	Pen	pen
Pen cartridge	Vulling/Inktpatroon	vuh-ling/ing-k't-pa-trōn
(Coloured) pencil	(Kleur)potlood	(klœr)-pot-lōt

Pencil sharpener	**Puntenslijper**	puhn-tuh-sly-puhr
Postcard	**Ansichtkaart/ Prentbriefkaart**	an-zikht-kārt/ prent-breef-kārt
Rubber	**Vlakgom**	vlak-khom
Sellotape	**Plakband**	plak-bant
String	**Touw**	tow

OPTICIAN

I have broken my glasses	**Ik heb mijn bril gebroken**	ik heb muh bril khuh-brō-kuhn
The frame/arm is broken	**Het montuur/De poot is kapot**	uht mon-tür/duh pōt is ka-pot
Can you repair them?	**Kunt u hem repareren?**	kunt ü uhm ray-pa-ray-ruh
I'd like a new pair of glasses to the same prescription	**Ik wou graag een nieuwe bril op het zelfde recept**	ik wow khrākh uhn nee-wuh bril op uht zel-luhv-duh ruh-sept
I have difficulty reading	**Ik heb moeite met lezen**	ik heb mooee-tuh met lay-zuhn
Please test my eyes	**Wilt u mijn ogen testen**	wilt ü muhn ō-khuhn tes-t'n
I have lost one of my contact lenses	**Ik ben een van mijn contact lenzen kwijt**	ik ben ayn van muh kon-takt-len-zuhn kwyt

I should like to have contact lenses	**Ik wou graag contactlenzen**	ik wow khrākh kon-takt-len-zuhn
Hard/soft lenses	**Harde/zachte lenzen**	har-duh/zakh-tuh len-zuhn
I am short-sighted/far-sighted	**Ik ben bijziend/verziend**	ik ben by-zeent/ver-zeent

PHOTOGRAPHY

I want to buy a (cine) camera	**Ik zoek een (film) camera**	ik zook uhn (fil-luhm)-kā-muh-rā
Have you a film/cartridge for this camera?	**Hebt u film/cassette voor deze camera?**	hebt ü uhn fil-luhm/ka-set vor day-zuh kā-muh-rā
A 120/126 spool film	**Een honderdtwintig/honderdzes-entwintig**	uhn hon-duhrt-twin-tuhkh/hon-duhrt-zes-en- twin-tuhkh
A film with 24/36 exposures	**Een film van vierentwintig/zesendertig opnamen**	uhn fil-luhm van veer-en-twin-tuhkh/zes-en-der-tuhkh op-nā-muhn
Give me an 8/16/35 mm film, please	**Mag ik een acht/zestien/vijfendertig mm film?**	makh ik uhn akht/zes-teen/vyv-en-der-tuhkh mee-lee-may-t'r fil-luhm
A 100/400/1000 ASA film	**Een honderd/tweehonderd/duizend ASA film**	uhn hon-duhrt/tway-hon-duhrt/dui-zuhnt ā es ā fil-luhm

What is your fastest film?	Wat is uw snelste film?	wat is üw snel-stuh fil-luhm
I want a (fast) colour film/black-and-white film	Ik zoek een (snelle) kleurenfilm/ zwart-wit film	ik zook uhn (snel-luh) kloe-ruhn-fil-luhm/ zwart-wit fil-luhm
Film for slides/prints	Film voor dia's/foto's	fil-luhm vōr dee-yās/fō-tōs
What film speed is this?	Welke snelheid heeft deze film?	wel-kuh snel-hyt hayft day-zuh fil-luhm
Would you fit the film in the camera for me, please?	Kunt u de film voor me in de camera doen?	kunt ü duh fil-luhm vōr muh in duh kā-muh-rā doon
Does the price include processing?	Is ontwikkelen in de prijs inbegrepen?	is ont-wi-kuh-luh in duh prys in-buh-khray-puh
I'd like this film developed and printed	Kunt u deze film ontwikkelen en afdrukken?	kuhnt ü day-zuh fil-luhm ont-wi-kuh-luh en av-druh-kuh
Can I have ... prints/enlargements of this negative?	Mag ik ... afdrukken/ vergrotingen van dit negatief?	makh ik ... av-druh-kuhn/vuhr-khrō-ting-uhn van dit nay-khā-teef
When will they be ready?	Wanneer zijn ze klaar?	wan-nayr zyn zuh klār
Will they be done tomorrow?	Kunnen ze morgen klaar zijn?	kun-nuh zuh mor-ruh-khuh klār zyn
Do you have flash bulbs?	Hebt u ook flitslampjes?	hebt ü ōk flits-lamp-yuhs

My camera's not working, can you mend it?	Mijn camera is kapot, kunt u hem repareren?	Myn kā-muh-rā is ka-pot, kuhnt ü uhm ray-pa-ray-ruh
There is something wrong with the flash light meter shutter	Er is iets mis met de flitser lichtmeter sluiter	d'r is eets mis met duh flit-suhr likht-may-t'r slui-t'r
The film is jammed	De film zit vast	duh fil-luhm zit vast
Battery	Batterij	ba-tuh-ry
Cine film	Smalfilm	smal-fil-luhm
Film winder	Filmtransport	fil-luhm-trans-port
Filter	Filter	fil-tuhr
Lens(cap)	Lens(dop)	lens-(dop)
Light meter	Lichtmeter	likht-may-t'r
Shutter	Sluiter	slui-t'r
Video camera	Video camera	vee-day-yō kā-muh-rā
Viewfinder	Zoeker	zoo-k'r

RECORDS AND CASSETTES

| Do you have any records/cassettes of Dutch music? | Hebt u platen/cassettes van nederlandse muziek? | hebt ü plā-tuh/ka-set-tuhs van nay-duhr-lant-suh mü-zeek |

Are there any new records by ...	Zijn er nieuwe platen van ...	zyn uhr nee-wuh plā-tuh van
Do you sell compact discs/video cassettes?	Verkoopt u compact discs/video cassettes?	vuhr-kōpt ü kom-pakt disks/vee-day-yō ka-set-tuhs
Can I listen to this record?	Mag ik deze plaat horen?	makh ik day-zuh plāt hō-ruhn

TOBACCONIST

Do you stock English/American cigarettes?	Hebt u ook engelse/amerikaanse sigaretten?	hebt ü ōk eng-uhl-suh/ā-may-ree-kān-suh see-kha-re-tuhn
What English cigarettes have you?	Wat voor engelse sigaretten hebt u?	wat vor eng-uhl-suh see-khā-re-tuhn hebt ü
Filter tip cigarettes/ cigarettes without filter	Sigaretten met/zonder filter	see-khā-re-tuhn met/zon-duhr fil-tuhr
Do you have any small cigars?	Hebt u ook kleine sigaartjes?	hebt ü ōk kly-nuh see-khār-tyuhs
Light/dark tobacco	Lichte/zware tabak	likh-tuh/zwā-ruh ta-bak
A box of matches, please	Een doosje lucifers, alstublieft	uhn dōs-yuh lü-see-fers, als-tü-bleeft
Do you have cigarette paper/pipe cleaners?	Hebt u sigarettenpapier/ pijpewissers?	hebt ü see-khā-re-tuh-pa-peer/py-puh-wis-suhrs

I want to buy a lighter	Ik zoek een aansteker	ik zook uhn ān-stay-kuhr
I want a gas refill for this lighter	Hebt u vullingen voor deze gasaansteker?	hebt ü vuh-ling-uhn vōr day-ze khas-ān-stay-kuhr

REPAIRS

This is broken; could somebody mend it?	Dit is stuk; kan iemand het maken?	dit is stuhk, kan ee-mant uht mā-k'n
Can you do it while I wait?	Kan ik er op wachten?	kan ik uhr op wakh-t'n
When should I come back for it?	Wanneer kan ik het halen?	wan-nayr kan ik uht hā-luh
Can you sole these shoes (with leather)?	Kunt u deze schoenen (met leer) verzolen?	kuhnt ü day-zuh skhoo-nuh (met layr) vuhr-zō-luhn
Can you heel these shoes (with rubber)?	Kunt u hier (rubber)hakken onder zetten?	kuhnt ü heer (ruh-buhr)-ha-k'n on-duhr ze-t'n
I have broken the heel; can you put on a new one?	Ik heb de hak gebroken; kunt u er een nieuwe aanzetten?	ik heb duh hak khuh-brō-kuh, kuhnt ü uhr uhn nee-wuh ān-ze-t'n
My watch is broken	Mijn horloge is kapot	myn hor-lō-zhuh is ka-pot

I have broken the glass/strap/spring	Het glas/de band/de veer is kapot	uht khlas/duh bant/duh vayr is ka-**pot**
How much would a new one cost?	Wat zou een nieuwe kosten?	wat zow uhn **nee**-wuh **kos**-t'n
The stone/charm/ screw has come loose	De steen/het be- deltje/de schroef is los geraakt	duh stayn/uht **bay**-duhl- tyuh/duh skhroof is los khuh-**rākt**
The fastener/clip/ chain is broken	De sluiting/clip/ ketting is gebro- ken	duh **slui**-ting/klip/**ke**-ting is khuh-**brō**-kuhn
How much will it cost?	Wat gaat dat kosten?	wat khāt dat **kos**-t'n
It can (not) be repaired	*Het kan (niet) gere- pareerd/ gemaakt worden	uht kan (neet) khuh-ray- pa-**rayrt**/khuh-**mākt** wor-duh
You need a new one	*U moet een nieuwe hebben	ü moot uhn **nee**-wuh **he**-buh

POST OFFICE

Where's the (main) post office?	**Waar is het (hoofd) postkantoor?**	wār is uht (hōft)-pos-kan-tōr
Where's the nearest post office?	**Is hier een postkantoor in de buurt?**	is heer uhn pos-kan-tōr in duh bürt
What time does the post office open/close?	**Hoe laat gaat het postkantoor open/dicht?**	hoo lāt khāt uht pos-kan-tōr ō-puh/dikht
Where's the post box?	**Waar is de brievenbus?**	wār is duh bree-vuh-buhs
Which window do I go to for stamps?	**Aan welk loket krijg ik postzegels?**	ān wel-luhk lō-ket krykh ik pos-say-khuhls
Where do I go for telegrams/money orders?	**Waar kan ik telegrammen/ postwissels versturen?**	wār kan ik tay-luh-khram-muhn/post-wis-suhls vuhr-stü-ruhn

LETTERS AND TELEGRAMS

How much is a letter/postcard to England?	**Wat moet er op een brief/kaart naar Engeland?**	wat moot uhr op uhn breef/kărt năr **Eng**-uh-lant
What's the airmail/surface mail to the U.S.A.?	**Wat kost luchtpost/gewone post naar Amerika?**	wat kost **lukht**-post/khuh-wō-nuh post năr A-may- ree-kă
It's inland	**Dit is binnenland**	dit is **bin**-nuh-lant
Three ... cent stamps	**Mag ik drie postzegels van ...**	makh ik dree **pos**-say-khuhls van ...
I want to send this letter express	**Ik wil deze brief per expres versturen**	ik wil **day**-zuh breef per eks-**pres** vuhr-**stü**-ruhn
I want to register this letter	**Wilt u deze brief aantekenen?**	wilt ü **day**-zuh breef **ăn**-tay-kuh-nuh
Two airmail forms, please	**Twee luchtpost-formulieren, alstublieft**	tway **luhkht**-post-for-mü-lee-ruhn, als-tü-bleeft
Where is the poste restante section?	**Waar is het poste restante loket?**	wăr is uht post res-**tant** lō-ket
Are there any letters for me?	**Is er post voor mij?**	is uhr post vōr my
What is your name?	***Wat is uw naam?/ Hoe heet u?**	wat is üw năm/hoo hayt ü

Have you any means of identification?	*Hebt u een legitimatiebewijs/ paspoort?	hebt ü uhn lay-khee-tee-mā-tsee-buh-wys/pas-pōrt
I want to send a telegram/night letter	Ik wil een telegram/ brieftelegram opgeven	ik wil uhn tay-luh-khram/breef-tay-luh-khram op-khay-vuhn
Reply paid	Met betaald antwoord	met buh-tālt ant-wort
How much does it cost per word?	Wat kost het per woord?	wat kost uht per wōrt
Write the message here and your own name and address there	*Schrijft u de tekst hier, en uw eigen naam en adres daar	skhryft ü duh tekst heer, en üw y-khuhn nām en a-dres dār
Can I send a telex/fax	Kan ik een telex/fax sturen?	kan ik uhn tay-leks/faks stü-ruhn
I want to send a parcel	Ik wou een pakje versturen	ik wow uhn pak-yuh vuhr-stü-ruhn

TELEPHONING

Where's the nearest phone box?	Is hier ergens een telefooncel?	is heer er-ruh-khuhns uhn tay-luh-fōn-sel
I want to make a phone call	Ik wilde graag telefoneren	ik wil-duh khrākh tay-luh-fō-nay-ruhn
May I use your phone?	Mag ik uw telefoon gebruiken?	makh ik üw tay-luh-fōn khuh-brui-kuh

Do you have a telephone directory for ...?	**Hebt u een telefoonboek van ...?**	hebt ü uhn tay-luh-fōn-book van
Please get me ...	**Kunt u ... voor me bellen?**	kuhnt ü ... vōr muh bel-luh
I want to telephone to England	**Ik wil met Engeland telefoneren**	ik wil met Eng-uh-lant tay-luh-fō-nay-ruhn
What do I dial to get the international operator?	**Wat moet ik draaien om een internationaal gesprek aan te vragen?**	wat moot ik drā-yuh om uhn in-tuhr-nat-syo-nāl khuh-sprek ān tuh vrā-khuh
What is the code for ...?	**Wat is het kengetal voor ...?**	wat is uht ken-khuh-tal vōr
I want to make a personal (person-to-person) call	**Ik wil een gesprek met voorbericht**	ik wil uhn khuh-sprek met vōr-buh-rikht
Could you give me the cost (time-and-charges) afterwards?	**Kunt u me na afloop de kosten opgeven?**	kuhnt ü muh nā av-lōp duh kos-tuhn op-khay-vuh
I was cut off, can you reconnect me?	**Ik werd verbroken; kunt u me opnieuw verbinden?**	ik wert vuhr-brō-kuh, kuhnt ü muh op-neew vuhr-bin-duhn
I want extension ...	**Toestel ..., alstublieft**	too-stel ..., als-tü-bleeft
May I speak to ...	**Zou ik ... kunnen spreken?**	zow ik ... kuh-nuh spray-kuhn

The number is out of order	*Het nummer is gestoord	uht nuhm-muhr is khuh-stōrt
The subscriber number is ...	*Het abonné nummer is ...	uht a-bon-nay nuhm-muhr is
Who's speaking?	*Met wie spreek ik?	met wee sprayk ik
Hold the line, please	*Blijft u aan het toestel	blyft ü ān uht too-stel
He/She is not here	*Hij/Zij is niet hier	hy/zy is neet heer
You can reach him/her at ...	*U kunt hem/haar bereiken onder nummer ...	ü kuhnt uhm/hār buh-ry-kuhn on-duhr nuhm-muhr
When will he be back?	Wanneer komt hij terug?	wan-nayr komt hy truhkh
Will you take a message?	Kan ik een boodschap achterlaten?	kan ik uhn bōt-skhap akh-tuhr-lā-tuhn
Tell him that ... phoned	Wilt u hem zeggen dat ... gebeld heeft?	wilt ü uhm ze-khuhn dat ... khuh-belt hayft
Please ask her to phone me	Wilt u haar vragen mij te bellen?	wilt ü hār vrā-khuhn my tuh bel-luhn
What's your number?	*Wat is uw nummer?	wat is üw nuhm-muhr
My number is ...	Mijn nummer is ...	myn nuhm-muhr is
I can't hear you	Ik kan u niet verstaan	ik kan ü neet vuhr-stān
The line is engaged	*De lijn is bezet	duh lyn is buh-zet

There's no reply	***Er is geen antwoord/ gehoor**	d'r is khayn ant-wŏrt/khuh-hōr
You have the wrong number	***U bent verkeerd verbonden/U hebt een verkeerd nummer**	ü bent vuhr-kayrt vuhr-bon-duhn/ü hebt uhn vuhr-kayrt nuhm-muhr
Telephone directory/ number	**Telefoonboek/ nummer**	tay-luh-fōn-book/nuhm-muhr
Telephone operator	**Telefonist(e)**	tay-luh-fō-nist/tay-luh-fō-nis-tuh

SIGHTSEEING[1]

Where is the tourist office?	Waar is de V.V.V.?	wār is duh vay-vay-vay
What should we see here?	Wat valt er hier te zien?	wat valt uhr heer tuh zeen
Is there a map/plan of the places to visit?	Is er een kaart van de beziens- waardigheden?	is uhr uhn kārt van duh buh-zeens-wār-duhkh-hay-duhn
I want a good guidebook	Ik wou graag een goede gids	ik wow khrākh uhn khoo-yuh khits
Is there a sightseeing tour/boat ride?	Is er een rondrit/rondvaart?	is uhr uhn **ront-rit/ront-vārt**
Does the coach stop at the ... hotel?	Stopt de bus bij het ... hotel?	stopt duh buhs by uht ... hō-tel
Is there an excursion to ...?	Is er een excursie naar ...?	is uhr uhn eks-kuhr-see nār

1. See also TRAVEL (Bus, tram and underground) (p. 33), and DIRECTIONS (p. 37).

How long does the tour take?	**Hoe lang duurt de rondrit/rondvaart?**	hoo lang dürt duh ront-rit/ront-vārt
Does the guide speak English?	**Spreekt de gids Engels?**	spraykt duh khits eng-uhls
We don't need a guide	**Wij hebben geen gids nodig**	wy he-buh khayn khits nō-duhkh
I would prefer to go round by myself; is that all right?	**Ik wou graag in mijn eentje gaan; kan dat?**	ik wow khrākh in muhn ayn-tyuh khān, kan dat
How much does the tour cost?	**Wat kost de tocht?**	wat kost duh tokht
Are all admission fees included?	**Zijn alle entrées inbegrepen?**	zyn al-luh an-trays in-buh-khray-puh
Does it include lunch?	**Is lunch inbegrepen?**	is lunsh in-buh-khray-puh

MUSEUMS AND ART GALLERIES

When does the museum open/close?	**Wanneer gaat het museum open/dicht?**	wan-nayr khāt uht mü-zay-yuhm ō-puh/dikht
Is it open every day?	**Is het iedere dag open?**	is uht ee-duh-ruh dakh ō-puh
The gallery is closed on Mondays	***De galerie is 's maandags dicht/gesloten**	duh khal-luh-ree is smān-dakhs dikht/khuh-slō-t'n

Are there guided tours?	Zijn er rondleidingen?	zyn uhr ront-ly-ding-uhn
How much is it to get in?	Wat is de toegangsprijs?	wat is duh too-khangs-prys
Are there reductions for children/students/the elderly?	Zijn er kortingen voor kinderen/studenten/65-plussers?	zyn uhr kor-ting-uhn vōr kin-duh-ruh/stü-den-tuh/ vyf-en-zes-tuhkh- pluhs-suhrs
Are admission fees lower on any special day?	Is er een dag met lagere entrées?	is uhr uhn dakh met lā-khuh-ruh an-trays
Admission free	*Toegang vrij	too-khang vry
Have you got a ticket?	*Hebt u een kaartje?	hebt ü uhn kār-tyuh
Where do I buy a ticket?	Waar kan ik een kaartje krijgen?	wār kan ik uhn kār-tyuh kry-khuh
Please leave your bags/umbrellas/cameras in the cloakroom	Tassen/paraplu's/camera's in de garderobe, alstublieft	tas-suh/pa-rā-plüs/kā-muh-rās in du khar-duh-ro-buh, als-tü-bleeft
It's over there	*Het is daar	tis dār
Where is the . . . collection/exhibition?	Waar is de verzameling/tentoonstelling van . . .	wār is duh vuhr-zā-muh- ling/ten-tōn-stel-ling van
Can I get a catalogue/postcards somewhere?	Kan ik ergens een catalogus/prentbriefkaarten kopen?	kan ik e-ruh-khuhs uhn ka-tā-lō-khus/prent-breef- kār-tuh kō-p'n

Can I take photographs?	**Mag ik fotograferen?**	makh ik fō-tō-khrā-fay-ruhn
Can I use a tripod?	**Mag ik een statief gebruiken?**	makh ik uhn stā-teef khuh-brui-kuh
Photographs are not allowed	***Fotograferen verboden**	fō-tō-khrā-fay-ruhn vuhr- bō-duhn
Will you make photocopies?	**Kunt u fotocopieën maken?**	kuhnt ü fō-tō-kō-pee-yuhn mā-k'n
Could you make me a transparency of this painting?	**Kunt u me een dia laten maken van dit schilderij?**	kuhnt ü muh uhn dee-yā lā-tuh mā-k'n van dit skhil-duh-ry
How long will it take?	**Hoe lang duurt dat?**	hoo lang dürt dat

HISTORICAL SITES

We want to visit ...	**We wilden naar ...**	wuh wil-duhn nār
Can we get there by car?	**Kunnen we daar met de auto heen?**	kuh-nuh wuh dār met duh ō-tō hayn
Is that far to walk	**Is dat ver lopen?**	is dat ver lō-puh
Is it an easy walk/ride?	**Is het een makkelijke weg?**	is uht uhn ma-kuh-luh-kuh wekh
Is there access for wheelchairs?	**Is er ingang voor rolstoelen?**	is uhr in-khang vōr rol-stoo-luhn

Is it far to	Is het ver naar	is uht ver nār
the aquaduct?	het aquaduct?	uht ā-kwā-dukt
the castle?	het kasteel?	uht kas-tayl
the fort?	het fort?	uht fort
the fountain?	de fontein?	duh fon-tyn
the gate?	het hek?	uht hek
the walls?	de wallen?	duh wal-luhn

When was it built?	Wanneer werd het gebouwd?	wan-nayr wert uht khuh-bowt
Who built it?	Wie heeft het gebouwd?	wee hayft uht khuh-bowt
Where is the old part of the city?	Waar is de oude wijk van de stad?	wār is duh ow-duh wyk van duh stat
What is this building?	Wat is dit voor een gebouw?	wat is dit vōr uhn khuh-bow
What is the name of this house/ churchyard/ church/ street?	Hoe heet dit huis/ kerkhof/deze kerk/ straat?	hoo hayt dit huis/ ke-ruhk-hof/day-ze ke-ruhk/strāt

GARDENS, PARKS AND ZOOS

Where is the botanical garden/zoo?	Waar is de botanische tuin/dierentuin?	war is duh bō-tā-nee-suh tuin/dee-ruh-tuin
How do I get to the park?	Hoe kom ik naar het park?	hoo kom ik nār uht pa-ruhk

Can we walk there?	**Kunnen we er heen lopen?**	kuh-nuh wuh d'r hayn lō-puh
Can we drive through the park?	**Kunnen we door het park rijden?**	kuh-nuh wuh dōr uht pa-ruhk ry-yuh
Are the gardens open to the public?	**Is de tuin open voor het publiek?**	is duh tuin ō-puh vōr uht pü-bleek
What time do the gardens/does the park close?	**Hoe laat gaat de tuin/het park dicht?**	hoo lāt khāt duh tuin/uht pa-ruhk dikht
Is there a plan of the gardens/zoo?	**Is er een plattegrond van de tuin/dierentuin?**	is uhr uhn pla-tuh-khront van duh tuin/dee-ruh-tuin
Who designed the gardens?	**Wie heeft de tuin aangelegd?**	wee hayft duh tuin ān-khuh-lekht
Where is the tropical plant house/the lake?	**Waar is de tropische kas/het meer?**	wār is duh trō-pee-suh kas/uht mayr

EXPLORING

| I'd like to walk around in the old town | **Ik wou een beetje wandelen in de oude stad** | ik wow uhn bay-tyuh wan-duh-luh in duh ow-wuh stat |
| Is there a good street plan showing the buildings? | **Is er een goede plattegrond met de gebouwen er op?** | is uhr uhn khoo-yuh pla-tuh-khront met duh khuh-bow-wuhn d'r op |

We want to visit	**We wilden naar**	wuh **wil**-duhn nār
the cathedral	**de kathedraal**	duh ka-tuh-**drāl**
the fortress	**het fort**	uht fort
the library	**de bibliotheek**	duh bee-blee-yō-tayk
the monastery	**het klooster**	uht klōs-t'r
the palace	**het paleis**	uht pa-lys
the ruins	**de ruïnes**	duh rü-wee-nuhs
Can we walk there?	**Kunnen we daar heen lopen?**	kuh-nuh wuh dār hayn lō-puh
Is there a bus/tram to ...?	**Gaat er een bus/tram naar ...?**	khāt uhr uhn buhs/trem nār
May we walk around the walls?	**Kunnen we om de wallen lopen?**	kun-nuh wuh om duh wal-luh lō-puh
Can we go up the tower?	**Kunnen we de toren op?**	kun-nuh wuh duh tō-ruhn op
Where is the antiques market/flea market?	**Waar is de antiekmarkt/vlooienmarkt?**	wār is duh an-teek-ma-ruhkt/vlō-yuh-ma-ruhkt

GOING TO CHURCH

Is there a Catholic church?	**Is er een katholieke kerk?**	is uhr uhn ka-tō-lee-kuh ke-ruhk
a Protestant church?	**een protestante kerk?**	uhn pro-tuh-stan-tuh ke-rukh
a mosque?	**een moskee?**	uhn mos-kay
a synagogue?	**een synagoge?**	uhn see-nā-khō-khuh

What time is mass? the service?	Hoe laat is de mis? de dienst?	hoo lāt is duh mis duh deenst
I'd like to look round the church	Ik wou graag de kerk bezichtigen	ik wow khrākh duh ke-ruhk buh-zikh-tuh-khuh
When was this church built?	Wanneer is deze kerk gebouwd?	wan-nayr is day-zuh ke-ruhk khuh-bowt
Who was the architect?	Wie was de architect?	wee was duh ar-khee-tekt

ENTERTAINMENT

Is there an entertainment guide?	Bestaat er hier een theatergids?	buh-**stāt** uhr heer uhn tay-yā-tuhr-khits
What's on at the theatre/cinema?	Wat gaat er in het theater/in de bioscoop?	wat khāt uhr in uht tay-yā-tuhr/in duh bee-yos-kōp
Is there a concert on this evening?	Is er een concert vanavond?	is uhr uhn kon-**sert** van-ā-vont
Can you recommend a good ballet/film/musical?	Kunt u een goed ballet/een goede film/musical aanbevelen?	kuhnt ü uhn khoot bal-let/uhn khoo-yuh fil-luhm/myoo-see-kuhl ān-buh-vay-luh
Who is directing/conducting/singing/the soloist?	Wie is de regisseur/dirigent/zanger(es)/solist?	wee is duh ray-khee-sœr/dee-ree-khent/zang-uhr-(es)/sō-list

I want two seats for tonight/the matinee tomorrow	**Ik wou graag twee plaatsen voor vanavond/voor de middagvoorstelling van morgen**	ik wow khrākh tway plāt-suhn vōr van-ā-vont/ vōr duh mi-dakh-vōr-stel-ling van mo-ruh-khuhn
I want to book two seats for Thursday	**Kan ik twee plaatsen bespreken voor donderdag?**	kan ik tway plāt-suhn buh-spray-kuhn vōr don-duhr-dakh
Is the matinee sold out?	**Is de middagvoorstelling uitverkocht?**	is duh mi-dakh-vōr-stel-ling uit-vuhr-kokht
I'd like … seats in the stalls/circle/gallery	**Ik wou graag … stalles/balkon/ tweede balkon**	ik wow khrākh … stal-luhs/bal-kon/ tway-duh bal-kon
The cheapest seats, please	**De goedkoopste plaatsen, alstublieft**	duh khoot-kōp-stuh plāt-suhn, als-tü-bleeft
We're sold out (for that performance)	***We zijn uitverkocht (voor die voorstelling)**	wuh zyn uit-vuhr-kokht (vōr dee vōr-stel-ling)
Where are these seats?	**Waar zijn deze plaatsen?**	wār zyn day-zuh plāt-suhn
What time does the performance start?	**Hoe laat begint de voorstelling?**	hoo lāt buh-khint duh vōr-stel-ling
What time does it end?	**Hoe laat loopt de voorstelling af?**	hoo lāt lōpt duh vōr-stel-ling af
Is evening dress necessary?	**Is avondkleding vereist?**	is ā-vont-klay-ding vuhr-yst

Where is the cloakroom?	**Waar is de vestiaire/ garderobe?**	wār is duh ves-tee-yè-ruh/khar-duh-ro-buh
This is your seat	***Dit is uw plaats**	dit is üw plāts
A programme, please	**Mag ik een programma van u?**	makh ik uhn prō-khram-mā van ü
Where are the best nightclubs?	**Waar zijn de beste nachtclubs?**	wār zyn duh bes-tuh nakht-kluhps
What time is the floorshow?	**Wanneer begint het cabaret?**	wan-nayr buh-khint uht ka-bā-ret
Where can we go dancing?	**Waar kunnen we gaan dansen?**	wār kuh-nuh wuh khān dan-suh
Where is the best disco?	**Waar is de beste disco?**	wār is duh bes-tuh dis-kō
Would you like to dance?	**Wil je dansen?**	wil yuh dan-suh
Is there a good jazz club?	**Is er een goede jazzclub?**	is uhr uhn khoo-yuh dyez-kluhp

SPORTS & GAMES

Where is the nearest tennis court/golf course?	**Is hier in de buurt een tennisbaan/ golflinks?**	is heer in duh bürt uhn ten-nuhs-bān/ golf-links
What is the charge per game/hour/day?	**Wat kost het per spel/uur/dag?**	wat kost uht per spel/ür/dakh
Is it a club?	**Is het een club?**	is uht uhn kluhp
Do I need temporary membership?	**Moet ik lid worden?**	moot ik lit **wor**-duh
Where can we go swimming/fishing?	**Waar kunnen we zwemmen/vissen?**	wār kuh-nuh wuh zwem-muh/vis-suh
Can I hire a racket/ clubs/fishing tackle?	**Kan ik een racket/ sticks/vistuig huren?**	kan ik uhn re-ket/stiks/vis-tuikh hü-ruh
Do I need a permit?	**Heb ik een vergunning nodig?**	heb ik uhn vuhr-khuh-ning nō-dukh

Where do I get a permit?	**Waar kan ik een vergunning krijgen?**	wār kan ik uhn vuhr-khuh-ning kry-khuh
Is there a skating rink?	**Is er een kunstijsbaan?**	is uhr uhn **kunst**-ys-bān
Can I hire skates?	**Kan ik schaatsen huren?**	kan ik skhāt-suh hü-ruh
Can I take lessons here?	**Kan ik hier les krijgen?**	kan ik heer les kry-khuh
Where is the stadium?	**Waar is het stadion?**	wār is uht stā-dee-yon
We want to go to a football match/the tennis tournament	**We wilden naar een voetbal-wedstrijd/ het tennis tournooi gaan**	wuh wil-duhn nār uhn voot-bal-wet-stryt/uht ten-nuhs toor-**nōee** khān
Can you get us tickets?	**Kunt u ons kaartjes bezorgen?**	kuhnt ü ons kār-tyuhs buh-zo-ruh-khuhn
Are there still any seats in the grandstand?	**Zijn er nog plaatsen op de hoofdtribune?**	zyn uhr nokh plāt-suhn op duh hōft-tree-bü-nuh
Are they covered?	**Zijn ze overdekt?**	zyn zuh ō-vuhr-dekt
How much are they?	**Wat kosten ze?**	wat kos-t'n zuh
Which are the cheapest seats?	**Wat zijn de goedkoopste plaatsen?**	wat zyn duh khoot-kōp-stuh plāt-suh
Who's playing?	**Wie spelen er?**	wie spay-luhn uhr
When does it start?	**Hoe laat begint het?**	hoo lāt buh-khint uht
Who is winning?	**Wie wint er?**	wee wint uhr

What is the score?	Wat is de stand?	wat is duh stant
Where's the race course?	Waar is de renbaan?	wār is duh ren-bān
When's the next meeting?	Wanneer is de volgende race?	wan-nayr is duh vol-luh-khuhn-duh rays
Which is the favourite?	Wie is de favoriet?	wee is duh fa-vō-reet
Who is the jockey?	Wie is de jockey?	wee is duh zho-kee
Do you play cards?	Kaart u?	kārt ü
Would you like a game of chess?	Wilt u een partijtje schaken?	wilt ü uhn par-ty-tyuh skhā-k'n
I'd like to ride	Ik wou graag paardrijden	ik wow khrākh pārt-ry-duhn
Is there a riding stable nearby?	Is er een manege in de buurt?	is uhr uhn mā-nay-zhuh in de bürt
Do you give lessons?	Geeft u ook les?	khayft ü ōk les
I am an inexperienced rider/a good rider	Ik ben een beginner/ een goede ruiter	ik ben uhn buh-khi-nuhr/ uhn khoo-yuh rui-t'r
Can I hire a rowing boat/canoe/ windsurfer/motor boat?	Kan ik een roeiboot/ kano/surfplank/ motorboot huren?	kan ik uhn rooee-bōt/ kā-nō/suh-ruhf-plank/ mō-t'r-bōt hü-ruhn
What does it cost by the hour?	Hoeveel kost dat per uur?	hoo-vayl kost dat per ür
Is there a map of the river?	Is er een kaart van de rivier?	is uhr uhn kārt van duh ree-veer

Are there many locks to pass?	**Moet ik veel sluizen door?**	moot ik vayl slui-zuh dōr
Can we get fuel here?	**Kunnen we hier brandstof krijgen?**	kun-nuh wuh heer brant-stof kry-khuh

ON THE BEACH

Where are the best beaches?	**Waar is het beste strand?**	wār is uht **bes**-tuh strant
Is there a quiet beach near here?	**Is er een rustig strand in de buurt?**	is uhr uhn **ruhs**-tuhkh strant in duh bürt
Can we walk or is it too far?	**Kunnen we lopen of is het te ver?**	kun-nuh wuh lō-puhn ov is uht tuh ver
Is there a bus to the beach?	**Is er een bus naar het strand?**	is uhr uhn buhs nār uht strant
Is it safe for swimming here?	**Is het hier veilig om te zwemmen?**	is uht heer vy-luhkh om tuh zwem-muh
Is it safe for small children?	**Is het veilig voor kleine kinderen?**	is uht vy-luhkh vor kly-nuh kin-duh-ruh
Is the sea very rough here?	**Is de zee hier erg ruw?**	is duh zay heer e-ruhkh rüw
Is there a lifeguard?	**Is er een strandwacht?**	is uhr uhn **strant**-wakht

What time is high/low tide?	Hoe laat is het vloed/eb?	hoo lāt is uht vloot/eb
Bathing prohibited	*Verboden te zwemmen/baden	vuhr-bō-duhn tuh zwem-muhn/bā-duhn
It's dangerous	*Het is gevaarlijk	uht is khuh-vār-luhk
There's a strong current here	*Er is een sterke stroom hier	d'r is uhn ste-ruh-kuh strōm heer
Are you a strong swimmer?	*Bent u een goede zwemmer?	bent ü uhn khoo-yuh zwem-muhr
Is it deep?	Is het diep?	is uht deep
How's the water?	Hoe is het water?	hoo is uht wā-t'r
It's warm/cold	Het is warm/koud	uht is wa-ruhm/kowt
Can one swim in the lake/river?	Kun je in het meer/in de rivier zwemmen?	kuhn yuh in uht mayr/in duh ree-veer zwem-muhn
Is there an indoor/outdoor swimming pool?	Is er een overdekt/openlucht zwembad?	is uhr uhn ō-vuhr-dekt/ō-puh-lukht zwem-bat
Is it heated?	Is het verwarmd?	is uht vuhr-wa-ruhmt
Are there showers?	Zijn er douches?	zyn uhr doo-shus
I want a cabin	Kan ik een kabine huren	kan ik uhn ka-bee-nuh hü-ruhn
for the day for the morning for two hours	voor de hele dag voor de ochtend voor twee uur?	vōr duh hay-luh dakh vōr duh okh-tuhnt vōr tway ür
I want to hire a deckchair/sunshade	Kan ik een ligstoel/parasol huren?	kan ik uhn likh-stool/pa-rā-sol hü-ruhn

Can we water-ski here?	Kunnen we hier waterskieën?	kuh-nuh wuh heer wā-tuhr-skee-yuhn
I haven't waterskied before	Ik heb nooit eerder gewaterskied	ik heb nōeet ayr-duhr khuh-wā-tuhr-skeet
Can I rent/borrow a wetsuit?	Kan ik een surfpak huren/lenen?	kan ik uhn suh-ruhf-pak hü-ruh/lay-nuh
Should I wear a life jacket?	Moet ik een zwemvest dragen?	moot ik uhn zwem-vest drā-khuhn
Can we hire the equipment?	Kunnen we de uitrusting huren?	kuh-nuh wuh duh uit-ruhs-ting hü-ruhn
Where's the harbour?	Waar is de haven?	wār is duh hā-vuhn
Can we go out in a fishing boat?	Kunnen we met een vissersboot mee?	kuh-nuh wuh met uhn vis-suhrs-bōt may
We want to go fishing	We wilden gaan vissen	wuh wil-duhn khān vis-suhn
Is there any underwater fishing	Wordt er hier aan onderwater vissen gedaan?	wort uhr heer ān on-duhr-wā-tuhr vis-suhn khuh-dān
Where can I buy a snorkel flippers a bucket and spade?	Waar krijg ik een snorkel zwemvliezen een emmertje en schepje?	wār krykh ik uhn snor-kuhl zwem-vlee-zuhn uhn em-muhr-tyuh en skhep-yuh
ball	bal	bal
crab	krab	krab
rowing/motor/sailing boat	roei/motor/zeil boot	rooee/mō-t'r/zyl bōt

first aid	eerste hulp	ayr-stuh hul-luhp
jellyfish	kwal	kwal
lighthouse	vuurtoren	vür-tō-ruhn
sand(-castle)	zand(kasteel)	zant(-kas-tayl)
sun	zon	zon
sunburn	zonnebrand	zon-nuh-brant
sun cream/lotion	zonnebrand crème/olie	zon-nuh-brant krèm/ō-lee
sunglasses	zonnebril	zon-nuh-bril
surf	branding	bran-ding
swimsuit	badpak	bat-pak
swimming trunks	zwembroek	zwem-brook
towel	handdoek	han-dook
waves	golven	khol-vuhn

IN THE COUNTRY

Is there a scenic route to …?	**Is er een toeristische route naar …?**	is uhr uhn too-ris-tee-suh roo-tuh nār
Can you give me a lift to …?	**Kunt u me een lift geven naar …?**	kuhnt ü muh uhn lift khay-vuh nār
Is there a footpath/cycle track to …?	**Is er een wandelpad/ fietspad naar …?**	is uhr uhn wan-duhl-pat/feets-pat nār
Is it possible to go across country?	**Is het mogelijk om door het veld te gaan?**	is uht mō-khuh-luhk om dōr uht velt tuh khān
Is there a shortcut?	**Is er een kortere weg?**	is uhr uhn kor-tuh-ruh wekh
Is this a public footpath?	**Is dit een openbaar wandelpad?**	is dit uhn ō-puhn-bār wan-duhl-pat
Is there a bridge across the river/stream?	**Is er een brug over de rivier/beek?**	is uhr uhn bruhkh ō-vuhr duh ree-veer/bayk

Can we walk there?	Kunnen we het lopen?	kuh-nuh wuh uht lō-puh
How far is the next village?	Hoe ver is het volgende dorp?	hoo ver is uht vol-luh-khuhn-duh do-ruhp
It's an hour's walk	*Het is een uur lopen	tis uhn ür lō-p'n

THE WEATHER

Is it usually as cold as this?	Is het hier altijd zo koud?	is uht heer al-tyt zō kowt
It's going to be hot/cold today	Het wordt warm/koud vandaag	uht wort war-ruhm/kowt van-dākh
This mist will clear later	De mist trekt later op	duh mist trekt lā-t'r op
Will it be fine tomorrow?	Wordt het morgen goed weer?	wort uht mo-ruh-khuh khoot wayr
What is the weather forecast?	Wat is de weersverwachting?	wat is duh wayrs-vuhr-wakh-ting
Do you think it will rain?	Denkt u dat het gaat regenen?	denkt ü dat uht khāt ray-khuh-nuh
What lovely/awful weather!	Wat een prachtweer/rotweer!	wat uhn prakht-wayr/rot-wayr

TRAVELLING WITH CHILDREN

Can you put a child's bed in our room?	Kunt u een kinder ledikant in onze kamer laten zetten?	kuhnt ü uhn kin-duhr lay-dee-kant in on-zuh kā-muhr lā-tuh zet-tuh
Can you give us adjoining rooms?	Kunt u ons kamers naast elkaar geven?	kuhnt ü ons kā-muhrs nāst muh-kār khay-vuhn
Is there a babysitting service?	Is er een babysit/ oppas centrale?	is uhr uhn bay-bee-sit/op-pas sen-trā-luh
Can you find me a babysitter?	Kunt u een babysitter voor me vinden?	kuhnt ü uhn bay-bee-si-tuhr vŏr muh vin-duh
We shall be out for a couple of hours	We gaan een paar uur uit	wuh khān uhn pār ür uit
We shall be back at ...	We zijn om ... terug	wuh zyn om ... truhkh
Is there a children's menu?	Is er een kindermenu?	is uhr uhn kin-duhr-muh-nü

Do you have half portions for children?	**Zijn er kinderporties?**	zyn uhr **kin**-duhr-por-sees
Have you got a high chair?	**Is er een kinderstoel?**	is uhr uhn **kin**-duhr-stool
Are there any organized activities for children?	**Wordt er iets georganiseerd voor kinderen?**	wort uhr eets khuh-**or**-khā-nee-sayrt vŏr **kin**-duh-ruh
Is there a paddling pool? children's swimming pool? playground? games room?	**Is er een pierebadje? kinder zwembad? speeltuin? speelkamer?**	is uhr uhn pee-ruh-ba-tyuh **kin**-duhr zwem-bat **spayl**-tuin **spayl**-kā-muhr
Is there an amusement park nearby?	**Is er een pretpark in de buurt?**	is uhr uhn **pret**-pa-ruhk in duh bürt
I'd like a beach ball a bucket and spade a doll flippers goggles playing cards roller skates a skipping rope a snorkel	**Ik zoek een strandbal een emmertje en schepje een pop zwemvliezen een duikbril speelkaarten rolschaatsen een springtouw een snorkel**	ik zook uhn **strant**-bal uhn **em**-muhr-tyuh en **skhep**-yuh uhn pop **zwem**-vlee-zuhn uhn **duik**-bril **spayl**-kār-tuhn **rol**-skhāt-suhn uhn **spring**-tow uhn **snor**-kuhl
Toy shop	**Speelgoedwinkel**	**spayl**-khoot-wing-kuhl
Zoo	**Dierentuin**	**dee**-ruh-tuin

Where can I feed/change my baby?	**Waar kan ik de baby voeden/ verschonen?**	wār kan ik duh bay-bee voo-duhn/ vuhr-skhō-nuhn
Can you heat this bottle?	**Kunt u deze fles opwarmen?**	kuhnt ü day-zuh fles op-war-ruh-muh
I want some (disposable) nappies	**Ik zoek (wegwerp) luiers**	ik zook (wekh-werp) lui-yuhrs
Feeding bottle	**Fles**	fles
Baby food	**Baby voeding**	bay-bee voo-ding
My daughter suffers from travel sickness	**Mijn dochter heeft last van reisziekte**	muhn dokh-t'r hayft last van rys-zeek-tuh
She has hurt herself	**Ze heeft zich bezeerd**	zuh hayft zikh buh-zayrt
My son is ill	**Mijn zoon is ziek**	myn zōn is zeek
He has lost his toy	**Hij heeft zijn speeltje verloren**	hy hayft zuhn spayl-tyuh vuhr-lō-ruhn
I'm sorry if they have bothered you	**Het spijt me als u last van ze gehad heeft**	uht spyt muh als ü last van zuh khuh-hat hayft

BUSINESS MATTERS

I would like to make an appointment with ...	Ik wou graag een afspraak maken met ...	ik wow khrākh uhn af-sprāk mā-k'n met
I have an appointment	Ik heb een afspraak	ik heb uhn af-sprāk
My name is ...	Mijn naam is ...	myn nām is
Here is my card	Hier is mijn kaartje	heer is myn kār-tyuh
This is our catalogue	Dit is onze catalogus	dit is on-zuh ka-tā-lō-khuhs
I would like to see your products/factory	Ik zou graag uw producten/fabriek zien	ik zow khrākh üw prō-duhk-tuhn/fa-breek zeen
Could you send me samples?	Kunt u me monsters sturen?	kuhnt ü muh mon-stuhrs stü-ruhn
Can you provide an interpreter/secretary?	Kunt u me een tolk/secretaresse bezorgen?	kuhnt ü muh uhn tolk/si-kruh-tā-res-suh buh-zo-ruh-khuhn

| Where can I make photocopies? | **Waar kan ik fotocopieën maken?** | wār kan ik fō-tō-kō-pee-yuhn mā-k'n |
| Where can I send a telex/fax? | **Waar kan ik een telex/ (tele)fax versturen?** | wār kan ik uhn tay-leks/(tay-luh-)faks vuhr-stü-ruhn |

AT THE DOCTOR'S

Is there a doctor's surgery near here?	Woont hier een dokter in de buurt?	wónt heer uhn **dok**-t'r in de bürt
I must see a doctor; can you recommend one?	Ik heb een dokter nodig; weet u een goede?	ik heb uhn **dok**-t'r nō-duhk, wayt ü uhn **khoo**-yuh
Please call a doctor	Kunt u een dokter roepen?	kuhnt ü uhn **dok**-t'r **roo**-p'n
When can the doctor come?	Wanneer kan de dokter komen?	wan-nayr kan duh **dok**-t'r kō-muhn
Does the doctor speak English	Spreekt de dokter Engels?	spraykt duh **dok**-t'r **eng**-uhls
Can I make an appointment for as soon as possible?	Kan ik zo gauw mogelijk een afspraak krijgen?	kan ik zō khow **mō**-khuh-luhk uhn af-sprāk **kry**-khuhn

AILMENTS

I take ...; can you give me a new prescription?	Ik neem ...; kunt u me een nieuw recept geven?	ik naym ...; kuhnt ü muh uhn neew ruh-**sept** khay-vuhn
I have high/low blood pressure	Ik heb hoge/lage bloeddruk	ik heb hō-khuh/lā-khuh bloot-druhk
I am pregnant	Ik ben zwanger	ik ben zwang-uhr
I am allergic to ...	Ik ben allergisch voor ...	ik ben a-**ler**-khees vōr
I think it is infected	Ik denk dat het ontstoken is	ik denk dat uht ont-**stō**-kuhn is
I feel ill	Ik voel me ziek	ik vool muh ̇zeek
I have a pain in my right arm	Ik heb pijn in mijn rechterarm	ik heb pyn in muh **rekh**-tuhr-arm
My left wrist hurts	Mijn linkerpols doet pijn	myn **lin**-kuhr-pols doot pyn
I have pulled/strained a muscle	Ik heb een spier verrekt	ik heb uhn speer vuh-**rekt**
I think I have sprained/ broken my ankle	Ik geloof dat ik mijn enkel verstuikt/ gebroken heb	ik khuh-**lōf** dat ik myn eng-kuhl vuhr-**stuikt**/ khuh-**brō**-kuhn heb
I fell down and hurt my back	Ik ben gevallen en heb mijn rug bezeerd	ik ben khuh-**val**-luh en heb muh ruhkh buh-**zayrt**
My feet are swollen	Mijn voeten zijn gezwollen	muh **voo**-t'n zyn khuh-**zwol**-luhn

I've burned/cut/ bruised/ wounded myself	Ik heb me gebrand/ gesneden/ gestoten/verwond	ik heb muh khuh-**brant**/ khuh-**snay**- duhn/ khuh-stō-t'n/vuhr-**wont**
My stomach is upset	Ik heb last van mijn maag	ik heb last van muh mākh
My appetite's gone	Ik ben mijn eetlust kwijt	ik ben muhn ayt-lust kwyt
I think I've got food poisoning	Ik geloof dat ik voedselvergiftig- ing heb	ik khuh-lōf dat ik voot-suhl-vuhr-khif- tuh-khing heb
I can't eat sleep swallow	Ik kan niet eten slapen slikken	ik kan neet ay-tuhn slā-puhn sli-kuhn
My nose keeps bleeding	Mijn neus blijft bloeden	muh nœs blyft **bloo**-duh
I have earache toothache headache a sore throat	Ik heb oorpijn kiespijn hoofdpijn keelpijn	ik heb ōr-pyn kees-pyn hōft-pyn kayl-pyn
I have difficulty breathing	Ik kan moeilijk ademhalen	ik kan **mooee**-luhk ā-duhm-hā-luhn
I feel dizzy sick shivery	Ik ben duizelig misselijk huiverig	ik ben dui-zuh-luhkh mis-suh-luhk hui-vuh-ruhkh
I keep vomiting	Ik moet steeds overgeven	ik moot stayts ō-vuhr- khay-vuh

I have a temperature/fever	Ik heb verhoging/koorts	ik heb vuhr-hō-khing/kōrts
I think I've caught 'flu	Ik denk dat ik griep heb	ik denk dat ik khreep heb
I've got a cold	Ik ben verkouden	ik ben ver-kow-duh
I've had it since yesterday/a few hours	Ik heb het sinds gisteren/sinds een paar uur	ik heb uht sints khis-tuh-ruh/sints uhn pār ür
abscess	ontsteking	ont-stay-king
ache	pijn	pyn
allergy	allergie	a-ler-khee
appendicitis	blindedarm ontsteking	blin-duh-darm ont-stay-king
asthma	asthma	as-mā
back (pain)	(pijn in de) rug	(pyn in duh) rukh
blister	blaar	blār
boil	zweer	zwayr
bruise	kneuzing	knœ-zing
burn	brandwond	brant-wont
cardiac condition	hartaandoening	hart-ān-doo-ning
chill, cold	verkoudheid	vuhr-kowt-hyt
constipation	verstopping	vuhr-sto-ping
cough	hoest	hoost
cramp	kramp	kramp
diabetic	suikerziek	sui-kuhr-zeek
diarrhoea	diarree	dee-a-ray
earache	oorpijn	ōr-pyn
fever	koorts	kōrts
food poisoning	voedselvergiftiging	voot-suhl-vuhr-khif-tuh-khing

fracture	**breuk**	brœk
hay fever	**hooikoorts**	hōee-kŏrts
headache	**hoofdpijn**	hŏft-pyn
high blood pressure	**hoge bloeddruk**	hō-khuh bloot-druhk
ill, sick	**ziek**	zeek
illness	**ziekte**	zeek-tuh
indigestion	**indigestie**	in-dee-khes-tee
infection	**infectie**	in-fek-see
influenza	**griep**	khreep
insect bite	**insectenbeet**	in-sek-tuh-bayt
insomnia	**slapeloosheid**	slā-puh-lŏs-hyt
itch	**jeuk**	yœk
nausea	**misselijkheid**	mis-suh-luhk-hyt
nosebleed	**neusbloeding/**	nœs-bloo-ding/
	bloedneus	bloot-nœs
pain	**pijn**	pyn
rheumatism	**rheumatiek**	rœ-mā-teek
sore throat	**keelpijn**	kayl-pyn
sprain	**verstuiking**	vuhr-stui-king
sting	**steek**	stayk
stomach ache	**maagpijn**	mākh-pyn
stroke	**beroerte**	buh-roor-tuh
sunburn	**zonnebrand**	zon-nuh-brant
sunstroke	**zonnesteek**	zon-nuh-stayk
swelling	**zwelling**	zwel-ling
tonsillitis	**keelontsteking**	kayl-ont-stay-king
toothache	**kiespijn**	kees-pyn
ulcer	**maagzweer**	mākh-zwayr
wound	**wond**	wont

TREATMENT

You're hurting me	**U doet me pijn**	ü doot muh pyn
Must I stay in bed?	**Moet ik in bed blijven?**	moot ik in bet bly-vuh
Will you come and see me again?	**Komt u nog terug?**	komt ü nokh truhkh
How much do I owe you?	**Wat ben ik u schuldig?**	wat ben ik ü skhuhl-duhkh
When do you think I can travel again?	**Wanneer kan ik weer reizen?**	wan-nayr kan ik wayr ry-zuhn
Do you have a temperature?	***Hebt u verhoging?**	hebt ü vuhr-hō-khing
Does that hurt?	***Doet dat pijn?**	doot dat pyn
A lot?/A little?	***Erg?/Een beetje?**	e-ruhkh/uhn bay-tyuh
I feel better now	**Ik voel me weer beter**	ik vool muh wayr bay-t'r
Where does it hurt?	***Waar doet het pijn/zeer?**	wār doot uht pyn/zayr
Have you a pain here?	***Hebt u hier pijn?**	hebt ü heer pyn
How long have you had ...?	***Hoe lang hebt u al ...?**	hoo lang hebt ü al ...
Open your mouth	***Doet uw mond eens open**	doot üw mont uhs ō-puh

Put out your tongue	*Steekt uw tong eens uit	staykt üw tong uhs uit
Breathe in/out	*Ademt u in/uit	ā-duhmt ü in/uit
Hold your breath	*Adem inhouden	ā-duhm in-how-duhn
Please lie down	*Gaat u even liggen	khāt ü ay-vuh li-khuh
What medicines have you been taking?	*Wat voor medicijnen hebt u?	wat vōr may-dee-sy-nuhn hebt ü
I take this medicine – could you give me another prescription?	Ik neem deze medicijnen; kunt u me een nieuw recept geven?	ik naym day-zuh may-dee-sy-nuhn, kunt ü muh uhn neew ruh-sept khay-vuhn
I will give you an antibiotic/sedative	*Ik zal u antibiotica/ een kalmerend middel geven	ik zal ü an-tee-bee-yō-tee-kā/uhn kal-may-ruhnt mi-duhl khay-vuhn
Take these pills/this medicine	*Neemt u deze pillen/medicijnen	naymt ü day-zuh pil-luhn/may-dee-sy-nuhn
Take this prescription to the chemist's	*Brengt u dit recept naar de apotheek	brengt ü dit ruh-sept nār duh a-pō-tayk
Take this three times a day	*Neemt u dit drie keer per dag	naymt ü dit dree kayr per dakh
I'll give you an injection	*Ik zal u een injectie geven	ik zal ü uhn in-yek-see khay-vuhn
Roll up your sleeve	*Rolt u uw mouw even op	rolt ü üw mow ay-vuhn op

You should stay on a diet for a few days	*U moet een paar dagen diëet houden	u moot uhn pār dā-khuhn dee-yayt how-d'n
Come and see me again in two days' time	*Komt u over twee dagen weer terug	komt ü ō-vuhr tway dā-khuhn wayr truhkh
You must be x-rayed	*Er moet een röntgenfoto gemaakt worden	d'r moot uhn ruhnt-zuhn-fō-tō khuh-mākt wor-duhn
You must go to hospital	*U moet naar het ziekenhuis	ü moot nār uht zee-kuhn-huis
You must stay in bed (for a few days)	*U moet (een paar dagen) in bed blijven	u moot (uhn pār dā-khuhn) in bet bly-vuhn
You should not travel until ...	*U mag niet reizen tot ...	ü makh neet ry-zuhn tot ...
Nothing to worry about	*Niks om ongerust over te zijn	niks om on-khuh-ruhst ō-vuhr tuh zyn
I'd like a receipt for the health insurance	Mag ik een kwitantie voor de verzekering	makh ik uhn kwee-tan-tsee vor de vuhr-zay-kuh-ring
ambulance	ziekenwagen/ambulance	zee-kuh-wā-khuh/am-bü-lan-suh
anaesthetic	verdoving	vuhr-dō-ving
aspirin	aspirine	as-pee-ree-nuh
bandage	verband (n)	vuhr-bant
chiropodist	pedicuur	pay-dee-kür
hospital	ziekenhuis (n)	zee-kuhn-huis
injection	injectie	in-yek-see

laxative	laxeermiddel (*n*)	lak-**sayr**-mi-duhl
nurse	verpleegster/ verpleger	vuhr-**playkh**-stuhr/ vuhr-**play**-khuhr
operation	operatie	ō-puh-**rā**-tsee
optician	opticien	op-tee-**shen**
osteopath	osteopaat	os-tay-yō-**pāt**
pill	pil	pil
(adhesive) plaster	pleister	**ply**-stuhr
prescription	recept (*n*)	ruh-**sept**
X-ray	röntgen foto	**ruhnt**-zyuhn-fō-tō

PARTS OF THE BODY

ankle	enkel	**eng**-kuhl
arm	arm	arm
back	rug	ruhkh
bladder	blaas	blās
blood	bloed (*n*)	bloot
body	lichaam (*n*)	**li**-khām
bone	bot (*n*)	bot
bowels	darmen	**dar**-muhn
brain	hersenen	**her**-suh-nuh
breast	borst	borst
cheek	wang	wang
chest	borst	borst
chin	kin	kin
collar-bone	sleutelbeen (*n*)	**slœ**-tuhl-bayn
ear	oor (*n*)	ōr
elbow	elleboog	el-luh-**bōkh**

eye	oog (*n*)	ōkh
eyelid	ooglid (*n*)	ōkh-lit
face	gezicht (*n*)	khuh-zikht
finger	vinger	ving-uhr
foot	voet	voot
forehead	voorhoofd (*n*)	vōr-hoft
gums	tandvlees (*n*)	tant-vlays
hand	hand	hant
head	hoofd (*n*)	hōft
heart	hart (*n*)	hart
heel	hiel	heel
hip	heup	hœp
jaw	kaak	kāk
joint	gewricht (*n*)	khuh-wrikht
kidney	nier	neer
knee	knie	knee
knee-cap	knieschijf	knee-skhyf
leg	been (*n*)	bayn
lip	lip	lip
liver	lever	lay-vuhr
lung	long	long
mouth	mond	mont
muscle	spier	speer
nail	nagel	nā-khuhl
neck	nek	nek
nerve	zenuw	zay-nü
nose	neus	nœs
rib	rib	rib
shoulder	schouder	skhow-duhr
skin	huid	huit

spine	**ruggegraat**	ruh-khuh-khrāt
stomach	**maag**	mākh
temple	**slaap**	slāp
thigh	**dij**	dy
throat	**keel**	kayl
thumb	**duim**	duim
toe	**teen**	tayn
tongue	**tong**	tong
tonsils	**amandelen**	a-man-duh-luh
tooth	**tand**	tant
vein	**ader**	ā-duhr
wrist	**pols**	pols

AT THE DENTIST'S

I must see a dentist	**Ik moet naar de tandarts**	ik moot nār duh tant-arts
Can I make an appointment?	**Kan ik een afspraak maken?**	kan ik uhn af-sprāk mā-k'n
As soon as possible	**Zo gauw mogelijk**	zo khow mō-khuh-luhk
I have toothache	**Ik heb kiespijn**	ik heb kees-pyn
This tooth/molar hurts	**Deze tand/kies doet pijn**	day-zuh tant/kees doot pyn
I've lost a filling	**Ik heb een vulling verloren**	ik heb uhn vuhl-ling vuhr-lō-ruhn
I have a broken tooth/molar	**Ik heb een tand/kies gebroken**	ik heb uhn tant/kees khuh-brō-kuh
Can you fill it?	**Kunt u hem vullen?**	kuhnt u uhm vuhl-luhn
Can you do it now?	**Kunt u het nu dadelijk doen?**	kuhnt ü uht nü dā-duh-luhk doon

Must you take the tooth out?	**Moet die kies er uit?**	moot dee kees uhr uit
Please give me an injection first	**Kan ik eerst een injectie/verdoving krijgen?**	kan ik ayrst uhn in-yek-see/vuhr-dō-ving kry-khuhn
My gums are swollen keep bleeding	**Mijn tandvlees is gezwollen blijft bloeden**	muhn tant-vlays is khuh-zwol-luh blyft bloo-duhn
I've broken my plate, can you repair it?	**Ik heb mijn prothese gebroken, kunt u hem repareren?**	ik heb muh prō-tay-zuh khuh-brō-kuhn, kuhnt ü uhm ray-pa-ray-ruhn
You're hurting me	**U doet me pijn**	ü doot muh pyn
How much do I owe you?	**Wat ben ik u schuldig?**	wat ben ik ü skhuhl-duhkh
When should I come again?	**Wanneer moet ik terugkomen?**	wan-nayr moot ik truhkh kō-muhn
Please rinse your mouth	***Wilt u even spoelen**	wilt ü ay-vuh spoo-luhn
I will X-ray your teeth	***Ik zal een (röntgen)foto nemen**	ik zal uhn (ruhnt-zyuhn) -fō-tō nay-muhn
You have an abscess	***U hebt een ontsteking**	ü hebt uhn ont-stay-king
The nerve is exposed	***De zenuw ligt bloot**	duh zay-nü likht blōt
This tooth can't be saved	***Deze tand/kies is niet meer te redden**	day-zuh tant/kees is neet mayr tuh re-duhn

Don't eat on this side for the next ... hours	*Aan deze kant de volgende ... uur niet kauwen/eten	ān day-zuh kant de vol-khuhn-duh ... ür neet kow-wuhn/ay-t'n
Anaesthetic	Verdoving	vuhr-dō-ving
Crown	Kroon	krōn
Filling	Vulling	vuhl-ling
Gum	Tandvlees	tant-vlays
Molar	Kies	kees
Plate (upper/lower)	Prothese (boven/onder)	prō-tay-zuh (bō-vuhn/on-duhr)
Roof of the mouth	Verhemelte	vuhr-hay-muhl-tuh
Tooth	Tand	tant

PROBLEMS & ACCIDENTS

It's urgent	Het is dringend	tis **dring**-uhnt
There's a fire	Er is brand	d'r is brant
Where's the police station?	Waar is het politiebureau?	wār is uht pō-**lee**-tsee-bü-rō
Call the police/a doctor	Roep de politie/een dokter	roop duh pō-**lee**-tsee/uhn **dok**-t'r
Where is the British/American consulate?	Waar is het britse/amerikaanse consulaat?	wār is uht **brit**-suh/a-may-ree-**kān**-suh kon-sü-lāt
Please let the consulate know	Wilt u het consulaat verwittigen?	wilt ü uht kon-sü-lāt vuhr-**wi**-tuh-khuhn
My bag/wallet has been stolen	Mijn tas/portefeuille is gestolen	myn tas/por-tuh-**fui**-yuh is khuh-**stō**-luh
I found this in the street	Ik heb dit op straat gevonden	ik heb dit op strāt khuh-**von**-duh

I have lost my luggage/passport/traveller's cheques	**Ik heb mijn bagage/ paspoort/ reischeques verloren**	ik heb myn ba-**khā**-zhuh/pas-**pōrt**/ rys-sheks vuhr-**lō**-ruh
I have missed my train	**Ik heb mijn trein gemist**	ik heb muh tryn khuh-**mist**
My luggage is (still) on board	**Mijn bagage is (nog) aan boord**	myn ba-**khā**-zhuh is (nokh) ān bōrt
Call an ambulance	**Roep een ziekenwagen**	roop uhn **zee**-kuh-**wā**-khuhn
There has been an accident	**Er is een ongeluk gebeurd**	d'r is uhn **on**-khuh-luhk khuh-**bœrt**
She's badly hurt	**Zij is ernstig gewond**	zuh is **ern**-stuhkh khuh-**wont**
He has fainted	**Hij is flauw gevallen**	hy is flow khuh-**val**-luh
She's losing blood	**Zij verliest bloed**	zuh vuhr-**leest** bloot
Her arm/leg is broken	**Haar arm/been is gebroken**	hār arm/bayn is khuh-**brō**-kuhn
Please get some water/a blanket/ some bandages	**Kunt u alstublieft water/ een deken/ verbandstof halen?**	kuhnt ü als-tü-bleeft **wā**-t'r/uhn **day**-k'n/vuhr-**bant**-stof **hā**-luh
I've broken my glasses	**Mijn bril is kapot**	muh bril is ka-**pot**
I can't see	**Ik kan niets zien**	ik kan niks zeen
A child has fallen in the water	**Er is een kind in het water gevallen**	d'r is uhn kint in uht **wā**-t'r khuh-**val**-luh
Driving licence	**Rijbewijs**	**ry**-buh-wys

I didn't understand the sign	**Ik begreep het bord niet**	ik buh-**khrayp** uht bort neet
How much is the fine?	**Hoeveel is de boete?**	hoo-vayl is duh **boo**-tuh
May I see your insurance certificate?	**Mag ik uw verzeke-ringspapieren zien?**	makh ik üw vuhr-**zay**-kuh-rings-pa-pee-ruhn zeen
Apply to the insurance company	***U moet zich tot de verzekering wenden**	ü moot zikh tot duh vuhr-**zay**-kuh-ring **wen**-duhn
Can you help me?	**Kunt u mij helpen?**	kuhnt ü my **hel**-puhn
What is the name and address of the owner?	**Wat zijn de naam en het adres van de eigenaar?**	wat zyn duh nām en uht a-dres van duh **y**-khuh-nār
Are you willing to act as a witness?	**Wilt u getuigen?**	wilt ü khuh-**tui**-khuhn
Can I have your name and address, please?	**Mag ik uw naam en adres, alstublieft?**	makh ik üw nām en a-dres, als-tü-bleeft
I want a copy of the police report	**Mag ik een kopie van het politie rapport/ proces verbaal?**	makh ik uhn kō-pee van uht pō-**lee**-tsee ra-port/prō-ses vuhr-**bāl**
Our car has been broken into	**Onze auto is opengebroken**	on-zuh ō-tō is ō-puh-khuh-brō-kuh
I've been robbed/mugged	**Ik ben bestolen/aangerand**	ik ben buh-**stō**-luh/**ān**-khuh-rant
My son/daughter is lost	**Mijn zoon/dochter is zoek**	myn zōn/**dokh**-t'r is zook

TIME & DATES

TIME

What time is it?	**Hoe laat is het?**	hoo lāt is uht
It's one o'clock[1]	**Het is één uur**	uht is ayn ür
two o'clock	**twee uur**	tway ür
five past eight	**vijf over acht**	vyf ō-vuhr akht
quarter past five	**kwart over vijf**	kwart ō-vuhr vyf
twenty past four	**tien voor half vijf**	teen vōr hal-luhf vyf
half past four	**half vijf**	hal-luhf vyf
twenty to three	**tien over half drie/**	teen ō-vuhr hal-luhf dree/

1. The hour in Dutch usage is divided into quarters, and times are expressed as so many minutes **over heel** (past the hour), **voor half** (before half), **over half** (past the half hour) and **voor heel** (to the hour).

	twintig voor drie	twin-tuhkh vōr dree
quarter to ten	kwart voor tien	kwart vōr teen
Second	Seconde	suh-kon-duh
Minute	Minuut	mee-nüt
Hour	Uur (*n*)	ür
It's early/late	Het is vroeg/laat	uht is vrookh/lāt
My watch is slow/fast	Mijn horloge loopt achter/voor	muhn hor-lō-zhuh lōpt akh-tuhr/vōr
Sorry I'm late	Het spijt me dat ik zo laat ben	uht spyt muh dat ik zō lāt ben

DATE

What's the date?	De hoeveelste is het vandaag?	de hoo-vayl-stuh is uht van-dākh
It's December 9th	Het is de negende december	uht is de nay-khuhn-duh day-sem-buhr
We got here on July 27th	Wij zijn hier de zevenentwintigste juli gekomen	wuh zyn heer de zay-vuhn-en-twin-tuhkh-stuh yü-lee khuh-kō-muhn
We're leaving on January 5th	We vertrekken de vijfde januari	wuh vuhr-tre-kuhn duh vyv-duh ja-nü-wā-ree

DAY

morning	ochtend/morgen	okh-tuhnt/mor-khuhn
this morning	vanochtend	van-okh-tuhnt
tomorrow morning	morgenochtend	mor-khuhn-okh-tuhnt
in the morning	's morgens	smor-khuhns
midday, noon	twaalf uur	twā-l'f ür
at noon	om twaalf uur	om twā-l'f ür
afternoon	middag	mi-dakh
yesterday afternoon	gistermiddag	khis-tuhr-mi-dakh
in the afternoon	's middags	smi-dakhs
evening	avond	ā-vont
tomorrow evening	morgenavond	mor-khuhn-ā-vont
in the evening	's avonds	sā-vonts
midnight	middernacht	mi-duhr-nakht
night	nacht	nakht
in the night	's nachts	snakhts
sunrise	zonsopgang	zons-op-khang
dawn	morgenstond	mor-khuhn-stont
sunset	zonsondergang	zons-on-duhr-khang
dusk, twilight	schemering	skhay-muh-ring
today	vandaag	van-dākh
yesterday	gisteren	khis-tuh-ruhn
day before yesterday	eergisteren	ayr-khis-tuh-ruhn

tomorrow	**morgen**	mor-khuh
day after tomorrow	**overmorgen**	ō-vuhr-mor-khuh
in ten day's time	**over tien dagen**	ō-vuhr teen dā-khuhn
daily	**dagelijks**	dā-khuh-luhks

WEEK

Monday	**maandag**	mān-dakh
Tuesday	**dinsdag**	dins-dakh
Wednesday	**woensdag**	woons-dakh
Thursday	**donderdag**	don-duhr-dakh
Friday	**vrijdag**	vry-dakh
Saturday	**zaterdag**	zā-tuhr-dakh
Sunday	**zondag**	zon-dakh
on Tuesday	**op dinsdag**	op dins-dakh
every Tuesday	**dinsdags**	dins-dakhs
fortnight	**veertien dagen**	vayr-teen dā-khuhn
weekly	**wekelijks**	way-kuh-luhks

MONTH

January	**januari**	ja-nü-wā-ree
February	**februari**	fay-brü-wā-ree
March	**maart**	mārt
April	**april**	a-pril

May	**mei**	my
June	**juni**	jü-nee
July	**juli**	jü-lee
August	**augustus**	ow-khuhs-tuhs
September	**september**	sep-tem-buhr
October	**october**	ok-tō-buhr
November	**november**	nō-vem-buhr
December	**december**	day-sem-buhr
monthly	**maandelijks**	mān-duh-luhks

SEASON

spring	**voorjaar/lente**	vōr-yār/len-tuh
summer	**zomer**	zō-muhr
autumn	**najaar/herfst**	nā-yār/he-r'fst
winter	**winter**	win-tuhr
in spring	**in de lente**	in duh len-tuh
during the	**'s zomers/**	zō-muhrs/
summer/winter	**'s winters**	swin-tuhrs
quarterly	**ieder kwartaal**	ee-duhr kwar-tāl

YEAR

This year	**dit jaar**	dit yār
Last year	**vorig jaar**	vō-ruhkh yār
Next year	**volgend jaar**	vo-luh-khuhnt yar
yearly	**jaarlijks**	yār-luhks

PUBLIC HOLIDAYS

New Year's Day	Nieuwjaarsdag	neew-yārs-dakh
Happy New Year	Gelukkig Nieuwjaar	khuh-luh-kuhkh neew-yār
Good Friday (half day)	Goede Vrijdag	khoo-yuh vry-dakh
Easter	Pasen	pā-suhn
Easter Monday	Tweede Paasdag	tway-duh pās-dakh
30 April (Queen's birthday)	Koninginnedag	kō-ning-in-nuh-dakh
Ascension Day	Hemelvaartsdag	hay-muhl-vārts-dakh
Whitsun	Pinksteren	pink-stuh-ruhn
Whit Monday	Tweede Pinksterdag	tway-duh pink-stuhr-dakh
Christmas	Kerstmis	kers-muhs
Merry Christmas	Vrolijk Kerstfeest	rrō-luhk kers-fayst
Christmas Day	(Eerste) Kerstdag	(ayr-stuh) kers-dakh
Boxing Day	Tweede Kerstdag	tway-duh kers-dakh

Religious holidays which are only observed in catholic areas (i.e. roughly south of the Maas and Waal rivers and in Belgium):

6 January (Epiphany)	Driekoningen	dree-kō-ning-uhn
15 August (Ascension of the Virgin)	Maria Hemelvaart	ma-ree-yā hay-muhl-vārt
1 November (All Saints' Day)	Allerheiligen	al-luhr-hy-luh-khuhn

NUMBERS

CARDINAL

0	nul	nuhl
1	een	ayn
2	twee	tway
3	drie	dree
4	vier	veer
5	vijf	vyf
6	zes	zes
7	zeven	zay-vuh/zœ-vuhn
8	acht	akht
9	negen	nay-khuh
10	tien	teen
11	elf	e-l'f
12	twaalf	twā-l'f
13	dertien	der-teen
14	veertien	vayr-teen
15	vijftien	vyf-teen

16	zestien	zes-teen
17	zeventien	zay-vuhn-teen
18	achttien	akh-teen
19	negentien	nay-khuhn-teen
20	twintig	twin-tuhkh
21	een en twintig	ayn-en-twin-tuhkh
22	twee en twintig	tway-en-twin-tuhkh
30	dertig	der-tuhkh
31	een en dertig	ayn-en-der-tuhkh
40	veertig	vayr-tuhkh
50	vijftig	vyf-tuhkh
60	zestig	zes-tuhkh
70	zeventig	zay-vuhn-tuhkh
80	tachtig	takh-tuhkh
90	negentig	nay-khuhn-tuhkh
100	honderd	hon-duhrt
101	honderdeen	hon-duhrt-ayn
200	tweehonderd	tway-hon-duhrt
1,000	duizend	dui-zuhnt
2,000	tweeduizend	tway-dui-zuhnt
1,000,000	(een) miljoen	(uhn) mil-yoon

ORDINAL

1st	eerste	ayr-stuh
2nd	tweede	tway-duh
3rd	derde	der-duh
4th	vierde	veer-duh
5th	vijfde	vyv-duh

6th	**zesde**	**zes**-duh
7th	**zevende**	zay-vuhn-duh
8th	**achtste**	**akh**-stuh
9th	**negende**	nay-khuhn-duh
10th	**tiende**	teen-duh
11th	**elfde**	el-luhf-duh
12th	**twaalfde**	twā-luhf-duh
13th	**dertiende**	der-teen-duh
20th	**twintigste**	twin-tuhkh-stuh
21st	**een en twintigste**	ayn-en-twin-tuhkh-stuh
30th	**dertigste**	der-**tuhkh**-stuh
100th	**honderdste**	hon-**duhrt**-stuh
1000th	**duizendste**	dui-zuhnt-stuh
half	**half**	ha-l'f/**hal**-luhf
quarter	**kwart**	kwart
three quarters	**drie kwart**	dree kwart
a third	**een derde**	uhn **der**-duh
two thirds	**twee derde**	tway **der**-duh

WEIGHTS & MEASURES

DISTANCE

kilometres – miles

km	miles or km	miles	km	miles or km	miles
1·6	1	0·6	14·5	9	5·6
3·2	2	1·2	16·1	10	6·2
4·8	3	1·9	32·2	20	12·4
6·4	4	2·5	40·2	25	15·3
8	5	3·1	80·5	50	31·1
9·7	6	3·7	160·9	100	62·1
11·3	7	4·3	804·7	500	310·7
12·9	8	5·0			

A rough way to convert from miles to kms: divide by 5 and multiply by 8;
to convert kms to miles divide by 8 and multiply by 5.

LENGTH AND HEIGHT

centimetres – inches

cm	inch or cm	inch	cm	inch or cm	inch
2·5	1	0·4	17·8	7	2·8
5·1	2	0·8	20·3	8	3·1
7·6	3	1·2	22·9	9	3·5
10·2	4	1·6	25·4	10	3·9
12·7	5	2·0	50·8	20	7·9
15·2	6	2·4	127	50	19·7

A rough way to convert from inches to cm: divide by 2 and multiply by 5; to convert cm to inches divide by 5 and multiply by 2.

metres – feet

m	ft or m	ft	m	ft or m	ft
0·3	1	3·3	2·4	8	26·2
0·6	2	6·6	2·7	9	29·5
0·9	3	9·8	3	10	32·8
1·2	4	13·1	6·1	20	65·6
1·5	5	16·4	15·2	50	164
1·8	6	19·7	30·5	100	328·1
2·1	7	23	152·5	500	1,690·5

A rough way to convert from ft to m: divide by 10 and multiply by 3; to convert m to ft divide by 3 and multiply by 10.

metres – yards

m	yds or m	yds	m	yds or m	yds
0·9	1	1·1	7·3	8	8·7
1·8	2	2·2	8·2	9	9·8
2·7	3	3·3	9·1	10	10·9
3·7	4	4·4	18·3	20	21·9
4·6	5	5·5	45·7	50	54·7
5·5	6	6·6	91·4	100	109·4
6·4	7	7·7	457·2	500	546·8

A rough way to convert from yds to m: subtract 10 per cent from the number of yds; to convert m to yds add 10 per cent to the number of metres.

LIQUID MEASURES

litres – gallons

litres	galls. or litres	galls.	litres	galls. or litres	galls.
4·6	1	0·2	36·4	8	1·8
9·1	2	0·4	40·9	9	2·0
13·6	3	0·7	45·5	10	2·2
18·2	4	0·9	90·9	20	4·4
22·7	5	1·1	136·4	30	6·6
27·3	6	1·3	181·8	40	8·8
31·8	7	1·5	227·3	50	11

1 pint = 0·6 litre   1 litre = 1·8 pint

A rough way to convert from galls. to litres: divide by 2 and multiply by 9; to convert litres to galls. divide by 9 and multiply by 2.

WEIGHT

kilogrammes – pounds

kg	lb. or kg	lb.	kg	lb. or kg	lb.
0·5	1	2·2	3·2	7	15·4
0·9	2	4·4	3·6	8	17·6
1·4	3	6·6	4·1	9	19·8
1·8	4	8·8	4·5	10	22·0
2·3	5	11·0	9·1	20	44·1
2·7	6	13·2	22·7	50	110·2

A rough way to convert from lb. to kg: divide by 11 and multiply by 5; to convert kg to lb. divide by 5 and multiply by 11.

grammes – ounces

grammes	oz.	oz.	grammes
100	3·5	2	57·1
250	8·8	4	114·3
500	17·6	8	228·6
1,000 (1 kg)	35	16 (1 lb.)	457·2

TEMPERATURE

centigrade °C	fahrenheit °F
− 10	14
− 5	23
0	32
5	41
10	50
15	59
20	68
25	77
30	86
35	95
37	98·4
38	100·5
39	102
40	104
100	212

To convert °F to °C: deduct 32, divide by 9 and multiply by 5; to convert °C to °F multiply by 9, divide by 5 and add 32.

BASIC GRAMMAR

CASES

Present-day Dutch has no cases in active use, except in the personal pronouns, and in a few archaic expressions with the dative or locative:

> ter plaatse – *on the spot*

and most frequently in the ending **-s** of the names of the days or seasons which gives them (as in English) the meaning of *every* or *during*:

> vrijdags – (*on*) *Fridays*; 's avonds – *evenings, in the evening*; 's zomers – *in summer*

GENDERS

Genders are not very strongly expressed any more except for living beings where the sex is clearly defined in the context; otherwise the only difference is in the use of the definite article, and the terms **de**-words and **het**-words are now used rather than the old genders.

DEFINITE ARTICLE

de for both masculine and feminine singular

> de man – *man*; de vrouw – *woman*

het for neuter nouns and for all dimunutives in the singular

het huis – *house*; het vrouwtje – (*dim.*) *woman*

de for all plurals

de mannen; de vrouwen; de huizen

INDEFINITE ARTICLE

een for all genders

een man; een vrouw; een huis

geen is the negative form, meaning no (none)

geen werk – *no work*

NOUNS

Nouns have either the common gender with the definite article **de**, or they are neuter and take **het**. Neuter nouns are indicated by (*n*) in the vocabulary.
The plural is normally formed by adding the ending **-en**. Some words change their stem vowel as well:

boek, boeken – *book*; stad, steden – *town*

The plural of all diminutives is formed by adding **-s** at the end:

hapje, hapjes – *snack*

Other groups of words which add **-s** to form the plural are those ending in

-en jongen, jongens – *boy*
-el boekhandel, boekhandels – *bookshop*
-er bakker, bakkers – *baker*

and most words borrowed from other languages

acteur, acteurs – *actor*; garage, garages – *garages*

except Latin words in **-um**: museum, musea

DIMINUTIVES

Dutch uses diminutives very frequently, and with a total disregard for relative size. They are formed by adding **-je** to the end of a word, or **-tje** after a voiced consonant or a vowel. Quite often they change the meaning of the word, and always they change the gender: a *de* word becomes a *het* word in the diminutive form.

> de stoel, het stoeltje – *chair*; de hap (*bite*) – het hapje (*snack*); de sla (*lettuce*) – het slaatje (*salad*)

ADJECTIVES

Adjectives take the ending **-e**

(a) when they are used after the definite article or demonstrative pronouns

> het oude huis – *the old house*
> de nieuwe jas – *the new coat*
> dat dure boek – *that expensive book*

(b) after the indefinite article and its negation (**geen**), if the noun is a **de**-word

> een oude man – *an old man*
> **but** een jong kind (*n*) *a young child*
> geen goede stof – *not a good cloth*
> **but** geen goed woord (*n*) – *not a good word*

(c) if no article at all is used and the noun is a **de**-word

> goede wijn – *good wine*
> **but** rood haar (*n*) – *red hair*

(d) in the plural

> de jonge kinderen – *the young children*
> oude huizen – *old houses*
> geen goede woorden – *no good words*

COMPARATIVES

Comparatives are always formed by adding **-er** to the adjective (**-der** for words ending in **-r**). To form the superlative add **-st**:

hoog	hoger	hoogst	*high*	*higher*	*highest*
ver	verder	verst	*far*	*farther*	*farthest*

The most common irregular forms are

goed	beter	best	*good*	*better*	*best*
veel	meer	meest	*much*	*more*	*most*
weinig	minder	minst	*little*	*less*	*least*

ADVERBS

Adverbs have the same form as adjectives, but do not decline. A peculiarity of Dutch is the use of diminutives even here:

>   zachtjes – *softly* (**from** zacht – *soft*)

PERSONAL PRONOUNS

Subject functions and all other functions

ik	*I*		me, mij	*me, to me, etc.*
je, jij	*you (familiar)*		je, jou	
u	*you (polite)*		u	
hij	*he*		hem	
ze, zij	*she*		ze, haar	
het	*it*		het	
we, wij	*we*		ons	
jullie	*you (pl., familiar)*		jullie	
u	*you (pl., polite)*		u	
ze, zij	*they*		ze	

The forms ending in **-e** are much more common than those ending in **-ij**. The latter are now mainly used to give emphasis to the word.

The polite form of address **u** is used to all strangers, and to people considered superior either in age or status.

het and plural **ze** are never used after a preposition; the following forms are used instead:

> ervan (**not** van het/ze) – *of it/them (thereof)*
> eraan (**not** aan het/ze) – *to it/them (thereto)*
> ermee (**not** met het/ze) – *with it/them (therewith)*

REFLEXIVE PRONOUNS

Reflexive pronouns follow the forms of the personal pronoun (to which **-zelf** can be added for greater emphasis), except in the third person singular and plural, where the form is **zich**:

> ik verweer me – *I defend myself*
> ik heb mezelf gesneden – *I've cut myself*
> hij scheert zich – *he shaves (himself)*

POSSESSIVE PRONOUNS

mijn	*my, mine*
jouw	*your, yours (familiar)*
uw	*your, yours (polite)*
zijn	*his*
haar	*her, hers*
ons, onze	*our, ours* (this is the only possessive pronoun which declines: **ons** changes to **onze** before a **de** noun and before any noun in the plural)
jullie	*your, yours (familiar)*
uw	*your, yours (polite)*
hun	*their, theirs*

DEMONSTRATIVE PRONOUNS

die	*that (one)*	for de-words

dat	*that (one)*	for **het**-words
die	*those*	for all plurals
deze	*this (one)*	for **de**-words
dit	*this (one)*	for **het**-words
deze	*these*	for all plurals

RELATIVE PRONOUNS

die	*who, which*	with **de**-words
dat	*who, which*	with **het**-words
die	*who, which*	for all plurals

INTERROGATIVE PRONOUNS

wie?	*who?*
wat?	*what?*
welk?	*which?*
wiens?	*whose?*

NEGATIVES

Negatives are generally formed by putting **niet** (not) after the word or phrase to be negated.

VERBS

Dutch verbs fall into two groups, strong and weak verbs, depending on the way they form their imperfect tense and past participle. Strong verbs also change their stem vowel and these changes are indicated in the vocabulary:

infinitive	*imperfect*	*past participle*	
breken	brak	gebroken	*to break*

Weak verbs form the imperfect tense by adding **-te** to the stem if it ends with **-ch, -f, -k, -p, -s, -t**, and by adding **-de** in all other cases. Both weak and strong verbs form the past participle by adding the prefix **ge-** to the stem, and the suffix **-t** or **-d** for weak verbs, **-en** for strong verbs. The latter sometimes revert to a weak form either in the vowel or the ending.

wachten	wachtte	gewacht	*to wait*
horen	hoorde	gehoord	*to hear*
lopen	liep	gelopen	*to walk*
brengen	bracht	gebracht	*to bring*

The pronoun of formal address, u, whether singular or plural, takes the verb in the second person singular, although in daily speech there is a tendency to use the third person of the auxiliary verb **hebben** – both are now considered correct:

| u hebt | u heeft | *you have (sing. or pl.)* |
| u bent | u is | *you are (sing. or pl.)* |

WEAK VERBS

infinitive	tellen	*to count*
pres. part.	tellend	*counting*
past part.	geteld	*counted*
imperative	tel	*count*

present		***future***[1]	
ik tel	I count	ik zal tellen	*I shall count, etc.*
jij telt	you count	jij zult tellen	
hij telt	he counts	hij zal tellen	
wij tellen	we count	*pl.* zullen tellen	
jullie tellen	you count		
zij tellen	they count		

perfect

| ik heb geteld | *I have counted, etc.* | hij heeft geteld |
| jij hebt geteld | | *pl.* hebben geteld |

---

1. In daily speech this tense is seldom used (except to denote a definite promise): the present tense is used instead.

imperfect		*pluperfect*	
sing. telde	*I counted, etc.*	*sing.* had geteld	*I had counted, etc.*
pl. telden		*pl.* hadden geteld	

STRONG VERBS

infinitive	roepen	*to call*
pres. part.	roepend	*calling*
past part.	geroepen	*called*
imperative	roep	*call*

present		*future*	
ik roep	*I call, etc.*	ik zal roepen	*I shall call, etc.*
jij roept		jij zult roepen	
hij roept		hij zal roepen	
wij roepen		*pl.* zullen roepen	
jullie roepen			
zij roepen			

imperfect		*pluperfect*	
sing. riep	*I called, etc.*	*sing.* had geroepen	*I had called, etc.*
pl. riepen		*pl.* hadden geroepen	

perfect
ik heb geroepen   *I have called, etc.*
jij hebt geroepen
hij heeft geroepen
pl. hebben geroepen

AUXILIARY VERBS

zijn – *to be (active sense)*

present	*imperfect*	*perfect*
ik ben	ik was	ik ben geweest
I am, etc.	*I was, etc.*	*I have been, etc.*

jij bent	jij was	jij bent geweest
hij is	hij was	hij is geweest
pl. zijn	*pl.* waren	*pl.* zijn geweest

worden – *to be (passive sense), to become*

present	*imperfect*	*perfect*
ik word I *become, etc.*	werd *I became, etc.*	ben geworden *I have become, etc.*
jij wordt	werd	bent geworden
hij wordt	werd	is geworden
pl. worden	werden	zijn geworden

This verb is used where we would use 'to be' to denote the passive – hy werd gezien – *he was seen.*

hebben – *to have*

present	*imperfect*	*perfect*
ik heb *I have, etc.*	had *I had, etc.*	heb gehad *I have had, etc.*
jij hebt	had	hebt gehad
hij heeft	had	heeft gehad
pl hebben	hadden	hebben gehad

zullen–*to be going to*

present	*imperfect*
ik zal *I shall/will, etc.*	zou *I should/would, etc.*
jij zult	zou
hij zal	zou
pl. zullen	zouden

kunnen—*to be able to*

present	*imperfect*
ik kan *I can, etc.*	kon *I could, etc.*
jij kunt	kon
hij kan	kon
pl. kunnen	konden

willen—*to want to*

present	*imperfect*
ik wil *I want, etc.*	wou/wilde *I wanted, etc.*
jij wilt	wou/wilde
hij wil	wou/wilde
pl. willen	wouden/wilden

mogen—*to be allowed to*

present	*imperfect*
sing. mag *I may, etc.*	mocht *I was allowed to, etc.*
pl. mogen	mochten

SEPARABLE VERBS

In Dutch, as in German, many verbs are modified in meaning by the addition of a prefix:

komen   *to come*; aankomen   *to arrive*
geven   *to give*; afgeven   *to deliver* **or** *to stain* (*give off*)

When these verbs are conjugated they split up into their component parts: the verb is used in its normal place and the prefix goes to the end of the sentence:

de trein komt aan   *the train arrives*

In the past participle the adverb remains a prefix:

de trein is aangekomen   *the train has arrived*

SENTENCE STRUCTURE

Sentence structure follows more or less the same pattern as in English, with a few important exceptions:

(1) indications of time usually precede those of place (in English the reverse is usual):

   ik ga morgen naar Amsterdam   *I am going to Amsterdam tomorrow*

and both these indications would precede the direct object

   ik ga morgen in Amsterdam een tentoonstelling zien   *I am going to Amsterdam to see an exhibition tomorrow*

(2) when a sentence starts with an adverb the verb precedes the subject:

   morgen ga ik een tentoonstelling zien   *I am going to see an exhibition tomorrow*

The last two examples illustrate also how the verb group is split in Dutch so that the main verb comes after the direct obect (which usually means that it comes at the end of the sentence):

   ik heb gisteren in Amsterdam een tentoonstelling gezien   *I saw an exhibition in Amsterdam yesterday*

VOCABULARY

Neuter nouns, the so-called **het** words, are indicated by (**n**) in the vocabulary and word lists. All other nouns take **de** as the definite article.

Various groups of specialized words are given elsewhere in this book and these words are not usually repeated in the vocabulary:

A

a, an	**een**	uhn
able (to be)	**kunnen (kon, gekund)**	kuh-nuhn (kon, khuh-kuhnt)
about	**ongeveer**	on-khuh-vayr
above	**boven**	bō-vuhn
abroad	**in het buitenland**	in uht bui-tuh-lant
accept (to)	**aannemen/ accepteren**	ān-nay-muhn/ak-sep-tay-ruhn
accident	**ongeluk** (*n*)	on-khuh-luhk
ache (to)	**pijn hebben**	pyn he-buhn
acquaintance	**kennis/bekende**	ke-nuhs/buh-ken-duh
across	**over**	ō-vuhr
act (to)	**handelen**	han-duh-luhn
add (to) *numbers*	**optellen**	op-tel-luhn
add (to) *things*	**toevoegen**	too-voo-khuhn
address	**adres** (*n*)	a-dres
admire (to)	**bewonderen**	buh-won-duh-ruhn
admission	**toegang**	too-khang
advice	**raad/advies** (*n*)	rāt/at-vees
aeroplane	**vliegtuig** (*n*)	vleekh-tuikh
afford (to)	**(zich) permitteren**	(zikh) per-mee-tay-ruhn
afraid (to be)	**bang zijn**	bang zyn
after	**na**	nā

again	weer/opnieuw	wayr/op-neew
against	tegen	tay-khuhn
age *period*	tijdperk (*n*)	tyt-perk
age *personal*	leeftijd	layf-tyt
ago	geleden	khuh-lay-duhn
agree (to) *to*	toestemmen	too-stem-muhn
agree (to) *with*	het eens zijn met ...	uht ayns zyn met
ahead (of)	voor	vōr
air	lucht	luhkht
alarm clock	wekker	we-k'r
alike	hetzelfde	uht-zel-luhv-duh
all *adj.*	alle	al-luh
all *noun*	alles	al-luhs
all right	in orde	in or-duh
allow (to)	toestaan	too-stān
almost	bijna	by-nā
alone	alleen	al-layn
along	langs	langs
already	al	al
also	ook	ōk
alter (to)	veranderen	vuhr-an-duh-ruhn
alternative	alternatief (*n*)	al-tuhr-nā-teef
although	hoewel	hoo-wel
always	altijd	al-tyt
ambulance	ambulance/ ziekenwagen	am-bü-lan-suh/zee-kuh- wā-khuhn
America	Amerika	a-may-ree-kā
American *adj.*	Amerikaans	a-may-ree-kāns

America *noun*	Amerikaan/ Amerikaanse	a-may-ree-kān/a-may- ree-kān-suh
among	tussen	tuh-suhn
amuse (to)	amuseren	a-mü-say-ruhn
amusing	amusant/leuk	a-mü-sant/lœk
ancient	(oer)oud	(oor)-owt
and	en	en
angry	boos/kwaad	bōs/kwāt
animal	dier (*n*)	deer
anniversary	trouwdag (*marriage*)/ jubileum (*gen.*)	trow-dakh/jü-bee-lay- yuhm
annoy (to)	ergeren	er-khuh-ruhn
another	een ander	uhn an-duhr
(one) another	elkaar/elkander	el-kār/el-kan-duhr
answer	antwoord (*n*)	ant-wōrt
answer (to)	antwoorden	ant-wōr-duhn
antique	antiek	an-teek
any	een of ander	ayn ov an-duhr
anyone	iemand	ee-mant
anything	iets	eets
anyway	in ieder geval	in ee-duhr khuh-val
anywhere	ergens	er-khuhns
apartment	woning	wō-ning
apologize (to)	zich verontschuldigen	zikh vuhr-ont-skhuhl- duh-khuhn
appetite	eetlust	ayt-luhst
appointment	afspraak	af-sprāk
architect	architect	ar-khee-tekt
architecture	architectuur	ar-khee-tek-tür

area	gebied (*n*)	khuh-**beet**
argument	argument (*n*)	ar-khü-ment
arm	arm	a-ruhm
armchair	leunstoel	lœn-stool
army	leger (*n*)	lay-khuhr
around	rond(om)	ront-(om)
arrange (to)	arrangeren	a-ran-zhay-ruhn
arrival	aankomst	ān-komst
arrive (to)	aankomen	ān-kō-muhn
art	kunst	kuhnst
art gallery	kunsthandel/ museum (*n*)	kuhnst-han-duhl/ mü-zay-yuhm
artist	kunstenaar/artiest	kuhn-stuh-nār/ar-teest
as	(zo)als	(zō)-als
as much as	zo veel als	zō vayl als
as soon as	zo gauw als	zō khow als
as well/also	ook	ōk
ashtray	asbak	as-bak
ask (to)	vragen (vroeg, gevraagd)	vrā-khuhn (vrookh, khuh-vrākht)
asleep	slapend/in slaap	slā-puhnt/in slāp
at *person's*	bij	by
at *place/time*	in/om	in/om
at last	eindelijk	yn-duh-luhk
at once	onmiddellijk	om-mi-duhl-luhk
atmosphere	atmosfeer	at-mos-fayr
attention	aandacht/attentie	ān-dakht/a-ten-tsee
attractive	aantrekkelijk	ān-tre-kuh-luhk
auction	veiling	vy-ling

audience	**publiek**	pü-bleek
aunt	**tante**	tan-tuh
Australia	**Australië**	ō-strā-lee-yuh
Australian *adj.*	**Australisch**	ō-strā-lees
Australian *noun*	**Australiër**	ō-strā-lee-yuhr
author	**schrijver**	skhry-vuhr
available	**beschikbaar**	buh-**skhik**-bār
average	**gemiddeld**	khuh-**mi**-duhlt
awake	**wakker**	wa-kuhr
away	**weg**	wekh
awful	**afschuwelijk**	af-skhü-wuh-luhk

B

baby	**baby**	bay-bee
bachelor	**vrijgezel**	vry-khuh-zel
back	**terug**	truhkh
bad	**slecht**	slekht
bad *food*	**bedorven**	buh-**dor**-vuhn
bag	**tas**	tas
baggage	**bagage**	ba-khā-zhuh
bait	**aas** (*n*)	ās
balcony	**balkon** (*n*)	bal-kon
ball	**bal**	bal
ballet	**ballet** (*n*)	bal-let
band *music*	**orkest** (*n*)	or-kest
bank	**bank**	bank
bar	**bar/café** (*n*)**/kroeg**	bār/ka-fay-/krookh
barbecue	**barbecue**	**bār**-buh-kyoo
bare	**bloot**	blōt

basket	**mand**	mant
bath	**bad** (*n*)	bat
bathe (to)	**baden**	bā-duhn
bathing cap	**badmuts**	bat-muhts
bathing costume	**badpak** (*n*)	bat-pak
bathing trunks	**zwembroek**	zwem-brook
bathroom	**badkamer**	bat-kā-muhr
battery	**batterij**	ba-tuh-ry
be (to)	**zijn** (was, geweest)	zyn (was, khuh-wayst)
beach	**strand** (*n*)	strant
beard	**baard**	bārt
beautiful	**mooi**	mōee
because	**omdat**	om-dat
become (to)	**worden** (werd, geworden)	wor-duhn (wert, khuh-wor-duhn)
bed	**bed** (*n*)	bet
bedroom	**slaapkamer**	slāp-kā-muhr
before	**voor**(dat)	vōr-(dat)
begin (to)	**beginnen** (begon, begonnen)	buh-khin-nuhn (buh-khon, buh-khon-nuhn)
beginning	**begin** (*n*)	buh-khin
behind	**achter**	akh-tuhr
Belgian *adj.*	**Belgisch**	bel-khees
Belgian *noun*	**Belg**	belkh
Belgium	**België**	bel-khee-yuh
believe (to) in	**geloven** (aan)	khuh-lō-vuhn (ān)
belong (to)	**(toe)behoren aan**	(too)-buh-hō-ruhn ān
below	**onder**	on-duhr

belt	**riem**	reem
bench	**bank**	bank
bend	**bocht**	bokht
beneath	**onder**	on-duhr
berth	**couchette**	koo-shet
beside	**naast**	nāst
best	**best**	best
bet	**weddenschap**	we-duhn-skhap
better	**beter**	bay-tuhr
between	**tussen**	tuhs-suhn
beyond	**voorbij**	vōr-by
bicycle	**fiets/rijwiel**	feets/ry-weel
big	**groot**	khrōt
bill	**rekening**	ray-kuh-ning
binoculars	**kijker**	ky-kuhr
bird	**vogel**	vō-khuhl
birthday	**verjaardag**	vuhr-jār-dakh
bit	**stukje** (*n*)	stuhk-yuh
bite (to)	**bijten** (beet, gebeten)	by-t'n (bayt, khuh-bay-t'n)
bitter	**bitter**	bi-t'r
blanket	**deken**	day-k'n
bleach	**bleekmiddel** (*n*)	blayk-mi-duhl
bleed (to)	**bloeden**	bloo-duhn
blind	**blind**	blint
blond	**blond**	blont
blood	**bloed** (*n*)	bloot
blouse	**blouse**	bloo-zuh
blow	**klap**	klap

blow (to)	**blazen (blies, geblazen)**	blā-zuhn (blees, khuh-**blā**-zuhn)
(on) board	**(aan) boord**	(ān) bōrt
boarding house	**pension (n)**	pen-syon
boat	**boot**	bōt
body	**lichaam (n)**	li-khām
bolt	**grendel**	khren-duhl
bone	**been (n)/bot (n)**	bayn/bot
bonfire	**(kamp)vuur (n)**	kamp-vür
book	**boek (n)**	book
book (to)	**boeken/bespreken**	boo-k'n/buh-**spray**-k'n
boot	**laars**	lārs
border	**grens**	khrens
borrow (to)	**lenen**	lay-nuhn
both	**allebei**	al-luh-by
both ... and ...	**zowel ... als ...**	zō-wel ... als
bottle	**fles**	fles
bottle opener	**(fles)opener**	(fles)-ō-puh-nuhr
bottom	**bodem**	bō-duhm
bowl	**schaal**	skhāl
box *container*	**doos**	dōs
box *theatre*	**loge**	lo-zhuh
box office	**(theater) kassa**	(tay-yā-tuhr) kas-sā
boy	**jongen**	yong-uhn
bracelet	**armband**	arm-bant
braces	**bretels**	bruh-tels
brain	**verstand (n)**	vuhr-stant
branch *tree*	**tak**	tak
branch *office*	**bijkantoor (n)**	by-kan-tōr

brand	merk (*n*)	me-ruhk
brassière	b.h./bustehouder	bay-hā/büs-tuh-how-duhr
break (to)	breken (brak, gebroken)	bray-k'n (brak, khuh-brō-k'n)
breakfast	ontbijt (*n*)	ont-byt
breathe (to)	ademen	ā-duh-muhn
bridge	brug	bruhkh
briefs	onderbroek	on-duhr-brook
bright	licht/helder	likht/hel-duhr
bring (to)	brengen (bracht, gebracht)	breng-uhn (brakht, khuh-brakht)
British	Brits	brits
broken	gebroken/kapot	khuh-brō-k'n/ka-pot
brooch	broche/speld	bro-shuh/spelt
broom	bezem	bay-zuhm
brother	broer	broor
bruise (to)	kneuzen	knœ-zuhn
brush	borstel	bor-stuhl
brush (to) *hair*	borstelen	bor-stuh-luhn
brush (to) *floor*	vegen	vay-khuhn
bucket	emmer	em-muhr
buckle	gesp	khesp
build (to)	bouwen	bow-wuhn
building	gebouw (*n*)	khuh-bow
bunch	bundel	buhn-duhl
buoy	boei	booee
burn (to)	branden	bran-duhn
burn down (to)	verbranden	vuhr-bran-duhn

burst (to)	**barsten**	bar-stuhn
bus	**bus**	buhs
bus stop	**bushalte**	buhs hal-tuh
business	**zaken**	zā-k'n
busy	**druk**	druhk
but	**maar**	mār
button	**knoop**	knōp
buy (to)	**kopen (kocht, gekocht)**	kō-puhn (kokht, khuh-kokht)
by *means, via*	**door**	dōr
by *near*	**(na)bij**	(nā)-by

C

cab	**taxi**	tak-see
cabin	**hut**	huht
call *visit*	**bezoek (*n*)**	buh-zook
call (to) *summon*	**roepen (riep, geroepen)**	roo-puhn (reep, khuh-roo-puhn)
call (to) *telephone*	**opbellen**	op-bel-luhn
call (to) *visit*	**bezoeken (bezocht, bezocht)**	buh-zoo-kuhn (buh-zokht)
calm	**kalm**	kalm
camp (to)	**kamperen**	kam-pay-ruhn
camp site	**kampeerterrein**	kam-payr-tuh-ryn
can *to be able*	**kunnen (kon, gekund)**	kuhn-nuhn (kon, khuh-kuhnt)
can *tin*	**blik (*n*)**	blik
Canada	**Canada**	ka-nā-dā
Canadian	**Canadees**	ka-nā-days

cancel (to)	annuleren	a-nü-lay-ruhn
candle	kaars	kārs
canoe	kano	kā-nō
can opener	blikopener	blik-ō-puh-nuhr
cap	pet	pet
capable of	in staat om	in stāt om
capital city	hoofdstad	hōft-stat
car	auto	ō-tō
car park	parkeerplaats	par-kayr-plāts
caravan	caravan	ke-ruh-ven
card	kaart	kārt
care	zorg	zo-ruhkh
careful	voorzichtig	vōr-zikh-tuhkh
careless	nalatig	nā-lā-tuhkh
carpenter	timmerman	tim-muhr-man
carry (to)	dragen (droeg, gedragen)	drā-khuhn (drookh, khuh-drā-khuhn)
cash	contant (geld)	kon-tant (khelt)
cashier	kassier	kas-seer
casino	casino/speelclub	kā-see-nō/spayl-kluhp
cassette player	cassette recorder	kas-set ree-kōr-duhr
castle	kasteel (*n*)	kas-tayl
cat	kat	kat
catalogue	catalogus	ka-tā-lō-khuhs
catch (to)	vangen (ving, gevangen)	vang-'n (ving, khuh-vang-'n)
cathedral	kathedraal	ka-tuh-drāl
catholic	katholiek	ka-tō-leek
cause	(oor)zaak	ōr-zāk

cave	**grot**	khrot
ceiling	**plafond** (*n*)	pla-**fon**
central	**centraal**	sen-**trāl**
centre	**centrum** (*n*)/**midden** (*n*)	sen-truhm/**mi**-duhn
century	**eeuw**	ayw
ceremony	**plechtigheid**	**plekh**-tuhkh-hyt
certain	**zeker**	**zay**-kuhr
chair	**stoel**	stool
chambermaid	**kamermeisje** (*n*)	**kā**-muhr-my-shuh
chance	**kans**	kans
by chance	**bij toeval**	by **too**-val
(small) change	**kleingeld** (*n*)/**wisselgeld** (*n*)	**klyn**-khelt/**wis**-suhl-khelt
change (to)	**wisselen**	**wis**-suh-luhn
charcoal	**houtskool**	**howts**-kōl
charge (to) *account*	**op de rekening schrijven**	op duh **ray**-kuh-ning **skhry**-vuhn
charge (to) *battery*	**opladen**	op-**lā**-duhn
cheap	**goedkoop**	khoot-**kōp**
check (to)	**nakijken**	nā-**ky**-k'n
cheque	**cheque**	shek
child(ren)	**kind(eren)** (*n*)	kint/**kin**-duh-ruhn
chill	**kou**	kow
chilly	**huiverig**	**hui**-vuh-ruhkh
chimney (breast)	**schoorsteen(mantel)**	**skhōr**-stayn-(man-t'l)
china	**porcelein** (*n*)	por-suh-**lyn**
choice	**keuze**	**kœ**-zuh

choose (to)	**kiezen (koos, gekozen)**	kee-zuhn (kōs, khuh-kō-zuhn)
chop (to)	**hakken**	ha-k'n
chopping board	**snijplank**	sny-plank
church	**kerk**	ke-ruhk
cigarette case	**sigaretten-koker**	see-khā-re-tuh-kō-kuhr
cinema	**bioscoop**	bee-yos-kōp
circle *theatre*	**balkon (n)**	bal-kon
circus	**circus (n)**	sir-kuhs
city	**stad**	stat
class *school*	**klas**	klas
class *social*	**klasse/stand**	klas-suh/stant
clean	**schoon**	skhōn
clean (to)	**schoonmaken**	skhō-mā-kuhn
clear *reason*	**duidelijk**	dui-duh-luhk
clear *substance*	**helder**	hel-duhr
clerk	**bediende**	buh-deen-duh
climb (to)	**klimmen**	klim-muhn
cloakroom	**garderobe/vestiaire**	khar-duh-rō-buh/ves-tee-yè-ruh
clock	**klok**	klok
close (to)	**sluiten/dichtmaken**	slui-t'n/dikht-mā-k'n
closed	**gesloten**	khuh-slō-tuhn
cloth	**stof**	stof
clothes	**kleren**	klay-ruhn
clothes line/pegs	**waslijn/(was)knijpers**	was-lyn/(was-)kny-puhrs
cloud	**wolk**	wol-luhk
coach	**touringcar**	too-ring-kār
coast	**kust**	kuhst

coat	jas/mantel	yas/man-t'l
coat hanger	klerenhanger	klay-ruh-hang-uhr
coin	munt	muhnt
colander	vergiet (*n*)	vuhr-kheet
cold	koud	kowt
collar	kraag	krākh
collect (to)	verzamelen	vuhr-zā-muh-luhn
colour	kleur	klœr
comb	kam	kam
come (to)	komen (kwam, gekomen)	kō-muhn (kwam, khuh-kō-muhn)
come in!	binnen!	bin-nuh
comfortable	gemakkelijk	khuh-ma-kuh-luhk
common	algemeen	al-khuh-mayn
company	gezelschap (*n*)	khuh-zel-skhap
compartment *train*	compartiment (*n*)	kom-par-tee-ment
complain (to)	klagen	klā-khuhn
complaint	klacht	klakht
complete	compleet/volledig	kom-playt/vol-lay-duhkh
concert	concert (*n*)	kon-sert
condition	staat/toestand	stāt/too-stant
conductor *bus*	conducteur	kon-duhk-tœr
conductor *orchestra*	dirigent	dee-ree-khent
congratulations	gefeliciteerd!	khuh-fay-lee-see-tayrt
connect (to)	verbinden	vuhr-bin-duhn
connection *train, etc.*	aansluiting	ān-slui-ting
consul	consul	kon-suhl
consulate	consulaat (*n*)	kon-sü-lāt
contain (to)	bevatten	buh-va-t'n

contrast	tegenstelling	tay-khuhn-stel-ling
convenient	makkelijk	ma-kuh-luhk
conversation	gesprek (*n*)	khuh-sprek
cook	kok	kok
cook (to)	koken	kō-k'n
cooker *gas*	fornuis (*n*)	for-nuis
cooker *electric*	kookplaat	kōk-plāt
cool	koel	kool
copper	koper	kō-puhr
copy	exemplaar (*n*)	ek-sem-plār
copy (to)	kopiëren	kō-pyay-ruhn
cork	kurk	kuh-ruhk
corkscrew	kurketrekker	kuh-ruh-kuh-tre-kuhr
corner	hoek	hook
correct	juist	yuist
corridor	gang	khang
cosmetics	toiletartikelen	twa-let-ar-tee-kuh-luhn
cost	prijs	prys
cost (to)	kosten	kos-t'n
cot	kinderbed (*n*)	kin-duhr-bet
cottage	(land)huisje (*n*)	(lant)-**huis**-yuh
cotton	katoen (*n*)	ka-toon
cotton wool	watten	wa-tuhn
couchette	slaapplaats	slāp-plāts
cough (to)	hoesten	hoos-tuhn
count (to)	tellen	tel-luhn
country	land (*n*)	lant
couple	paar (*n*)	pār
course *dish*	gang	khang

courtyard	erf (n)	e-ruhf
cousin *female*	nicht	nikht
cousin *male*	neef	nayf
cover *general*	dek	dek
cover *book*	omslag (n)	om-slakh
cover *pot*	deksel (n)	dek-suhl
cover (to)	bedekken	buh-de-kuhn
cow	koe	koo
crease	vouw	vow
creased	gekreukeld	khuh-krœ-kuhlt
credit	krediet (n)	kruh-deet
crew	bemanning	buh-man-ning
cross	boos	bōs
cross (to)	oversteken	ō-vuhr-stay-kuhn
crossroads	kruispunt (n)	kruis-puhnt
crossword	kruiswoordpuzzel	kruis-wōrt-puh-zuhl
crowd	menigte	may-nuhkh-tuh
crowded	vol	vol
cry (to)	huilen	hui-luhn
cry (to) *call*	roepen	roo-puhn
cuff (links)	manchet(knopen)	man-shet-(knō-puhn)
cup	kopje	kop-yuh
cup *trophy*	beker	bay-kuhr
cupboard	kast	kast
cure (to)	genezen (genas, genezen)	khuh-nay-zuhn (khuh-nas, khuh-nay-zuhn)
curious	nieuwsgierig	neews-khee-ruhkh
current	stroom	strōm
curtain	gordijn (n)	khor-dyn

curve	**bocht**	bokht
cushion	**kussen** (*n*)	kuhs-suhn
customs (officer)	**douane (beambte)**	doo-wā-nuh (buh-am-tuh)
cut	**snee**	snay
cut (to)	**snijden (sneed, gesneden)**	sny-duhn (snayt, khuh-snay-duhn)

D

daily	**dagelijks**	dā-khuh-luhks
damaged	**beschadigd**	buh-skhā-duhkht
damp	**vochtig**	vokh-tuhkh
dance	**dans**	dans
dance (to)	**dansen**	dan-suhn
danger	**gevaar** (*n*)	khuh-vār
dangerous	**gevaarlijk**	khuh-vār-luhk
dark	**donker**	dong-kuhr
date *appointment*	**afspraak**	af-sprāk
date *calendar*	**datum**	dā-tuhm
daughter	**dochter**	dokh-t'r
day	**dag**	dakh
dead	**dood**	dōt
deaf	**doof**	dōf
dear *expensive*	**duur**	dür
decide (to)	**besluiten (besloot, besloten)**	buh-slui-t'n (buh-slōt, buh-slō-tuhn)
deck	**dek** (*n*)	dek
deckchair	**ligstoel**	likh-stool
declare (to)	**aangeven**	ān-khay-vuhn

deep	**diep**	deep
delay	**vertraging/uitstel**	vuhr-trā-khing/uit-stel
deliver (to)	**afgeven/bestellen**	af-khay-vuhn/ buh-stel-luhn
delivery	**bestelling**	buh-stel-ling
demi-pension	**half pension**	hal-luhf pen-syon
dentures	**prothese**	prō-tay-zuh
deodorant	**deodorant**	day-ō-do-rant
depart (to)	**vertrekken (vertrok, vertrokken)**	vuhr-tre-kuhn (vuhr-trok, vuhr-tro-kuhn)
department	**afdeling**	av-day-ling
department store	**warenhuis** (*n*)	wā-ruhn-huis
departure	**vertrek** (*n*)	vuhr-trek
dessert	**dessert** (*n*)	des-sert
detergent	**wasmiddel** (*n*)	was-mi-duhl
detour	**omweg**	om-wekh
dial (to)	**draaien**	drā-yuhn
diamond	**diamant**	dee-yā-mant
dice	**dobbelsteen**	do-buhl-stayn
dictionary	**woordenboek** (*n*)	wōr-duh-book
diet	**diëet** (*n*)	dee-yayt
diet (to)	**op diëet zijn**	op dee-yayt zyn
different	**anders**	an-duhrs
difficult	**moeilijk**	mooee-luhk, moo-yuh-luhk
dine (to)	**dineren**	dee-nay-ruhn
dining room	**eetkamer**	ayt-kā-muhr
dinner	**diner** (*n*)	dee-nay
direct	**rechtstreeks**	rekht-strayks

direction	**richting**	rikh-ting
dirty	**vuil/smerig**	vuil/smay-ruhkh
disappointed	**teleurgesteld**	tuh-loer-khuh-stelt
discotheque	**discotheek**	dis-kō-tayk
discount	**korting**	kor-ting
dish *meal*	**gerecht** (*n*)	khuh-rekht
dish *plate*	**schotel**	skhō-t'l
disinfectant	**ontsmettingsmiddel** (*n*)	ont-sme-tings-mi-duhl
distance	**afstand**	af-stant
disturb (to)	**storen**	stō-ruhn
ditch	**greppel**	khre-p'l
dive (to)	**duiken (dook, gedoken)**	dui-k'n (dōk, khuh-dō-k'n)
diving board	**duikplank**	duik-plank
divorced	**gescheiden**	khuh-skhy-duhn
do (to)	**doen (deed, gedaan)**	doon (dayt, khuh-dān)
dock (to)	**dokken/aanleggen**	do-k'n/ān-le-khuhn
doctor	**dokter**	dok-t'r
dog	**hond**	hont
doll	**pop**	pop
door (bell/knob)	**deur (bel/knop)**	dœr-(bel/knop)
double	**dubbel**	duh-b'l
double bed	**tweepersoonsbed** (*n*)	tway-per-sōns-bet
double room	**tweepersoonskamer**	tway-per-sōns-kā-muhr
down(stairs)	**beneden**	buh-nay-duhn
dozen	**dozijn** (*n*)	dō-zyn
drawer	**la**	lā
dream	**droom**	drōm

dress	jurk/japon	yœrk/ya-**pon**
dressing gown	peignoir/kamerjas	pen-**wār**/kā-muhr-yas
dressmaker	naaister	nāee-stuhr
drink (to)	drinken (dronk, gedronken)	dring-kuhn (drongk, khuh-**drong**-khun)
drinking water	drinkwater (*n*)	dringk-**wā**-t'r
drive (to)	rijden (reed, gereden)	ry-duhn (rayt, khuh-**ray**-duhn)
driver	bestuurder	buh-**stür**-duhr
drop (to)	laten vallen	lā-tuh val-luhn
drunk	dronken	**drong**-kuhn
dry	droog	drōkh
during	gedurende/tijdens	khuh-dü-ruhn-duh/ty-duhns
dust	stof (*n*)	stof
dustbin	vuilnisbak	**vuil**-nis-bak
dustpan	(stoffer en) blik (*n*)	(stof-fuhr en) blik
Dutch	Hollands/Nederlands	hol-lants/nay-duhr-lants

E

each/per piece	ieder/per stuk	ee-duhr/per stuhk
early	vroeg	vrookh
earrings	oorbellen	ōr-bel-luhn
east	oost	ōst
easy	makkelijk	ma-kuh-luhk
eat (to)	eten (at, gegeten)	ay-t'n (at, khuh-**khay**-t'n)
edge	kant	kant
elastic	elastiek (*n*)	ay-las-**teek**
electric light bulb	lamp	lamp

electric point	**stopcontact** (*n*)	stop-kon-takt
electricity	**electriciteit**	ay-lek-tree-see-tyt
elevator	**lift**	lift
embarrass (to)	**in verlegenheid brengen**	in vuhr-lay-khuhn-hyt breng-uhn
embassy	**ambassade**	am-bas-sā-duh
emergency exit	**nooduitgang**	nōt-uit-khang
empty	**leeg**	laykh
end	**einde** (*n*)	yn-duh
engaged *people*	**verloofd**	vuhr-lōft
engaged *telephone*	**in gesprek**	in khuh-sprek
engaged *toilet*	**bezet**	buh-zet
engine	**motor**	mō-t'r
England	**Engeland**	eng-uh-lant
English	**Engels**	eng-uhls
enjoy (to)	**genieten van**	khuh-nee-tuhn van
enough	**genoeg**	khuh-nookh
enter (to)	**binnengaan/ binnenkomen**	bin-nuh-khān/bin-nuh-kō-muhn
entrance	**ingang**	in-khang
envelope	**envelop**	an-vuh-lop
equipment	**materiaal** (*n*)	ma-tuh-ree-yāl
escape (to)	**ontsnappen**	ont-sna-p'n
Europe	**Europa**	œ-rō-pā
even *not odd*	**even**	ay-vuhn
event	**gebeurtenis**	khuh-bœr-tuh-nis
ever	**ooit**	ōeet
every	**iedere**	ee-duh-ruh
everybody	**iedereen**	ee-duh-rayn

everything	**alles**	al-luhs
everywhere	**overal**	ō-vuh-ral
example	**voorbeeld** (*n*)	vōr-baylt
excellent	**uitstekend**	uit-stay-kuhnt
except	**behalve**	buh-hal-luh-vuh
excess	**over/teveel**	ō-vuhr/tuh-rayl
exchange bureau	**wisselkantoor** (*n*)	wis-suhl-kan-tōr
exchange rate	**wisselkoers**	wis-suhl-koors
excursion	**excursie**	ex-kuhr-see
excuse	**excuus** (*n*)	ex-küs
exhausted	**uitgeput**	uit-khuh-puht
exhibition	**tentoonstelling**	ten-tōn-stel-ling
exit	**uitgang**	uit-khang
expect (to)	**verwachten**	vuhr-wakh-t'n
expensive	**duur**	dür
explain (to)	**uitleggen**	uit-le-khuhn
express	**spoedbestelling**	spoot-buh-stel-ling
express train	**sneltrein**	snel-tryn
extra	**extra**	ek-strā
eye shadow	**oogschaduw**	ōkh-skhā-dü

F

fabric	**stof**	stof
face	**gezicht** (*n*)	khuh-zikht
face cream	**gezichtscrème**	khuh-zikhts-krèm
face powder	**poeder**	poo-yuhr
fact	**feit** (*n*)	fyt
factory	**fabriek**	fa-breek
fade (to)	**vervagen**	vuhr-vā-khuhn

faint (to)	**flauw vallen**	flow val-luhn
fair *colour*	**blond**	blont
fair *fête*	**kermis**	ker-muhs
fall (to)	**vallen (viel, gevallen)**	val-luhn (veel, khuh-val-luhn)
family	**familie/gezin (*n*)**	fa-mee-lee/khuh-zin
far	**ver**	ver
fare	**prijs**	prys
farm	**boerderij**	boor-duh-ry
farmer	**boer**	boor
farther	**verder**	ver-duhr
fashion	**mode**	mō-duh
fast	**snel**	snel
fat	**dik**	dik
father	**vader**	vā-d'r
fault	**fout**	fowt
fear	**angst**	angst
feed (to)	**voeden**	voo-duhn
feel (to)	**voelen**	voo-luhn
female *adj.*	**vrouwelijk**	vrow-wuh-luhk
fence	**hek (*n*)**	hek
ferry	**veer (*n*)**	vayr
fetch (to)	**halen**	hā-luhn
few (a)	**een paar**	uhn pār
fiancé(e)	**verloofde**	vuhr-lōv-duh
field	**veld (*n*)**	velt
fight (to)	**vechten (vocht, gevochten)**	vekh-tuhn (vokht, khuh-vokh-tuhn)
fill (to)	**vullen**	vuhl-luhn

film	film	fil-luhm
find (to)	vinden (vond, gevonden)	vin-d'n (vont, khuh-von-d'n)
fine *adj.*	mooi	mōee
fine *noun*	boete	boo-tuh
finish (to)	afmaken	af-mā-kuhn
finished	klaar	klār
fire (*as in a grate*)	vuur (*n*)	vür
fire (*as of a building*)	brand	brant
fire escape	brandtrap	bran-trap
fireplace	(open) haard	(ō-puhn) hārt
first	eerst	ayrst
first aid	eerste hulp	ayr-stuh huhl-luhp
first class	eerste klas	ayr-stuh klas
fish	vis	vis
fish (to)	vissen	vis-suhn
fisherman	visser	vis-suhr
fit	fit	fit
fit (to)	passen	pas-suhn
flag	vlag	vlakh
Flanders	Vlaanderen	vlān-duh-ruhn
flat *adj.*	plat/vlak	plat/vlak
flat *noun*	flat/woning	flet/wō-ning
Flemish	Vlaams	vlāms
flight	vlucht	vluhkht
flippers	zwemvliezen	zwem-vlee-zuhn
float (to)	drijven (dreet, gedreven)	dry-vuhn (drayt, khun-dray-vuhn)
flood	overstroming	ō-vuhr-strō-ming

floor *ground*	vloer	vloor
floor *storey*	verdieping	vuhr-dee-ping
floor show	cabaret (*n*)	ka-bā-ret
flower	bloem	bloom
fly *insect*	vlieg	vleekh
fly *trousers*	gulp	khuhlp
fly (to)	vliegen (vloog, gevolgen)	vlee-khuhn (vlōkh, khuh-vlō-khuhn)
fog	mist	mist
fold (to)	vouwen	vow-wuhn
follow (to)	volgen	vol-khuhn
food	eten (*n*)/voedsel (*n*)	ay-t'n/voot-suhl
foot	voet	voot
football	voetbal	voot-bal
footpath	voetpad (*n*)	voot-pat
for	voor	vōr
foreign	vreemd/buitenlands	vraymt/bui-tuh-lants
forest	bos (*n*)	bos
forget (to)	vergeten (vergat, vergeten)	vuhr-khay-t'n (vuhr-khat, vuhr-khay-t'n)
fork	vork	vo-ruhk
forward	vooruit	vōr-uit
forward (to)	nasturen	nā-stü-ruhn
fountain	fontein	fon-tyn
fragile	breekbaar	brayk-bār
free	vrij	vry
freezer	vrieskast	vrees-kast
freight	vracht	vrakht
fresh	vers	vers

fresh water	zoet water	zoot wā-t'r
friend	vriend	vreent
friendly	vriendelijk	vreen-duh-luhk
from	van	van
front	voorkant	vōr-kant
frontier	grens	khrens
frozen	bevroren	buh-vrō-ruhn
fruit	fruit (n)	fruit
fry (to)	bakken	ba-k'n
frying pan	koekepan	koo-kuh-pan
full	vol	vol
full board	vol pension	vol pen-syon
fun	pret	pret
funny	grappig	khra-puhkh
fur	bont (n)	bont
furniture	meubilair (n)	mœ-bee-lèr
further	verder	ver-duhr

G

gallery	galerij	khal-luh-ry
gamble (to)	gokken	kho-k'n
game	wedstrijd/spel (n)	wet-stryt/spel
garage	garage	kha-rā-zhuh
garbage	vuilnis (n)	vuil-nis
garden	tuin	tuin
gas	gas (n)	khas
gate	hek (n)	hek
gentlemen	heren	hay-ruhn

get (to)	krijgen (kreeg, gekregen)	kry-khuhn (kraykh, khuh-kray-khuhn)
get off (to)	uitstappen	uit-sta-p'n
get on (to)	instappen	in-sta-p'n
gift	geschenk (*n*)/cadeau (*n*)	khuh-skhenk/ka-dō
girdle	corset (*n*)	kor-set
girl	meisje (*n*)	my-shuh
give (to)	geven (gaf, gegeven)	khay-vuhn (khaf, khuh-khay-vuhn)
glad	blij	bly
glass	glas (*n*)	khlas
glasses	bril	bril
gloomy	somber	som-buhr
glorious	prachtig	prakh-tuhkh
glove	handschoen	hant-skhoon
go (to)	gaan (ging, gegaan)	khān (khing, khuh-khān)
goal	goal	gōl
god	god	khot
gold	goud	khowt
good	goed	khoot
government	regering	ruh-khay-ring
granddaughter	kleindochter	klyn-dokh-tuhr
grandfather	grootvader	khrōt-vā-duhr
grandmother	grootmoeder	khrōt-moo-duhr
grandson	kleinzoon	klyn-zōn
grass	gras (*n*)	khras
grateful	dankbaar	dank-bār
gravel	grint (*n*)	khrint

great	enorm	ay-no-ruhm
groceries	kruidenierswaren	krui-duh-neers-wā-ruhn
ground	grond	khront
grow (to)	groeien	khroo-yuhn
guarantee	garantie	kha-ran-tsee
guard	wacht	wakht
guard *museum*	suppoost	suh-pōst
guest	gast	khast
guide	gids	khits
guide book	handleiding	hant-ly-ding

H

hail	hagel	hā-khuhl
hair	haar (*n*)	hār
hair brush	borstel	bor-st'l
hairpin	haarspeld	hār-spelt
half	half	hal-luhf
half board	half pension	hal-luhf pen-syon
half fare	half geld	hal-luhf khelt
hammer	hamer	hā-muhr
hand	hand	hant
handbag	handtas	han-tas
handkerchief	zakdoek	zak-dook
hang (to)	(op)hangen	op-hang-uhn
hanger	kleerhanger	klayr-hang-uhr
happen (to)	gebeuren	khuh-bœ-ruhn
happy	gelukkig	khuh-luh-kuhkh

happy birthday	**gefeliciteerd (met je verjaardag)**	khuh-fay-lee-see-tayrt (met yuh vuhr-yār-dakh)
harbour	**haven**	hā-vuhn
hard	**hard**	hart
hardly	**nauwelijks**	now-wuh-luhks
hat	**hoed**	hoot
have (to)	**hebben (had, gehad)**	he-buhn (hat, khuh-hat)
he	**hij**	hy
head	**hoofd (*n*)**	hōft
health	**gezondheid**	khuh-zont-hyt
hear (to)	**horen**	hō-ruhn
heart	**hart (*n*)**	hart
heat	**hitte**	hi-tuh
heating	**verwarming**	vuhr-war-ming
heavy	**zwaar**	zwār
heel *shoe*	**hak**	hak
height	**hoogte**	hōkh-tuh
height *people*	**lengte**	leng-tuh
help	**hulp**	huh-luhp
help (to)	**helpen (hielp, geholpen)**	hel-puhn (hee-luhp, khuh-hol-puhn)
hem	**zoom**	zōm
her	**haar**	hār
here	**hier**	heer
hers	**van haar**	van hār
high	**hoog**	hōkh
hike (to)	**trekken (trok-getrok- ken)**	tre-kuhn (trok, khuh-tro-kuhn)

hill	heuvel	hœ-vuhl
him	hem	hem/uhm
hinge	scharnier	skhar-neer
hire (to)	huren	hü-ruhn
his	zijn/van hem	zyn/van hem
hitch-hike (to)	liften	lif-tuhn
hold (to)	(vast)houden	vast-how-duhn
hole	gat (*n*)	khat
holiday	vrije dag	vry-yuh dakh
holidays	vakantie	va-kan-tsee
Holland	Holland/Nederland	hol-lant/nay-duhr-lant
hollow	hol	hol
(at) home	thuis	tuis
honeymoon	huwelijksreis	hü-wuh-luhks-rys
hope	hoop	hōp
hope (to)	hopen	hō-puhn
horse	paard (*n*)	pārt
horse races	paarderennen	pār-duh-ren-nuhn
horse riding	paardrijden	pārt-ry-duhn
hospital	ziekenhuis (*n*)	zee-kuh-huis
host/hostess	gastheer/gastvrouw	khast-hayr/khast-vrow
hot	heet	hayt
hot water bottle	kruik	kruik
hotel	hotel (*n*)	hō-tel
hotel keeper	hotelhouder	hō-tel-how-duhr
hour	uur (*n*)	ür
house	huis (*n*)	huis
how?	hoe	hoo

how much, many?	**hoeveel?**	hoo-vayl
(to be) hungry	**honger (hebben)**	hong-uhr he-buhn
hurry (to)	**(zich) haasten**	(zikh) hās-t'n
hurt (to)	**pijn doen**	pyn doon
husband	**man/echtgenoot**	man/**ekht**-khuh-nōt

I

I	**ik**	ik
if	**als**	als
immediately	**onmiddellijk**	om-**mi**-duh-luhk
immersion heater	**dompelaar**	dom-puh-lār
important	**belangrijk**	buh-**lang**-ryk
in	**in**	in
included	**inbegrepen**	in-buh-khray-puhn
inconvenient	**ongelegen**	on-khuh-lay-khuhn
incorrect	**onjuist**	on-yuist
indeed	**inderdaad**	in-duhr-**dāt**
indoors	**binnen**	bin-nuhn
information	**inlichtingen**	in-likh-ting-uhn
ink	**inkt**	ing-k't
inn	**herberg**	her-be-rukh
insect	**insect (n)**	in-sekt
insect bite	**insectenbeet**	in-sek-tuh-bayt
insect repellant	**insecticide**	in-sek-tee-see-duh
inside	**binnen**	bin-nuhn
instead	**inplaats daarvan**	in-plāts dār-van
instead of	**inplaats van**	in-plāts van
instructor	**instructeur**	in-struhk-tœr
insurance	**verzekering**	vuhr-zay-kuh-ring

insure (to)	**verzekeren**	vuhr-zay-kuh-ruhn
interested	**geïnteresseerd**	khuh-in-tuh-res-sayrt
interesting	**interessant**	in-tuh-res-sant
interpreter	**tolk**	tol-luhk
into	**in**	in
introduce (to)	**voorstellen**	vōr-stel-luhn
invitation	**uitnodiging**	uit-nō-duh-khing
invite (to)	**uitnodigen**	uit-nō-duh-khuhn
Ireland	**Ierland**	eer-lant
Irish	**Iers**	eers
(steam) iron	**(stoom) strijkijzer**	(stōm) stryk-y-zuhr
iron (to)	**strijken (streek, gestreken)**	stry-k'n (strayk, khuh-stray-kuhn)
island	**eiland (n)**	y-lant
it	**het**	het/uht

J

jar	**pot**	pot
jellyfish	**kwal**	kwal
jewellery	**juwelen/sieraden**	yü-way-luhn/see-rā-duhn
job	**baan/werk**	bān/we-ruhk
journey	**reis**	rys
jump (to)	**springen (sprong, gesprongen)**	spring-uhn (sprong, khuh-sprong-uhn)
jumper	**trui**	trui

K

keep (to)	**houden (hield, gehouden)**	how-duhn (heelt, khuh-how-duhn)
kettle	**ketel**	kay-t'l

key	sleutel	slœ-t'l
kick (to)	schoppen	skho-puhn
kind *nice*	aardig/lief	ār-duhkh/leef
king	koning	kō-ning
kiss (to)	zoenen/kussen	zoo-nuhn/kuhs-suhn
kitchen	keuken	kœ-kuhn
knickers/briefs	broekje (*n*)	brook-yuh
knife	mes (*n*)	mes
knock (to)	kloppen	klo-p'n
know (to) *fact*	weten (wist, geweten)	way-t'n (wist, khuh-way-t'n)
know (to) *person*	kennen	ken-nuhn

L

label	etiket (*n*)	ay-tee-ket
lace	kant	kant
ladies	dames	dā-muhs
lake	meer (*n*)	mayr
lamp	lamp	lamp
lampshade	lampekap	lam-puh-kap
land	land (*n*)	lant
landing *plane*	landing	lan-ding
landing *stairs*	overloop	ō-vuhr-lōp
landlord/lady	huisbaas/huisbazin	huis-bās/bā-zin
lane *road*	laan	lān
lane *traffic*	(rij)baan	(ry)-bān
language	taal	tāl
large	groot	khrōt
last	laatste	lāt-stuh

late	laat	lāt
laugh (to)	lachen	la-khuhn
laundry *clothes*	was	was
laundry *establishment*	wasserij	was-suh-ry
lavatory	toilet (*n*)/w.c.	twa-let/way-say
lavatory paper	toiletpapier (*n*)	twa-let-pa-peer
law	wet	wet
lead (to)	leiden	ly-duhn
leaf	blad (*n*)	blat
leak (to)	lekken	le-k'n
learn (to)	leren	lay-ruhn
least	minst	minst
leather	leer (*n*)	layr
leave (to) *abandon*	achterlaten	akh-tuhr-lā-t'n
leave (to) *go away*	vertrekken (vertrok, vertrokken)	vuhr-tre-k'n (vuhr-trok, vuhr-tro-k'n)
left *not right*	links	links
left luggage	gedeponeerde bagage	khuh-day-pō-nayr-duh bā-khā-zhuh
leg *animal*	been (*n*)	bayn
leg *object*	poot	pōt
lend (to)	lenen	lay-nuhn
length	lengte	leng-tuh
less	minder	min-duhr
lesson	les	les
let (to) *allow*	toestaan	too-stān
let (to) *rent*	verhuren	vuhr-hü-ruhn
letter	brief	breef

level crossing	**(spoorweg)overgang**	(spōr-wekh) ō-vuhr-khang
library	**bibliotheek**	bee-blee-yō-tayk
licence	**vergunning**	vuhr-khuhn-ning
life	**leven** (*n*)	lay-vuhn
lift	**lift**	lift
light	**licht** (*n*)	likht
light bulb	**(gloei)lamp**	(khlooee)-lamp
lighthouse	**vuurtoren**	vür-tō-ruhn
like (to) *to be fond of*	**graag mogen**	khrākh mō-khuhn
like (to) *enjoy*	**leuk vinden**	lœk vin-d'n
line	**streep**	strayp
linen	**beddegoed** (*n*)	be-duh-khoot
lingerie	**ondergoed** (*n*)	on-duhr-khoot
lipstick	**lipstift**	lip-stift
liquid *adj.*	**vloeibaar**	vlooee-bār
liquid *noun*	**vloeistof**	vlooee-stof
listen (to)	**luisteren**	luis-tuh-ruhn
little *small*	**klein**	klyn
little (a)	**een beetje**	uhn bay-tyuh
live (to)	**leven**	lay-vuhn
living room	**woonkamer**	wōn-kā-muhr
local	**plaatselijk**	plāt-suh-luhk
lock	**slot** (*n*)	slot
lock (to)	**op slot doen/afsluiten**	op slot doon/af-slui-t'n
long	**lang**	lang
look (to) *at*	**kijken (keek, gekeken)**	ky-k'n (kayk, khuh-kay-k'n)

look (to) *like*	er uitzien	uhr uit-zeen
look (to) *for*	zoeken (zocht, gezocht)	zoo-k'n (zokht, khuh-zokht)
loose	los	los
lorry	vrachtwagen	vrakht-wā-khuhn
lose (to)	verliezen (verloor, verloren)	vuhr-lee-zuhn (vuhr-lōr, vuhr-lō-ruhn)
lost property office	gevonden voorwerpen	khuh-von-duh vōr-wer-puhn
lot	(hele)boel	(hay-luh)-bool
loud	luid	luit
love (to)	houden (hield, gehouden) van	how-duhn (heelt, khuh-how-duhn) van
lovely	prachtig	prakh-tuhkh
low	laag	lākh
luggage	bagage	ba-khā-zhuh
lunch	lunch/middageten (*n*)	luhnsh/mi-dakh-ay-tuhn

M

mad	gek	khek
magazine	tijdschrift (*n*)	tyt-skhrift
maid	(dienst)meisje (*n*)	(deenst)-my-shuh
mail	post	post
main street	hoofdstraat	hōft-strāt
make (to)	maken	mā-k'n
make-up	make-up	mayk-uhp
male *adj.*	mannelijk	man-nuh-luhk
man	man	man
manage (to) to	klaarspelen	klār-spay-luhn

manager	**chef**	shef
manicure	**manicuur**	ma-nee-kür
many	**veel**	vayl
map	**kaart**	kārt
marble	**marmer** (*n*)	mar-muhr
market	**markt**	ma-ruhkt
married	**getrouwd**	khuh-trowt
Mass	**mis**	mis
massage	**massage**	mas-sā-zhuh
match *light*	**lucifer**	lü-see-fer
match *sport*	**wedstrijd**	wet-stryt
material	**materiaal** (*n*)	ma-tuh-ree-yāl
matinee	**matinee**	ma-tee-nay
mattress	**matras** (*n*)	ma-tras
maybe	**misschien**	muh-skheen
me	**mij**	my/muh
meal	**maaltijd**	māl-tyt
measurements	**maten**	mā-t'n
meet (to)	**ontmoeten**	ont-moo-t'n
mend (to)	**repareren**	ray-pa-ray-ruhn
mess	**rommel**	rom-muhl
message	**boodschap**	bōt-skhap
metal	**metaal** (*n*)	may-tāl
middle	**midden** (*n*)	mi-duhn
middle-aged	**van middelbare leeftijd**	van mi-duhl-bā-ruh layv-tyt
middle-class *adj.*	**middenstands**	mi-duhn-stants
mild	**mild/zacht**	milt/zakht
mine *pron.*	**mijn**	myn/muhn

minute *time*	**minuut**	mee-nüt
mirror	**spiegel**	spee-khuhl
Miss	**juffrouw**	yuhf-frow
miss (to) *train, etc.*	**missen**	mis-suhn
mistake	**vergissing**	vuhr-khis-sing
mix (to)	**mengen**	meng-uhn
mix (to) *with people*	**omgaan met**	om-khān met
mixed	**gemengd**	khuh-mengt
modern	**modern**	mō-de-ruhn
moment	**ogenblik (*n*)**	ō-khuhn-blik
money	**geld (*n*)**	khelt
month	**maand**	mānt
monument	**monument (*n*)**	mō-nü-ment
moon	**maan**	mān
mop	**ragebol**	rā-khuh-bol
more	**meer**	mayr
mosquito	**mug**	muhkh
most	**meest**	mayst
mother	**moeder**	moo-duhr
motor boat	**motorboot**	mō-t'r-bōt
motor cycle	**motorfiets**	mō-t'r-feets
motor racing	**motor racing**	mō-t'r ray-sing
motorway	**snelweg**	snel-wekh
mountain	**berg**	be-ruhkh
mouth	**mond**	mont
mouthwash	**mondspoeling**	mont-spoo-ling
move (to)	**bewegen (bewoog, bewogen)**	buh-way-khuhn (buh-wōkh, buh-wō-khuhn)
Mr	**De heer**	duh hayr

Mrs	**Mevr(ouw)**	muh-vrow
much	**veel**	vayl
museum	**museum** (*n*)	mu-zay-yuhm
music	**muziek**	mü-zeek
must *to have to*	**moeten**	moo-t'n
my, mine	**mijn**	myn/muhn
myself	**mijzelf**	muh-zel-luhf

N

nail *carpentry*	**spijker**	spy-k'r
nail polish	**nagellak**	nā-khuhl-lak
nailbrush	**nagelborsteltje** (*n*)	nā-khuhl-bor-stuhl-tyuh
nailfile	**nagelvijl**	nā-khuhl-vyl
name	**naam**	nām
napkin	**servet** (*n*)	ser-vet
nappy/diaper	**luier**	lui-yuhr
narrow	**nauw**	now
near	**dichtbij**	dikht-by
nearly	**bijna**	by-nā
necessary	**nodig**	nō-duhkh
necklace	**halsketting**	hals-ke-ting
need (to)	**nodig hebben**	nō-duhkh he-buhn
needle	**naald**	nālt
neither	**geen van beide**	khayn van by-duh
net	**net** (*n*)	net
never	**nooit**	nō-eet
new	**nieuw**	neew
news	**nieuws** (*n*)	neews
newspaper	**krant**	krant

next	**volgend**	vol-khuhnt
nice *people*	**aardig**	ār-duhkh
nice *objects*	**mooi**	mōee
nice *food*	**lekker**	le-kuhr
nightclub	**nachtclub**	nakht-kluhp
nightdress	**nachtjapon**	nakht-ya-pon
no *adj.*	**geen**	khayn
nobody	**niemand**	nee-mant
noisy	**lawaaiig**	la-wā-yuhkh
none	**geen**	khayn
north	**noord**	nōrt
not	**niet**	neet
note *money*	**(bank)biljet** (*n*)	(bank)-bil-yet
note *written*	**aantekening**	ān-tay-kuh-ning
notebook	**notitieboek** (*n*)	nō-tee-tsee-book
nothing	**niets**	neets
notice (to)	**merken**	mer-k'n
novel	**roman**	rō-man
now	**nu**	nü
nude	**bloot/naakt**	blōt/nākt
number	**nummer** (*n*)	nuhm-muhr
nylon	**nylon**	ny-lon
nylons	**nylons**	ny-lons

O

occasion	**gelegenheid**	khuh-lay-khuhn-hyt
occupation	**beroep** (*n*)	buh-roop
occupied	**bezet**	buh-zet
ocean	**oceaan**	ō-say-yān

odd *strange*	**vreemd**	vraymt
odd *not even*	**oneven**	on-ay-vuhn
of	**van**	van
offer	**aanbieding**	ān-bee-ding
offer (to)	**aanbieden (bood aan, aangeboden)**	ān-bee-duhn (bōt ān, ān-khuh-bō-duhn)
office	**kantoor (***n***)**	kan-tōr
officer	**ambtenaar**	am-tuh-nār
officer *military*	**officier**	of-fee-seer
official *adj.*	**officiëel**	of-fee-shayl
official *noun*	**beambte**	buh-am-tuh
often	**vaak**	vāk
ointment	**zalf**	zal-luhf
old	**oud**	owt
on	**op**	op
once	**eenmaal**	ayn-mal
only	**alleen**	al-layn
open	**open**	ō-puhn
open (to)	**openen**	ō-puh-nuhn
opening	**opening**	ō-puh-ning
opera	**opera**	ō-puh-rā
opportunity	**kans**	kans
opposite	**tegenovergesteld**	tay-khuhn-ō-vuhr-khuh-stelt
or	**of**	of
orchestra	**orkest (***n***)**	or-kest
order (to)	**bestellen**	buh-stel-luhn
ordinary	**gewoon**	khuh-wōn
other	**ander**	an-duhr

otherwise	**anders**	an-duhrs
our	**ons**	ons
ours	**van ons**	van ons
out(side)	**buiten**	bui-t'n
out of order	**buiten gebruik**	bui-t'n khuh-**bruik**
over	**over**	ō-vuhr
overnight	**de nacht over**	duh nakht ō-vuhr
over there	**daar(ginds)**	dār-(khints)
overcoat	**overjas**	ō-vuhr-yas
owe (to)	**schuldig zijn**	skhuhl-duhkh zyn
owner	**eigenaar**	y-khuh-nār

P

pack (to)	**(in)pakken**	(in)-pa-k'n
padlock	**hangslot (***n***)**	hang-slot
page	**bladzij**	blat-zy
paid	**betaald**	buh-tālt
pain	**pijn**	pyn
paint (brush)	**verf(kwast)**	ve-ruhf-(kwast)
paint (to)	**schilderen**	skhil-duh-ruhn
painting	**schilderij (***n***)**	skhil-duh-ry
pair	**paar**	pār
palace	**paleis (***n***)**	pa-lys
pale	**bleek**	blayk
pan	**pan**	pan
paper	**papier (***n***)**	pa-peer
parcel	**pakje (***n***)**	pak-yuh
park	**park (***n***)**	pa-ruhk
park (to)	**parkeren**	par-kay-ruhn

part	**deel** (*n*)/**gedeelte** (*n*)	dayl/khuh-dayl-tuh
party *fête*	**feest** (*n*)/**party**	fayst/pār-tee
party *political*	**partij**	par-ty
pass (to)	**passeren**	pas-say-ruhn
passenger	**passagier**	pas-sā-zheer
passport	**paspoort** (*n*)	pas-pōrt
past *adj.*	**vorig/verleden**	vō-ruhkh/vuhr-lay-duhn
past *noun*	**verleden** (*n*)	vuhr-lay-duhn
path	**pad** (*n*)	pat
patient *adj.*	**geduldig**	khuh-duhl-duhkh
patient *noun*	**patient**	pa-shent
pavement	**trottoir** (*n*)/**stoep**	trot-wār/stoop
pay (to)	**betalen**	buh-tā-luhn
peak	**top**	top
pearl	**parel**	pā-ruhl
pebble	**kiezel(steen)**	kee-zuhl-(stayn)
pedal	**pedaal** (*n*)	puh-dāl
pedestrian	**voetganger**	voot-khang-uhr
(fountain) pen	**(vul)pen**	(vuhl)-pen
pencil	**potlood** (*n*)	pot-lōt
penknife	**zakmes** (*n*)	zak-mes
people	**mensen**	men-suhn
per person	**per persoon**	per per-sōn
perfect	**perfect**	per-fekt
performance	**voorstelling**	vōr-stel-ling
perfume	**parfum** (*n*)	par-fuhm
perhaps	**misschien**	muh-skheen
perishable	**bederfelijk**	buh-der-fuh-luhk
permit	**vergunning**	vuhr-khuhn-ning

permit (to)	toestaan	too-stán
person	persoon	per-sōn
personal	persoonlijk	per-sōn-luhk
petticoat	onderrok	on-duhr-rok
photograph	foto	fō-tō
photographer	fotograaf	fō-tō-khrāf
piano	piano	pee-yā-nō
pick (to)	plukken	pluh-k'n
picnic	picnic	pik-nik
piece	stukje (*n*)	stuhk-yuh
pier	pier	peer
pillow	kussen (*n*)	kuhs-suhn
(safety) pin	(veiligheids)speld	(vy-luhkh-hyt)-spelt
pipe	pijp	pyp
pity!	jammer	yam-muhr
place	plaats	plāts
plain *clear*	duidelijk	dui-duh-luhk
plain *colour*	effen	ef-fuhn
plain *not fancy*	eenvoudig	ayn-vow-duhkh
plan *thought*	plan (*n*)	plan
plan *town*	plattegrond	pla-tuh-gront
plant	plant	plant
plastic	plastic	plas-teek
plate	bord (*n*)	bort
play *theatre*	(toneel)stuk (*n*)	(tō-nayl)-stuhk
play (to)	spelen	spay-luhn
player	speler	spay-luhr
please	alstublieft	als-tü-bleeft
plenty	genoeg	khuh-nookh

pliers	**tang**	tang
plug *bath*	**stop**	stop
plug *electric*	**stekker**	ste-kuhr
plug *wall*	**stopcontact (*n*)**	stop-kon-takt
pocket	**zak**	zak
point	**punt**	puhnt
poisonous	**vergiftig**	vuhr-khif-tuhkh
policeman	**(politie)agent**	(pō-lee-tsee)-ā-khent
police station	**politiebureau (*n*)**	pō-lee-tsee-bü-rō
poor	**arm**	a-ruhm
popular	**populair**	pō-pü-lèr
port	**haven**	hā-vuhn
possible	**mogelijk**	mō-khuh-luhk
post (to)	**posten**	pos-t'n
post box	**brievenbus**	bree-vuhn-buhs
post office	**postkantoor (*n*)**	pos-kan-tōr
(picture) postcard	**(prent)briefkaart**	(prent-)breef-kārt
postman	**postbode**	post-bō-duh
postpone (to)	**uitstellen**	uit-stel-luhn
pound	**pond (*n*)**	pont
powder	**poeder**	poo-yuhr
prefer (to)	**liever hebben**	lee-vuhr he-buhn
prepare (to)	**klaarmaken**	klār-mā-k'n
present *gift*	**geschenk (*n*)/cadeau (*n*)**	khuh-shkenk/ka-dō
press (to) *clothes*	**persen**	per-suhn
pretty	**aardig**	ār-duhkh
price	**prijs**	prys
priest *protestant*	**dominee**	dō-mee-nay

priest *catholic*	**priester**	**pree**-stuhr
print *picture*	**prent**	prent
print (to)	**drukken**	**druh**-kuhn
private	**privé**	pree-**vay**
problem	**probleem** (*n*)	prō-**blaym**
profession	**beroep** (*n*)	buh-**roop**
programme	**programma** (*n*)	prō-**khram**-mā
promise	**belofte**	buh-**lof**-tuh
promise (to)	**beloven**	buh-**lō**-vuhn
prompt	**prompt**	prompt
protestant	**protestant**	pro-tuh-**stant**
provide (to)	**voorzien**	**vōr**-zeen
public	**publiek** (*n*)	pü-**bleek**
pull (to)	**trekken** (trok, getrokken)	**tre**-k'n (trok, khuh-**tro**-kuhn)
pump	**pomp**	pomp
pure	**puur**	pür
purse	**portemonnaie**	por-tuh-**mō**-nay
push (to)	**duwen**	**dü**-wuhn
put (to)	**plaatsen**	**plāt**-suhn
pyjamas	**pyjama**	pee-**yā**-mā

Q

quality	**kwaliteit**	kwal-lee-**tyt**
quantity	**hoeveelheid**	**hoo**-vayl-hyt
quarrel	**ruzie**	**rü**-zee
quarter	**kwart**	kwart
queen	**koningin**	**kō**-ning-in
question	**vraag**	vrākh

queue	**rij**	ry
queue (to)	**in de rij staan**	in duh ry stān
quick(ly)	**vlug/snel**	vluhkh/snel
quiet(ly)	**rustig**	ruh-stuhkh
quite	**helemaal**	hay-luh-māl

R

race	**race**	rays
racecourse	**renbaan**	ren-bān
radiator	**radiator**	ra-dee-yā-tor
radio	**radio**	rā-dee-yō
railway	**spoorweg**	spōr-wekh
rain	**regen**	ray-khuhn
(it is) raining	**het regent**	uht ray-khuhnt
raincoat	**regenjas**	ray-khuhn-yas
rare	**zeldzaam**	zelt-sām
rather *more or less*	**min of meer**	min ov mayr
rather *preference*	**liever**	lee-vuhr
raw	**rauw**	row
razor	**scheermes (***n***)**	skhayr-mes
razor blade	**scheermesje (***n***)**	skhayr-me-shuh
reach (to) *destination*	**bereiken**	buh-ry-k'n
reach (for)	**reiken (naar)**	ry-k'n (nār)
read (to)	**lezen (las, gelezen)**	lay-zuhn (las, khuh-lay-zuhn)
ready	**klaar**	klār
real	**echt**	ekht
really	**werkelijk**	wer-kuh-luhk
reason	**reden**	ray-duhn

receipt	**kwitantie**	kwee-tan-tsee
receive (to)	**ontvangen (ontving, ontvangen)**	ont-vang-uhn (ont-ving, ont-vang-uhn)
recent	**recent**	ruh-sent
recipe	**recept** (*n*)	ruh-sept
recognize (to)	**herkennen**	her-ken-nuhn
recommend (to)	**aanbevelen**	ān-buh-vay-luhn
record	**plaat**	plāt
record *sport*	**record** (*n*)	re-kōr
refrigerator	**koelkast/ijskast**	kool-kast/ys-kast
(give my) regards	**(doe de) groeten**	(doo duh) khroo-t'n
register (to) *birth*	**aangeven**	ān-khay-vuhn
register (to) *mail*	**aantekenen**	ān-tay-kuh-nuhn
relatives	**familieleden**	fa-mee-lee-lay-duhn
religion	**religie**	ruh-lee-khee
remember (to)	**(zich) herinneren**	(zikh) her-in-nuh-ruhn
rent	**huur**	hür
rent (to)	**huren**	hü-ruhn
repair (to)	**repareren**	ray-pa-ray-ruhn
repeat (to)	**herhalen**	her-hā-luhn
reply (to)	**antwoorden**	ant-wōr-duhn
reservation	**reservering/boeking**	ray-ser-vay-ring/ boo-king
reserve (to)	**reserveren**	ray-ser-vay-ruhn
reserved	**gereserveerd**	khuh-ray-ser-vayrt
restaurant	**restaurant** (*n*)	res-tō-ran
return (to) *from*	**terugkomen** *van*	truhkh-kō-muhn van
return (to) *to*	**teruggaan** *naar*	truh-khān nār
return (to) *give back*	**teruggeven**	truh-khay-vuhn

reward	**beloning**	buh-lō-ning
ribbon	**lint** (*n*)	lint
rich	**rijk**	ryk
ride	**rit**	rit
ride (to)	**rijden (reed, gereden)**	ry-duhn (rayt, khuh-ray-duhn)
right *not left*	**rechts**	rekhts
right *not wrong*	**goed**	khoot
right (to be)	**gelijk hebben**	khlyk he-buhn
ring	**ring**	ring
ripe	**rijp**	ryp
rise (to)	**opstaan**	op-stān
river	**rivier**	ree-veer
road	**weg/straat**	wekh/strāt
rock	**rots**	rots
roll (to)	**rollen**	rol-luhn
roof	**dak** (*n*)	dak
room	**kamer**	kā-muhr
rope	**touw** (*n*)	tow
rotten	**(ver)rot**	(vuh)-rot
rough	**ruw**	rüw
round	**rond**	ront
rowing boat	**roeiboot**	rooee-bōt
rubber	**rubber** (*n*)	ruh-buhr
rubbish	**rommel**	rom-muhl
rucksack	**rugzak**	ruhkh-zak
rude	**onhebbelijk**	on-he-buh-luhk
ruin	**ruïne**	rü-wee-nuh
rule (to)	**regeren**	ruh-khay-ruhn

run (to)	**rennen**	ren-nuhn

S

sad	**triest/treurig**	treest/trœ-ruhkh
safe	**veilig**	vy-luhkh
sailor	**zeeman**	zay-man
sale *clearance*	**uitverkoop**	uit-vuhr-kōp
(for) sale	**(te) koop**	(tuh) kōp
salesman	**verkoper/ winkelbediende**	vuhr-kō-puhr/wing- kuhl-buh-deen-duh
saleswoman	**verkoopster/ winkeljuffrouw**	vuhr-kōp-stuhr/ wing-kuhl-yuhf-frow
salt	**zout** (*n*)	zowt
salt water	**zeewater** (*n*)	zay-wā-t'r
same	**zelfde**	zel-luhf-duh
sand	**zand** (*n*)	zant
sandals	**sandalen**	san-dā-luhn
sanitary towel	**maandverband** (*n*)	mānt-vuhr-bant
satisfactory	**bevredigend**	buh-vray-duh-khunt
saucer	**schotel**	skhō-t'l
save (to)	**sparen**	spā-ruhn
saw	**zaag**	zākh
saw (to)	**zagen**	zā-khuhn
say (to)	**zeggen**	ze-khuhn
scald (to) *oneself*	**zich branden**	zikh bran-d'n
scarf	**das/shawl**	das/shāl
scenery	**landschap** (*n*)	lant-skhap
scent	**luchtje** (*n*)	luhkh-yuh
school	**school**	skhōl

scissors	**schaar**	skhār
Scot	**Schot/Schotse**	skhot/**skhot-suh**
Scotland	**Schotland**	skhot-lant
Scottish	**Schots**	skhots
scratch (to)	**krabben**	kra-buhn
screw	**schroef**	skhroof
screwdriver	**schroevendraaier**	skhroo-vuh-drā-yuhr
sculpture	**beeldhouwwerk (*n*)**	baylt-how-we-ruhk
sea	**zee**	zay
seafood	**schaaldieren**	skhāl-dee-ruhn
seasick	**zeeziek**	zay-zeek
season	**seizoen (*n*)**	sy-zoon
seat	**(zit)plaats**	(zit)-plāts
second *time*	**seconde**	suh-kon-duh
see (to)	**zien (zag, gezien)**	zeen (zakh, khuh-zeen)
seem (to)	**schijnen (scheen, geschenen)**	skhy-nuhn (skhayn, khuh-skhay-nuhn)
self-service	**zelfbediening**	zel-luhf-buh-dee-ning
sell (to)	**verkopen (verkocht, verkocht)**	vuhr-kō-p'n (vuhr-kokht)
send (to)	**sturen**	stü-ruhn
separate(ly)	**afzonderlijk**	af-zon-duhr-luhk
serious	**ernstig**	ern-stuhkh
serve (to)	**bedienen**	buh-dee-nuhn
service	**bediening**	buh-dee-ning
service *church*	**dienst**	deenst
service charge	**bedieningsgeld (*n*)**	buh-dee-nings-khelt
several	**verscheidene**	vuhr-skhy-duh-nuh
sew (to)	**naaien**	nā-yuhn

shade *colour*	tint	tint
shade *shadow*	schaduw	skhā-dü
shallow	ondiep	on-deep
shape	vorm	vo-ruhm
share (to)	delen	day-luhn
sharp	scherp	skhe-ruhp
shave (to)	scheren (schoor, geschoren)	skhay-ruhn (skhōr, khuh-skhō-ruhn)
shaving brush	scheerkwast	skhayr-kwast
shaving cream/foam	scheerzeep/schuim (*n*)	skhayr-zayp/skhuim
she	zij	zy
sheet	laken (*n*)	lā-k'n
shelf	plank	plank
shell	schelp	skhel-luhp
shelter	toevlucht	too-vluhkht
shine (to)	schijnen (scheen, geschenen)	skhy-nuhn (skhayn, khuh-skhay-nuhn)
shingle	kiezel(steen)	kee-zuhl-(stayn)
ship	schip (*n*)	skhip
shipping line	scheepvaartmaat-schappij	skhayp-vārt māt-skha-py
shirt	(over)hemd (*n*)	(ō-vuhr)-hemt
shock	schok	skhok
shoe	schoen	skhoon
shoelace	veter	vay-t'r
shoe polish	schoensmeer	skhoon-smayr
shop	winkel	wing-k'l
shopping centre	winkelcentrum (*n*)	wing-kuhl-sen-truhm

shore	kust	kuhst
short	kort	kort
shortly	binnenkort	bin-nuh-kort
shorts	korte broek	kor-tuh brook
shoulder	schouder	skhow-duhr
show	show	shō
show (to)	laten zien	lā-t'n zeen
shower	douche	doosh
shut	gesloten	khuh-slō-t'n
shut (to)	sluiten (sloot, gesloten)/dicht doen	slui-t'n (slōt, khuh-slō-t'n)/ dikht doon
shutter	luik (*n*)	luik
side	zijkant	zy-kant
sieve	zeef	zayf
sights	bezienswaardigheden	buh-zeens-wār-duhkh-hay-duhn
sightseeing	bezichtiging	buh-zikh-tuh-khing
sign	teken (*n*)/bord (*n*)	tay-k'n/bort
sign (to)	tekenen	tay-kuh-nuhn
signpost	verkeersbord (*n*)	vuhr-kayrs-bort
silver	zilver	zil-vuhr
simple	eenvoudig	ayn-vow-duhkh
since	sinds	sints
sing (to)	zingen (zong, gezongen)	zing-uhn (zong, khuh-zong-uhn)
single *just one/not return*	enkel	eng-kuhl
single *unmarried*	ongehuwd	on-khuh-hüwt

single room	eenpersoonskamer	ayn-per-sōns-kā-muhr
sink	gootsteen	khōt-stayn
sister	zuster	zuhs-t'r
sit (to)	zitten (zat, gezeten)	zi-t'n (zat, khuh-zay-t'n)
sit down (to)	gaan zitten	khān zi-t'n
size	maat	māt
skid (to)	glijden (gleed, gegleden)	khly-duhn (khlayt, khuh-**khlay**-duhn)
skirt	rok	rok
sky	hemel/lucht	hay-muhl/luhkht
sleep (to)	slapen (sliep, geslapen)	slā-puhn (sleep, khuh-slā-puhn)
sleeper *train*	slaapwagen	slāp-wā-khuhn
sleeping-bag	slaapzak	slāp-zak
sleeve	mouw	mow
slice	sneetje (*n*)	snay-tyuh
slip	onderjurk	on-duhr-yuhrk
slippers	pantoffels	pan-tof-fuhls
slowly	langzaam	lang-zām
small	klein	klyn
smart	chic	sheek
smell	reuk	rœk
smell (to)	ruiken	rui-k'n
smile (to)	glimlachen	khlim-la-khuhn
smoke (to)	roken	rō-k'n
(no) smoking	(niet) roken	(neet) rō-k'n
snow	sneeuw	snayw
(it is) snowing	het sneeuwt	uht snaywt
so	zo	zō

soap	**zeep**	zayp
soap powder	**zeeppoeder**	zay-poo-yuhr
sober	**sober**	sō-buhr
sock	**sok**	sok
soft	**zacht**	zakht
sold	**verkocht**	vuhr-kokht
sole *shoe*	**zool**	zōl
solid	**stevig**	stay-vuhkh
solid *not liquid*	**vast**	vast
some *a few*	**sommige/enkele**	som-muh-khuh/eng-kuh-luh
some *a little*	**een beetje**	uhn bay-tyuh
somebody	**iemand**	ee-mant
somehow	**op de een of andere manier**	op duh ayn ov an-duh-ruh ma-neer
something	**iets**	eets
sometimes	**soms**	soms
somewhere	**ergens**	e-ruh-khuns
son	**zoon**	zōn
song	**lied** (*n*)	leet
soon	**gauw**	khow
sort	**soort** (*n*)	sōrt
sound	**geluid** (*n*)	khuh-luit
sour	**zuur**	zür
south	**zuid**	zuit
souvenir	**souvenier** (*n*)	soo-vuh-neer
space	**ruimte**	ruim-tuh
spanner	**(moer)sleutel**	(moor)-slœ-tuhl
spare	**reserve**	ruh-ser-vuh

speak (to)	spreken (sprak, gesproken)	spray-k'n (sprak, khuh-sprō-k'n)
speciality	specialiteit	spay-see-yā-lee-tyt
spectacles *glasses*	bril	bril
speed	snelheid	snel-hyt
speed limit	maximum snelheid	mak-see-muhm snel-hyt
spend (to)	uitgeven	uit-khay-vuhn
spoon	lepel	lay-p'l
sport	sport	sport
sprain (to)	verstuiken	vuhr-stui-k'n
spray	verstuiver	vuhr-stui-vuhr
spring *water*	bron	bron
square	vierkant	veer-kant
square *town*	plein (*n*)	plyn
stable *noun*	stal	stal
stage	toneel (*n*)	tō-nayl
stain	vlek	vlek
stained	gevlekt	khuh-vlekt
stairs	trap	trap
stalls	zaal/stalles	zāl/stal-luhs
stamp	postzegel	pos-say-khuhl
stand (to)	staan (stond, gestaan)	stān (stont, khuh-stān)
star	ster	ster
start (to)	beginnen (begon, begonnen)	buh-khin-nuhn (buh-khon, buh-khon-nuhn)
statue	beeld (*n*)	baylt

stay (to)	**blijven (bleef, gebleven)**	bly-vuhn (blayf, khuh-blay-vuhn)
step	**stap**	stap
steward(ess)	**steward(es)**	styoo-wart/styoo-war-des
stick	**stok**	stok
stiff	**stijf**	styf
still *not moving*	**stil**	stil
still *time*	**nog**	nokh
sting	**beet**	bayt
stocking	**kous**	kows
stolen	**gestolen**	khuh-stō-luhn
stone	**steen**	stayn
stool	**kruk**	kruhk
stop (to)	**stoppen/ophouden**	sto-p'n/op-how-duhn
store	**winkel**	wing-k'l
storm	**storm**	stō-ruhm
stove	**fornuis (*n*)**	for-nuis
straight	**recht**	rekht
straight on	**rechtuit**	rekht-uit
strange	**vreemd**	vraymt
strap	**riem**	reem
stream	**stroom**	strōm
street	**straat**	strāt
streetcar	**tram**	trem
stretch (to)	**rekken**	re-k'n
string	**touw**	tow
string *piece of*	**touwtje**	tow-tyuh
strong	**sterk**	ste-ruhk
student	**student**	stü-dent

stung (to be)	gestoken worden	khuh-stō-kuhn wor-duhn
style	stijl	styl
subject	onderwerp (n)	on-duhr-we-ruhp
suburb	buitenwijk	bui-tuh-wyk
such	zo (een)/zo'n	zō ayn/zōn
suede	suède	sü-wè-duh
suggestion	voorstel (n)	vōr-stel
suit	pak (n)/kostuum (n)	pak/kos-tüm
suitcase	koffer	kof-fuhr
sun	zon	zon
sunbathing	zonnebaden	zon-nuh-bā-duhn
sunburn	zonnebrand	zon-nuh-brant
sunglasses	zonnebril	zon-nuh-bril
sunhat	zonnehoed	zon-nuh-hoot
sunshade	zonnescherm (n)	zon-nuh-skhe-ruhm
suntan cream	zonnebrandolie	zon-nuh-brant-ō-lee
supper	avondeten (n)	ā-vont-ay-tuhn
supplementary charge	toeslag	too-slakh
sure	zeker	zay-k'r
surgery hours	spreekuur (n)	sprayk-ür
surprise	verrassing	vuh-ras-sing
surprise (to)	verrassen	vuh-ras-suhn
suspender belt	jarretel-gordel	zha-ruh-tel-khor-duhl
sweat	zweet (n)	zwayt
sweater	trui	trui
sweet adj.	zoet	zoot
sweet noun	snoepje (n)	snoop-yuh
swell (to)	opzwellen (zwol op, opgezwollen)	op-zwel-luhn (zwol op, op-khuh-zwol-luhn)

swim (to)	**zwemmen (zwom, gezwommen)**	zwem-muhn (zwom, khuh-zwom-muhn)
swimming pool	**zwembad (***n***)**	zwem-bat
swings	**schommel**	skhom-muhl
switch *light*	**schakelaar/(licht)- knopje (***n***)**	skhā-kuh-lār/(likht)- knop-yuh
synagogue	**synagoge**	see-na-**khō**-khuh

T

table	**tafel**	tā-fuhl
tablecloth	**tafellaken (***n***)**	tā-fuhl-lā-k'n
tablet	**tablet (***n***)/pil**	ta-blet/pil
tailor	**kleermaker**	klayr-mā-kuhr
take (to)	**(mee)nemen (nam, genomen)**	(may)-nay-muhn (nam, khuh-**nō**-muhn)
talk (to)	**praten**	prā-t'n
tall *person*	**lang**	lang
tall *object*	**hoog**	hōkh
tank	**tank**	tenk
tanned	**bruin**	bruin
tap	**kraan**	krān
taste	**smaak**	smāk
taste (to) *active*	**proeven**	proo-vuhn
taste (to) *passive*	**smaken**	smā-k'n
tax	**belasting**	buh-las-ting
taxi (rank)	**taxi(standplaats)**	tak-see(stant-plāts)
tea	**thee**	tay
tea towel	**theedoek**	tay-dook
teach (to)	**leren**	lay-ruhn

tear *cloth, etc.*	scheur	skhœr
tear *drop*	traan	trān
tear (to)	scheuren	skhœ-ruhn
telegram	telegram (*n*)	tay-luh-khram
telephone	telefoon	tay-luh-fōn
telephone (to)	telefoneren	tay-luh-fō-nay-ruhn
telephone box	telefooncel	tay-luh-fōn-sel
telephone call	telefoongesprek (*n*)	tay-luh-fōn-khuh-sprek
television	t.v./televisie	tay-vay/til-luh-vee-see
tell (to)	vertellen	vuhr-tel-luhn
temperature	temperatuur	tem-puh-rā-tür
temple	tempel	tem-puhl
temporary	tijdelijk	ty-duh-luhk
tennis	tennis	ten-nuhs
tent	tent	tent
tent peg	haring	hā-ring
tent pole	tentstok	tent-stok
terrace	terras (*n*)	tuh-ras
than	dan	dan
that	dat	dat
the	de/het	duh/het, uht
theatre	theater (*n*)	tay-yā-t'r
their	hun	huhn
theirs	van hun	van huhn
them	hen	hen
then	dan/toen	dan/toon
there	daar	dār
thermometer	thermometer	ter-mō-may-t'r

these	deze	day-zuh
they	zij	zy
thick	dik	dik
thin	dun	duhn
thing	ding (n)	ding
think (to)	denken (dacht, gedacht)	deng-kuhn (dakht, khuh-dakht)
thirsty (to be)	dorst hebben	dorst he-buhn
this	dit	dit
those	die	dee
though	hoewel	hoo-wel
thread	draad	drāt
through	door	dōr
throughout (the day)	de hele (dag)	de hay-luh (dakh)
throw (to)	gooien	khō-yuhn
thunderstorm	onweer (n)	on-wayr
ticket	kaartje (n)	kār-tyuh
tide	getij (n)	khuh-ty
tie	das	das
tie sport	gelijkspel (n)	khlyk-spel
tight	nauw	now
tights	panties	pen-tees
tile	tegel	tay-khuhl
time	tijd	tyt
timetable	dienstregeling	deenst-ray-khuh-ling
timetable railway	spoorboekje (n)	spōr-book-yuh
tin	blik (n)	blik
tin opener	blikopener	blik-ō-puh-nuhr
tip in restaurant	fooi	fōee

tip (to)	een fooi geven	uhn fōee khay-vuhn
tired	moe	moo
to	naar/aan	nār/ān
tobacco	tabak	ta-bak
tobacco pouch	tabakszak	ta-bak-sak
together	samen	sā-muhn
toilet	toilet (*n*)/WC	twa-let/way-say
toilet paper	toiletpapier (*n*)	twa-let-pa-peer
tongue	tong	tong
too *also*	ook	ōk
too *excessive*	te	tuh
too much/many	te veel	tuh vayl
toothbrush	tandeborstel	tan-duh-bor-stuhl
toothpaste	tandpasta	tam-pas-tā
toothpick	tandestoker	tan-duh-stō-kuhr
top	bovenkant	bō-vuh-kant
torch	(zak)lantaarn	(zak)-lan-tā-ruhn
torn	gescheurd	khuh-skhoert
touch (to)	aanraken	ān-rā-kuhn
tough	taai	tāee
tour	toer	toor
tourist	toerist	too-rist
towards	naar ... toe	nār ... too
towel	handdoek	han-dook
tower	toren	tō-ruhn
town	stad	stat
town hall	gemeentehuis (*n*)	khuh-mayn-tuh-huis
toy	speelgoed (*n*)	spayl-khoot
traffic	verkeer (*n*)	vuhr-kayr

traffic jam	verkeersopstopping	vuhr-kayrs-op-sto-ping
traffic lights	verkeerslichten	vuhr-kayrs-likh-t'n
trailer	oplegger	op-le-khuhr
train	trein	tryn
tram	tram	trem
transfer (to)	overdragen	ō-vuhr-drā-khuhn
transit	doorreis	dōr-rys
translate (to)	vertalen	vuhr-tā-luhn
translation	vertaling	vuhr-tā-ling
travel (to)	reizen	ry-zuhn
travel agent	reisbureau (*n*)	rys-bü-rō
traveller	reiziger	ry-zuh-khuhr
traveller's cheque	reischeque	rys-shek
treat (to)	behandelen	buh-han-duh-luhn
treatment	behandeling	buh-han-duh-ling
tree	boom	bōm
trip	reisje (*n*)	ry-syuh
trouble	moeilijkheden	moo-yuh-luhk-hay-duhn
trousers	broek	brook
true	waar	wār
trunk *luggage*	koffer	kof-fuhr
trunks	onderbroek	on-duhr-brook
truth	waarheid	wār-hyt
try (to)	proberen	prō-bay-ruhn
try on (to)	passen	pas-suhn
tunnel	tunnel	tuh-nuhl
turn (to)	draaien	drā-yuhn
turning	bocht/afslag	bokht/af-slakh
tweezers	pincet (*n*)	pin-set

twin beds	lits jumeaux	lee-shü-mō
twisted	gedraaid	khuh-drāeed

U

ugly	lelijk	lay-luhk
umbrella	paraplu	pa-rā-plü
uncle	oom	ōm
uncomfortable	ongemakkelijk	on-khuh-ma-kuh-luhk
under	onder	on-duhr
underground *train*	metro	may-trō
underneath	onder	on-duhr
understand (to)	begrijpen (begreep, begrepen)	buh-khry-puhn (buh-khrayp, buh-khray-puhn)
underwear	ondergoed (*n*)	on-duhr-khoot
university	universiteit	ü-nee-ver-see-tyt
unpack (to)	uitpakken	uit-pa-kuhn
until	tot	tot
unusual	ongewoon	on-khuh-wōn
upon	op	op
upstairs	boven	bō-vuhn
urgent	dringend	dring-uhnt
us	ons	ons
U.S.A.	Verenigde Staten	vuhr-ay-nuhkh-duh stā-t'n
use (to)	gebruiken	khuh-brui-kuhn
useful	bruikbaar	bruik-bār
useless	onbruikbaar	on-bruik-bār
usual(ly)	gewoon(lijk)	khuh-wōn-(luhk)

V

vacancies *job*	**vacatures**	va-kā-tü-ruhs
vacancies *hotel*	**kamers vrij**	kā-muhrs vry
vacant	**vrij**	vry
vacuum cleaner	**stofzuiger**	stof-zui-khuhr
valid	**geldig**	khel-duhkh
valley	**vallei**	val-ly
valuable	**kostbaar/waardevol**	kost-bār/wār-duh-vol
value	**waarde**	wār-duh
vase	**vaas**	vās
vegetables	**groente**	khroon-tuh
vegetarian *noun*	**vegetariër**	vay-khuh-tā-ree-yuhr
ventilation	**ventilatie**	ven-tee-lā-tsee
very	**erg/heel**	erkh/hayl
very little	**klein beetje**	klyn bay-tyuh
very much	**heel veel**	hayl vayl
vest	**hemdje** (*n*)	hem-pyuh
view	**uitzicht** (*n*)	uit-zikht
villa	**villa**	veel-lā
village	**dorp** (*n*)	do-ruhp
violin	**viool**	vee-yōl
visa	**visum** (*n*)	vee-zuhm
visibility	**zicht** (*n*)	zikht
visit	**bezoek** (*n*)	buh-zook
visit (to)	**bezoeken (bezocht, bezocht)**	buh-zoo-kuhn (buh-zokht)
voice	**stem**	stem
voltage	**voltage** (*n*)	vol-tā-zhuh
voyage	**reis**	rys

W

wait (to)	wachten	wakh-t'n
waiter	kelner	kel-nuhr
waiting room	wachtkamer	wakht-kā-muhr
waitress	dienster	deen-stuhr
wake (to)	wakker worden	wa-kuhr wor-duhn
Wales	Wales	wayls
walk	wandeling	wan-duh-ling
walk (to)	wandelen/lopen (liep, gelopen)	wan-duh-luhn/lō-p'n (leep, khuh-lō-p'n)
wall	muur	mür
wallet	portefeuille	por-tuh-fui-yuh
want (to)	willen	wil-luhn
wardrobe	klerenkast	klay-ruh-kast
warm	warm	wa-ruhm
wash (to)	wassen	was-suhn
washbasin	wasbak	was-bak
washing machine	wasmachine	was-mā-shee-nuh
washing powder	waspoeder (*n*)	was-poo-yuhr
washing-up liquid	afwasmiddel (*n*)	af-was-mi-duhl
waste	verspilling	vuhr-spil-ling
waste *garbage*	afval	af-fal
watch	horloge (*n*)	hor-lō-zhuh
water (fresh, salt)	(zoet, zout) water (*n*)	(zoot, zowt) wā-t'r
water ski-ing	waterskiën	wā-t'r-skee-yuhn
waterfall	waterval	wā-t'r-val
waterproof	waterproof	wā-t'r-proof
wave	golf	khol-luhf
way *road*	weg	wekh

way *manner*	**manier**	ma-neer
we	**wij**	wy/wuh
wear (to)	**dragen (droeg, gedragen)**	drā-khuhn (drookh, khuh-drā-khuhn)
weather	**weer (*n*)**	wayr
week	**week**	wayk
weigh (to)	**wegen (woog, gewogen)**	way-khuhn (wōkh, khuh-wō-khuhn)
weight	**gewicht (*n*)**	khuh-wikht
welcome	**welkom**	wel-kom
well	**goed**	khoot
Welsh	**Weels**	wayls
west	**west**	west
wet	**nat**	nat
what	**wat**	wat
wheel	**wiel (*n*)**	weel
when	**wanneer**	wan-nayr
where	**waar**	wār
whether	**of**	of
which	**welke**	wel-kuh
while	**terwijl**	ter-wyl
who	**wie**	wee
whole	**heel**	hayl
whose	**wiens**	weens
why	**waarom**	wā-rom
wide	**wijd**	wyt
widow	**weduwe**	way-dü-wuh
widower	**weduwnaar**	way-dü-nār
wife	**vrouw/echtgenote**	vrow/ekht-khuh-nō-tuh

wild	**wild**	wilt
win (to)	**winnen (won, gewonnen)**	win-nuhn (won, khuh-**won**-nuhn)
wind	**wind**	wint
window	**raam** (*n*)/**venster** (*n*)	rām/**ven**-stuhr
window catch	**haakje** (*n*)	**hāk**-yuh
window sill	**vensterbank**	**ven**-stuhr-bank
wing	**vleugel**	**vlœ**-khuhl
wire	**draad**	drāt
wish (to)	**wensen**	**wen**-suhn
with	**met**	met
within	**binnen**	**bin**-nuhn
without	**zonder**	**zon**-duhr
woman	**vrouw**	vrow
wood *forest*	**bos** (*n*)	bos
wood *timber*	**hout** (*n*)	howt
wool	**wol**	wol
word	**woord** (*n*)	wōrt
word processor	**tekstverwerker**	tekst-vuhr-**we**-ruh-kuhr
work	**werk** (*n*)	**we**-ruhk
work (to)	**werken**	**wer**-k'n
worry (to)	**zich zorgen maken**	zikh **zor**-khuhn mā-k'n
worse	**slechter**	**slekh**-tuhr
worth (to be)	**waard zijn**	wārt zyn
wrap (to)	**inpakken**	**in**-pa-kuhn
write (to)	**schrijven (schreef, geschreven)**	**skhry**-vuhn (skhrayf, khuh-**skhray**-vuhn)
writing paper	**schrijfpapier** (*n*)	**skhryf**-pa-peer
wrong	**verkeerd**	vuhr-**kayrt**

Y

yacht	**jacht (*n*)/zeilboot**	yakht/zyl-bōt
year	**jaar (*n*)**	yār
yet *time*	**nog**	nokh
yet *contrast*	**toch**	tokh
you	**jij/je**	yy/yuh
young	**jong**	yong
your, yours	**jouw**	yow
youth hostel	**jeugdherberg**	yœkht-her-be-ruhkh

Z

zip	**ritssluiting**	rits-slui-ting
zoo	**dierentuin**	dee-ruh-tuin

INDEX